THE GEORGE GUND FOUNDATION
IMPRINT IN AFRICAN AMERICAN STUDIES

The George Gund Foundation has endowed
this imprint to advance understanding of
the history, culture, and current issues
of African Americans.

The publisher and the University of California Press Foundation gratefully acknowledge the generous support of the George Gund Foundation Imprint in African American Studies.

Publication was also aided by the Hull Memorial Publication Fund of Cornell University.

Sporting Blackness

Sporting Blackness

Race, Embodiment, and Critical Muscle Memory on Screen

SAMANTHA N. SHEPPARD

University of California Press

University of California Press
Oakland, California

Library of Congress Cataloging-in-Publication Data

Names: Sheppard, Samantha N., author.
Title: Sporting blackness : race, embodiment, and critical muscle memory
   on screen / Samantha N. Sheppard.
Description: Oakland, California : University of California Press, [2020] |
   Includes bibliographical references and index.
Identifiers: LCCN 2019059432 (print) | LCCN 2019059433 (ebook) |
   ISBN 9780520307773 (cloth) | ISBN 9780520307797 (paperback) |
   ISBN 9780520973855 (ebook)
Subjects: LCSH: Sports in motion pictures. | African Americans in motion
   pictures. | Race in motion pictures.
Classification: LCC PN1995.9.S67 S54 2020 (print) |
   LCC PN1995.9.S67 (ebook) | DDC 791.43/6579—dc23
LC record available at https://lccn.loc.gov/2019059432
LC ebook record available at https://lccn.loc.gov/2019059433

Manufactured in the United States of America

29 28 27 26 25 24 23 22 21 20
10 9 8 7 6 5 4 3 2 1

For the home team:
Allen, Bayard, and Baldwin

Contents

Illustrations

Acknowledgments

The end of writing this book coincided with the 2019 Women's World Cup. As a former Division-1 soccer player, I was thrilled to watch the US Women's National Soccer Team (USWNT) win the international tournament in grand fashion, especially with Megan "I'm not going to the fucking White House" Rapinoe leading the charge. Following their victory, I soaked up every glimpse of their celebration, canvasing social media (shout out to Ashlyn Harris's Instagram) to revel in their unfiltered joy. I smiled when they danced to D.J. Khaled's "All I Do Is Win" during their champions' ceremony at city hall. And I chuckled admiringly when Rapinoe (while holding the championship trophy and a bottle of champagne) proclaimed: "I deserve this. I deserve this. Everything!" Overall, I just loved watching her and the USWNT own their success, praise themselves and each other, and advocate for equity and equality. I was particularly struck by a tweet of a dancing Rapinoe and her teammates with the caption: "This is how I want women to celebrate their successes. None of that 'humble' shit." I could not agree more with this sentiment. In fact, I want to keep that same energy in these acknowledgments and boldly celebrate everyone who made this book possible and supported me throughout the years. None of that humble shit. We did it. We deserve this. Everything!

It has been a privilege and pleasure to work with Raina Polivka and University of California Press. I have long admired UC Press and could not have imagined a better place for *Sporting Blackness*. Raina, you have been a dream editor to see this project through to the end with, and I am forever grateful for your collaborative spirit and perceptive suggestions. You have been patient, generous, supportive, and encouraging throughout the entire process, which has made the daunting task of book publishing much easier and more affirming than I ever expected. Special thanks to editorial assistant Madison Wetzell, the entire UC Press staff, Emilia Thiuri, Nicholle Robertson, and Gary J. Hamel for their efforts in bringing all the elements of this book together.

Sporting Blackness began as a dissertation at UCLA under the thoughtful guidance of Kathleen McHugh and Allyson Nadia Field. Thank you, Kathleen, for your astute feedback, unwavering support, impactful pedagogy, and enthusiastic mentorship. Thank you, Ally, for being a fierce advocate, inspiring teacher, constant friend, and generous interlocutor. Thank you both for encouraging me to take the time to develop the concept of critical muscle memory for the book. I am deeply appreciative of my committee members Chon Noriega, Richard Yarborough, and Toby Miller, all of whom provided thoughtful advice, support, resources, and comments that shaped my dissertation and guided the revision process. Special thanks to Chon, who, while grabbing breakfast at Dewitt Café during a visit to Ithaca, gave constructive feedback on the book's broader conceptual stakes and suggested the title of *Sporting Blackness*.

This book has been workshopped at various stages of its development, and I have benefited immensely from generous individuals and academic communities who have engaged forcefully and thoughtfully with my work. As a postdoctoral fellow at Cornell, I received timely feedback on the book's proposal during the seminar "Lived Worlds and Possible Futures." I am deeply appreciative of Leslie A. Adelson for her comments, warmth, and collegiality during the seminar and intervening years. My time as a "Skin" fellow with Cornell's Society for the Humanities was particularly transformative. The rigorous, substantive, and constructive criticism I received on an early draft of the introduction came at an especially critical time in thinking through the book's theories, methodology, and argument. Thank you Tim Murray, Naminata Diabate, Ricardo A. Wilson II, Emily Rials, Nancy Worman, Kevin Ohi, Andrea Bachner, Alicia Imperiale, Karmen MacKendrick, Elyse Semerdjian, Pamela Gilbert, Gloria Chan-Sook Kim, Gemma Angel, Alana Staiti, Stacey Langwick, Erik Born, Daniel Smyth, and Seçil Yilmaz.

With generous support from Cornell's Department of Performing and Media Arts, I was able to workshop the entire manuscript with cinema and media scholars par excellence. Thank you Aaron Baker, Michael Gillespie, and Sabine Haenni for convening what proved to be a rich discussion of the book filled with detailed feedback, sharp criticism, and invaluable suggestions that greatly improved the manuscript overall. Aaron, you have been supportive of me and my work since I was a graduate student. You have my deepest gratitude and respect for flying to Ithaca in February only to get stuck at the airport in Philadelphia because of the terrible weather. You never complained and were such a team player, doing the entire workshop via Skype from a hotel room. Your brilliance as a thinker is outshined only by your kindness as a person. Thank you for helping me clarify my prose and the book's conclusion. Michael, you are in a class of your own. You are one of the most astute and creative thinkers I have ever met. You are exceedingly generous with your time and expertise. Thank you for your detailed notes, wise edits, and unflinching encouragement to lift my voice in the work and put the rest in the footnotes.

Thank you to the Woodrow Wilson National Fellowship Foundation for awarding me the Career Enhancement Fellowship for Junior Faculty, which has afforded me much needed time to complete the final elements and edits of this book. I am especially thankful for the ever-fabulous and remarkable Miriam Petty for agreeing to serve as my fellowship mentor. You have provided wonderful guidance and sage advice on all things book, career, and life related.

I am grateful to have presented and received feedback on writing included in this book at the annual conferences for the Society for Cinema and Media Studies and the American Studies Association. I have published earlier sections of chapter 1 and chapter 2 as "Historical Contestants: African American Documentary Traditions in *On the Shoulders of Giants*" in the *Journal of Sport and Social Issues* 41, no. 6 (2017): 462–77; and "Boobie Miles: Failure and *Friday Night Lights*" in the *Journal of Sport and Social Issues* 43, no. 4 (2019): 319–40. Thank you to editors Travis Vogan and C.L. Cole for your suggestions and support. I am very appreciative to have been invited to present aspects of this work at the Barnard Center for Research on Women's Scholar and Feminist Conference, Lafayette College's Film and Media Studies Speaker Series, Skidmore College's American Studies Lecture Series, Cornell's Department of Performing and Media Arts Research Colloquium, University of Illinois–Champaign's Media and Cinema Studies program, and Cornell's Blackness and the Visual Symposium. I want to express sincere gratitude to Nancy Worman, Tina Campt, Katherine Groo, Julie Turnock, Dan Nathan, Rebecca Krefting, Sabine Haenni, and Naminata Diabate for extending the invitations and serving as generous hosts and interlocutors.

Writing about athletics has afforded me the opportunity to meet and learn from so many wonderful interdisciplinary sports media scholars, including Aaron Baker, Travis Vogan, Vicky Johnson, and Les Friedman. Special thanks to Travis for his camaraderie, humor, and support throughout the years. And so much gratitude to Daniel Nasset for his initial and sustained enthusiasm in this project.

I am grateful for all of the institutional support I have received at Cornell. Production of this book was aided by the Hull Memorial Publication Fund of Cornell University. In addition, thank you to the College of Arts and Sciences for bestowing upon me the inaugural endowed assistant professorship named in honor of Mary Armstrong Meduski, who has been immensely supportive of me and my research. It is also a pleasure to work with nurturing and encouraging colleagues and be assisted by kind and helpful staff in the Department of Performing and Media Arts. Special thanks to Nick Salvato, Sabine Haenni, and Christine Bacareza Balance for their generosity and friendship. My sincere gratitude goes to Amy Villarejo, a gifted thinker, outstanding mentor, and road trip buddy. Every new faculty member should come in with a colleague like Karen Jaime, a true and loyal friend who has seen me through it all (including being drunk with tiredness). I am constantly inspired by your scholarship, teaching, and advocacy. Thank you for supporting me, this book, my family, and my career. I also have been deeply enriched by many current and former Cornell colleagues: Oneka LaBennett, Cheryl Finley, Judith Byfield, Stacey Langwick, Noliwe Rooks, Bill Gaskins, Riché Richardson, Ella Diaz, C. Riley Snorton, Parisa Vaziri, Anna Haskins, Steven Alvarado, Leslie Adelson, Adrienne Clay, Veronica Fitzpatrick, Nelly Andarawis-Puri, Anna Bartel, and Dehanza Rogers. Thank you to all my undergraduate and graduate students and teaching assistants at Cornell, especially Sadé Ayorinde, Jon Cicoski, and Kriszta Pozsonyi.

While this book's subject was initially conceived during graduate school, my undergraduate years at Dartmouth were invaluable to my growth as a cinema and media studies scholar. I am especially grateful for Annabel Martín, Cirri Nottage, Mark Williams, Mary Desjardins, and Stephanie Boone. I am deeply indebted to the Mellon Mays Undergraduate Fellowship (MMUF) program, which has supported me throughout my undergraduate, graduate, and professorial careers. I am now the faculty director of Cornell's MMUF program, and I am honored to continue the legacy of supporting undergraduate research and careers in the professoriate. A special thank-you to the Cornell MMUF fellows that I have had the distinct pleasure to work with over the last few years, and a hearty thanks to my co-coordinator Ekaterina Pirozhenko.

A cohort of scholars make up the intellectual and disciplinary coordinates of this book. I owe a depth of gratitude to Nicole Fleetwood, Ben Carrington, Harvey Young, Aaron Baker, Jared Sexton, Michele Wallace, Judith Butler, Trinh T. Minh-ha, Allyson Nadia Field, Phyllis R. Klotman, Janet K. Cutler, Michael Gillespie, Stuart Hall, and Grant Farred for their inspiring scholarship. It has been a wonderful experience to think with and through your work. Any misunderstandings are faults of my own. Ricardo Bracho has been absolutely invaluable throughout the process of writing this book. As a developmental editor, you have pushed me as a writer and critical thinker to envision this book in ways that I never imagined but am forever grateful for. Thank you for your insights, suggestions, comments, trips to Ithaca for writing bootcamps, and almost encyclopedic knowledge of the *Friday Night Lights* television series.

I am blown away by the amount of generosity I have received from creative artists whose work I deeply admire. Thank you to Hank Willis Thomas for discussing *Overtime* with me and for allowing me to use an image of *Strange Fruit* in the book. My sincerest appreciation goes to Esmaa Mohamoud, a gifted artist whose astounding photo *Untitled, No Fields* serves as the book's cover image. And much love to Michael Gillespie for sharing Esmaa's remarkable work with me and suggesting the image for the cover.

I have been inspired by the fellowship, community, and camaraderie of colleagues near and far. Thank you to TreaAndrea M. Russworm, Karen Bowdre, Bambi Haggins, Brandy Monk Payton, Miriam Petty, Linde Murugan, Jan-Christopher Horak, Beretta E. Smith-Shomade, Michael Gillespie, Kristen Warner, Racquel Gates, Nina Bradley, Artel Great, Catherine Clepper, Rebecca Wanzo, Morgan Woosley, Jaimie Baron, Jonathan Cohn, Jennifer Moorman, Maya Montañez Smukler, Caetlin Benson-Allott, Nsenga Burton, Ellen Scott, Hunter Hargraves, Michael T. Martin, David J. Leonard, Zeinabu irene Davis, Brett Kashmere, Keith Corson, Jennifer Porst, Melynda Price, Sarah Florini, Monica White Ndounou, Jennifer McClearen, Evan Brody, Paula Massood, Khadijah Costley White, Aymar Jean Christian, Alfred Martin, Jeffrey Coleman, Regina Longo, Charlene Regester, Adrien Sebro, Kwanda Ford, Christine Acham, Eric Pierson, Anna Everett, B. Ruby Rich, Andy Owens, Rudy Mondragón, Elizabeth Patton, Aimee Meredith Cox, Mikal Gaines, Jehan Roberson, Roberto D. Sirvent, Dan Morgan, Matt Holtmeier, Chelsea Wessels, Andrew Utterson, and Jamie Rogers. All the love in the world to my golden grad school friends Mila Zuo and Ben Sher: "thank you for being a friend, travel down the road and back again—your heart is true; you're a pal and a confidante."

A special thanks to Miriam, Beretta, and Bambi for being such amazing, kindhearted, and no-nonsense role-models. Hugs to coconspirators Kristen Warner and Racquel Gates for their friendship, fun, support, and (for KW) reading lists. And my deep affection, respect, and gratitude to Jacqueline Stewart; you are #goals in so many ways. I am particularly thankful to my friends outside the academy who have encouraged, sustained, and cheered me on throughout the years. Much love to Jackie Thornton, RuDee

Lipscomb, Lenée Richards, Brandon Harrison, Vanessa Skällenäs, Michelle Courtney Berry, and the "Crew." Special love to Black Girls Run Los Angeles for all the miles and marathons run. I would not have gotten this far without my oldest, dearest, and best friend, Dr. Amanda Rossie Barroso, the Ann Perkins to my Leslie Knope. Two decades of friendship means we have seen each other through high school to college to grad school to jobs to weddings to motherhood. Thank you for everything, including always saying yes to my eleventh-hour editing request. You'll always be my favorite running buddy: Can't Stop, Won't Stop!

This book would have not been possible without my family, who have always championed me on and off the playing field and in and out of the classroom. George, you are a wonderous human being and you will always be my favorite athlete. I admire your fortitude and good humor. I could not have asked for a better brother. Mom, I am so proud to be Pat's daughter. Your belief in me is unparalleled and never taken for granted. I am (happily) my mother's daughter. I love you both deeply and unequivocally. I also am blessed with supportive extended family in Georgia, California, and New York, especially my Uncle Noel, Aunt Madge, Aunt Cheryl, and Uncle Lloyd, and many cousins. This book is written in honor and remembrance of my father, George Alfred Sheppard Sr., and my late grandparents: Noel and Myrtle "Joyce" Brown and Olivia and Lloyd Sheppard Sr.

I started writing this book in earnest after I gave birth to my first child, Bayard, and completed it just after my second child, Baldwin, was born. While writing a book can be a lonely and isolating venture, you two have been with me through it all. Whether in my belly or banging on my office door, you both have always reminded me of what (and who) matters most and made this work worth doing (if not, time sensitive). I love you two beyond words. Thank you both for reminding me that this book is *not* my baby; you two are my babies, and I am eternally and extraordinarily proud to be your mother. And special recognition goes out to all the daycare teachers at Cornell Child Care who have cared for Bayard and Baldwin and, thus, profoundly have contributed to making the completion of this work possible.

This book would not have been finished if not for Allen Holt, my favorite person. You are a fantastic husband, father, friend, reader, sports fan, computer genius, and every other thing I have ever needed or asked you to be. You make everything better. The word count limit prohibits me from doing justice to who you are to me, so I'll just tell you face-to-face, forever and ever all the ways you make everything worthwhile. I love you and I like you.

Thank you all. We did it. We deserve this. Everything!

Introduction

Sporting Blackness and Critical Muscle Memory on Screen

Yes, and the body has memory. The physical carriage hauls more than its weight. The body is the threshold across which each objectionable call passes into consciousness—all the unintimidated, unblinking, and unflappable resilience does not erase the moments lived through, even as we are eternally stupid or everlastingly optimistic, so ready to be inside, among, a part of the games.

—CLAUDIA RANKINE, *Citizen: An American Lyric*

In *Citizen*, Claudia Rankine poetically assesses the racial imaginary, detailing episodic transgressions, microaggressions, and violent acts that are endemic to Black quotidian experiences.[1] Composed of prose-poetry, images from popular culture, and work from Black artists such as David Hammons, Glenn Ligon, and Carrie Mae Weems, *Citizen* is visually punctuated and "thematically unified—its question one of intimacy, its fabric the intersection of social and personal realities, its bruising frame one of race."[2] Rankine reflects on tennis icon Serena Williams, who for many is the GOAT (Greatest [Athlete] of All Time). She examines Williams's on-court rage—her fury and frustration over sporting and other slights—that has her stereotyped as an "angry Black woman," among other racial tropes. Rankine calls attention to the overt racism and mocking Williams faced from officials, fans, and even her fellow tennis pro and friend Caroline Wozniacki. Williams, as well as her sister Venus, have been subject to an "ambivalent reception in the [white and wealthy] sporting world" of tennis because of their athletic dominance on the court, which has made them outliers as much as outsiders in the sport.[3] As Nicole Fleetwood further explicates, their public treatment "uncovers a serious divide in how race, gender, and physical prowess are perceived by black fans of the sisters and the majority of white sports journalists and tennis fans."[4] White athletes are thought to embody tennis's cultural and sporting norms. Through their participation, the Williams sisters contest and transform the narrow ideals associated with the sport in a dramatically public fashion. Rankine describes the years of Williams's strength and dignity on the court in the face of individual and institutional hostility as a "kind of resilience appropriate only for those who exist in celluloid."[5] Williams, she attests, dwells within representational and discursive spaces specific to Black women's experiences in American society.

Rankine assesses how Williams's sporting blackness in the tennis arena, historically an exclusively white space, becomes a site of racial projection, shaped by her identity and play as a kind of athletic enclosure bound by history, celebrity, politics, money, and fear.[6] Drawing on Zora Neale Hurston's words—"I feel most colored when I am thrown against a sharp white background"—Rankine's essay produces an affective mapping of Williams's experiences of "curious calls and oversights" throughout her career, including the incidents at the 2004 and 2009 US Opens.[7] Indexing a ledger of racial slights against the tennis pro, Rankine suggests that these moments are symptomatic of sporting and systemic issues that trap Williams's body in a racial imaginary, an unlevel playing field where the rules are applied discriminately against her. She also traces the projection of Williams's experiences outward: "Every look, every comment, every bad call blossoms out of history, through her, onto you. To understand is to see Serena as hemmed in as any other black body thrown against our American background."[8] With Williams, Rankine reminds us that sporting blackness—racial and athletic identity at play—operates within a signifying paradigm and functions as a mode and motor of experiential overlap between the extraordinary Black sports star and the everyday Black person. As the introductory epigraph claims, Williams's physicality and bearing can be read as historical, even if they are historically unprecedented. This is because the body has memory, carries more than its weight, and keeps score of its encounters. Rankine's description of race as epiphenomenal, lived largely in quotidian moments and yet experienced via phantasmic projection, suggests a kind of historiography, intra- and intertextuality, and sociality of the Black sporting body.

For example, in an interview with Rankine for the *New York Times Magazine*, Williams conveys a critical assessment of her own physicality, wherein she measures her faults and successes on the court in relation to other Black tennis players, stating: "Zina Garrison, Althea Gibson, Arthur Ashe and Venus opened so many doors for me. I'm just opening the next door for the next person."[9] Within her remarks, so lacking in braggadocio, is an enunciation and valorization of Black womanhood; Black sporting history; and the interventions made in, via, and by Black athletes and their skills on the professional tennis court. Williams reads her own athletic achievements and global recognition within a narrative of collective racial progress, one firmly situated within the genealogy of Black American tennis players, such "that in addition to being a phenomenon, she has come out of a long line of African-Americans who battled for the right to be excellent in such a space that attached its value to its whiteness and worked overtime to keep it segregated."[10]

I draw on Rankine's essay and interview with Williams because both demonstrate a way to think through not only the sporting and social measure of blackness but also the formal consequences of the Black body as an excessive force that, as evidenced by Williams, is in direct contradistinction to and complicates the overall impression of what sport (and specifically women's tennis) is and means. Her incantatory excellence—also known as "Black girl magic"—in the sport compulsively exceeds and revises the standards of play that have been established, a surpassing intensity that, as Williams explains, transformed tennis forever, "not because [she and Venus] were welcomed, but because [they] wouldn't stop winning."[11] As game changers, both sisters' bodies were cast as anomalous to the sport—not quite right/not quite white for women's tennis—and, in turn, altered expectations and set new standards for sports in general.[12] During her career, Williams specifically "made a decision to be excellent while still being Serena," an athletic morphogenesis that is outside the conventional gender and racial constitution and conditioning of the sport.[13] In other words, Williams's sporting blackness belies mythic notions of meritocracy and white superiority in tennis and beyond as well as dogged attempts to equate blackness with inferiority, failure, and cheating. She has achieved her stellar and unparalleled athletic career without conforming to white sporting conventions. Rather, she wins blackly, via a virtuosic Black body in all of its cornrowed, catsuited, and Crip-walking glory. As Fleetwood explains, "Williams's style of playing tennis, her 'grunting,' the musculature of her body, and her clothing produce affective responses that play into polarized discourses where such choices are embraced by many of her black and progressive fans while questioned by the normative American public as markers of the black figure's unwillingness, or even inability, to conform to American and European conventions of sporting, femininity, and social cues."[14] From her long-standing reign as the Women Tennis Association's World No. 1 player, her twenty-three and counting Grand Slams, her fashionista tennis outfits, her motherhood and sisterhood, and her most recent controversy at the 2018 US Open where she called the umpire a "liar" and "thief," Williams's body compels and challenges us to confront "our investments in the signs that we employ to make sense of her athleticism and embodiment."[15] In other words, her sporting blackness is a disruptive body-at-work and impresses upon, manipulates, and restructures codification and conventions (figure 1).

FIGURE 1.   Serena Williams in her Nike catsuit at the 2018 French Open at Roland Garros. Photo by Jean Catuffe/Getty Images.

In this book, I work within the celluloid, focusing on sports films to analyze their depictions of sporting blackness and to theorize the anatomy of shared embodied experiences in a manner that parallels both Rankine's critical assessment of Williams's embodied histories and the tennis star's assertion of Black lineages and collective achievement (and defeat) against the idea of athletic exceptionalism and a dehistoricized Black sporting body. I also demonstrate how the Black body, thrown against the sharp white background of generic and social conventions that shape pervasive ideas of racial identity, operates as a historical force that exceeds the formal structures and representational strictures of sports films. Because the body's "physical carriage hauls more than its weight," I attend to the freighted racial representations and formal consequences of a study of blackness and historiography grounded in and through the on screen Black sporting body. In doing so, I evaluate the practices of Black memory at work within individual characters, athletes, filmmakers, critics, and audiences/fans, even if they are often at odds with or occluded by dominant film modes and conventions specific to the sports film genre.

FROM SKIN IN THE GAME TO SKIN IN THE GENRE

My purpose in this book is to scrutinize the performative embodiment of blackness that is confirmed and contested by representations of Black athletes in film, specifically, but also sports media and culture more generally. Sports films are not simply narratives about athletes in rule-governed contests; they are also allegorical stories of physical racialization. The sports films under investigation here foreground the disciplined, competitive, excellent, and failing Black body across documentaries, feature-length melodramas and comedies, experimental short films and videos, television series, and music videos. *Sporting Blackness* offers macrocosmic as well as close reads of how narratives become embodied and examines how representations of Black athletes can intervene in and supersede their loaded iconography. I argue that representations of Black sporting bodies contain what I call "critical muscle memories," embodied, kinesthetic, and cinematic histories that go beyond a film's diegesis to index, circulate, reproduce, and/or counter broader narratives about Black sporting and non-sporting experiences in American society.

The sports film is an under-theorized genre, particularly in terms of race and representation. Much of the scholarship on blackness and sports films focuses on what I call "skin in the game," meaning narrative strategies for representing race in sports films and the stereotypes attached to representations of Black athletes, an already tropified and mythologized (and often male) body in the public imagination. There has been little attention to how blackness functions in sports films beyond an analysis of the politics of representation and the idea of positive or negative images. My concern for criticism that includes but also goes beyond studies of stereotyping as well as my broad interdisciplinary grounding—drawn from film and media, sports, gender, performance, critical race, and cultural studies—propels me to examine how racial representation impacts this film genre. I show how the portrayal of Black athletes in sports films has an important influence on pervasive ideas of racial identity and vice versa. I also consider the ways in which racial representations can be formally countered and, sometimes, revised in socially progressive ways.

I argue that we must conceptualize race in sports films not only in terms of content but also in terms of genre and film form. This is a charge predicated on the idea that we must, as Alessandra Raengo asserts, "think of blackness both as a challenge for film form and as a reservoir of surplus expressivity, mobility, affect, and pathos that has benefited film aesthetics since the cinema's inception."[16] I therefore pivot away from examining race in sports films solely in terms of "skin in the game" to include what I call "skin in the genre"—evaluating what Black characters, themes, and cinematic-athletic stylistics do to the sports film in terms of generic modes, codes, and conventions. As my opening exegesis on Serena Williams suggests, *Sporting Blackness* addresses how, despite stereotyping, the Black sporting body on screen is a threshold and a rendering force. It shapes, inflects, challenges, and upends sports cinema's ideologies, discourses, and conventions in order to make larger claims about the meanings, resonances, and intra- and intertextuality of the Black body in motion and contest in American cinema and society.

Race and *blackness* are not synonymous terms, nor are they on a chain of equivalence in sports films or my analysis of the genre. While *race* is often used to scientifically categorize differences among groups as naturalized, Henry Louis Gates Jr. explains that "race, in these usages, pretends to be an objective term of classification, when in fact it is a dangerous trope."[17] In American cinema, race has played and continues to play a significant role in the medium's development and textual systems. Daniel Bernardi argues that "race informed the inception and development of fictional narrative cinema—crossing audiences, authors, genres, studios, and styles."[18] In his trilogy on the "birth," "classical period," and "persistence" of whiteness in Hollywood films, Bernardi tracks how whiteness remains the norm; its cinematic pronouncements and permutations shape popular genre images and imaginings in visible and invisible ways.[19] Popular genres, then, "are perhaps the most obvious place to look for the reflection of ideologies and myths over cinematic time, mainly because they rely on reoccurring themes and motifs in order to play to viewer expectations."[20] As such a popular genre, classic and contemporary sports films represent and narrate ideologies of race (alongside other axes of identity including gender, sexuality, ability, ethnicity, nationality, etc.) in ways done previously by other popular genres such as the western, musical, and action film, making whiteness appear natural, seamless, and patriotic.[21] Hollywood sports films function in a similar manner to these other genres in popular culture. These mainstream works often discount and dissimulate the importance of race as they propagate predominately utopic, "color-mute" stories meant to affirm mythologies of excellence, individualism, and self-reliance in American society.[22]

My focus on Black representation in the genre locates race within and through the mediated sporting images, history, and achievements of Black diasporic peoples.[23] At the intersection of sports film and Black film criticism, *Sporting Blackness* examines American films about Black athletes in the United States, principally represented in the games of basketball and football. My attention to cinematic examples drawn primarily from these sporting worlds stems from the contemporary magnitude of these sports in popular culture and their importance (in terms of participation and cultural impact) to African American communities. While baseball *was* the Black national pastime and boxing has a long-standing sporting and cinematic history, basketball, even more so than football, "saturates popular culture and permeates our national identity."[24] As basketball players circulate as celebrities/ambassadors of US culture in domestic and global markets, this sport (which dominates the majority of the films discussed in this book) looms massively in our contemporary public imagination and the cultural production of sporting blackness. Additionally, given the national parameters of the genre and my project, soccer (fútbol), which globally is the most popular game among African nations and in South American countries such as Brazil (the country with the largest Black diasporic population), has been left out of consideration, as have films and videos made and funded outside US cinematic infrastructures (e.g., studios, graduate school, art galleries, grants, etc.).[25]

With *Sporting Blackness*, I use and expand existing scholarship on genre and Black representation in American cinema. Unlike more studied categories such as race films, Blaxploitation, and '90s urban films, sports films are not bound by a specific film movement, temporal period, or production culture. Focusing on the broad and loosely defined genre of sports cinema, this book contributes to the work of scholars engaged with concepts of "race" and "ethnicity" in genre criticism.[26] I categorize the sports films discussed here as a "Black body genre." My use of the term *body genre* nods toward but is distinct from Linda Williams's description of the forms, functions, and systems that structure the representational and spectatorial excesses evidenced in the body genres of pornography, horror, and melodrama.[27] By *Black body genre*, I mean that sports films centralize Black athletes' corporeal performance as a spectacle, such that blackness is realized, mitigated, succumbed to, and disavowed via cinema's regimes of representation. Black bodies' visual and racial excess organizes the representational forms, functions, and systems of the genre in various ways. The idea, then, of the Black body in this book is slippery and has shifting meanings that try to grapple with its materiality, abstractedness, psychic manifestations, gendering, and historical contexts. I reference and situate the Black body in time and space as a physical and corporeal being. But I also attend to how, as Harvey Young explicates, "when popular connotations of blackness are mapped across or internalized within black people, the result is the creation of *the black body*. This second body, an abstracted and imagined figure, shadows or doubles the real one."[28] In this case, the Black body becomes primarily a repository for discrimination, racism, terror, and violence. I recognize, as Young suggests, that "we always see ourselves from a distance and from the (imagined) vantage point of another. It is the imagined and, yet, highly (mis)recognizable figure who shadows the actual, unseen body."[29] In this register, the Black body is not a body at all but a psychic recognition of blackness by the Black subject, or what Frantz Fanon understood as the epidermalization of race and the colonial encounter.[30] Finally, as I consider in greater depth in chapter 3, gender is consequential to the rendering and effacing of the Black body. While I oscillate between these manifold connotations and dimensions of embodiment, I always ground my analysis of the Black body within specific generic, cultural, historical, social, and political contexts.

Through this categorization, I contend that contemporary sports films offer a vaulted if underappreciated viewpoint on the Black body given their racial representation concentration, mirroring the hypervisibility of Black athletes—particularly via televised and live games—in US competitive sports, specifically football, basketball, baseball (I am thinking Black Dominicans and Puerto Ricans here), and track and field. While using contemporary US film and critical race scholarship on the Black body, I locate and follow across these works the raced sporting body's historical and spectacular functions in service to and in excess of cinematic and national ideologies of value, self, and surplus. In my close readings throughout the book, I extend this consideration of the Black sporting body's sedimented meanings, which meld and overlay the symbolic and the historic, to Black sporting figures' representational schemas in media and to the production of resonant and shared experiences.

SPORTING BLACKNESS ON SCREEN

Sporting Blackness argues that sports films are an important genre for representing race in American cinema, particularly blackness as kinetic and kinesthetic movement, modes, and meanings.[31] As a genre, sports films blur cinematic and social worlds, drawing on real sports history, events, and figures to construct themselves as part of a recognizable reality. The formal verisimilitude (cinematography and editing conventions that mimic television sports coverage), actor's physical training (making them credible as athletes), and overall studio production infrastructure (location shooting, uniforms, technical consultants) work together to make these films assuredly plausible, pleasurable, and predictable. These elements cohere within Hollywood film genres, such as the biopic, in formulaic ways that recycle standard narratives about (white, male) athletic heroes whose hard work, self-sacrifice, and paternalistic coaches help them overcome obstacles to win the big game in the end. Issues of race and the histories of racialization often do not go beyond the surface and are easily constrained to the playing field. Remember, this is a conservative genre where structural inequalities can be overcome by a buzzer-beater or a dignified loss; the latter, of course, being punctuated by an emotionally (dis)ingenuous slow clap.[32]

As they manipulate athletes' histories into inspirational narratives and filter real events into sanitized sporting worlds, sports films are made to appear factual and intrinsic, grounded in the historicity of the genre's conventions. This documentary impulse engages sports films' historicity, and thus how the genre represents the sporting body as connected to situated histories, communities, and national contexts even as it effaces how these contexts shape social identity. "Blackness in motion," as James Snead explains, "is typically sensed as a threat on screen and so black movement in film is usually restricted to highly bracketed and containable activities, such as sports and entertainment."[33] Sports films blend these two enterprises. Whether drawing on nostalgia or realism, sports films' inscriptions of athletic verisimilitude into idealized narratives "offer a powerful and decidedly secure medium in which classed, gendered, and racialized ideas, bodies, and structures are constructed, circulated, and consumed."[34] The Black athletic body is constituted in sports films as (hyper)visible and the narrative containment of its physical and discursive spectacle and excess is a common narrative arc seen in films such as *Glory Road* (James Gartner, 2006) via control over playing style, *Coach Carter* (Thomas Carter, 2005) via paternal disciplining by the head coach, and *The Hurricane* (Norman Jewison, 2009) via incarceration of a boxer on the rise. In these conventional movies, Black athletes perform spectacular, stylized athletic feats that often reinforce the racial status quo whereby "every critique doubles as a celebration."[35]

As Aaron Baker has convincingly argued, sports films are not, like sports themselves, apolitical; they "contribute to the contested process of defining social identities" including race, gender, sexuality, class, and nationality.[36] Despite the overdetermined formulas that structure the genre, even the tritest narratives and most hegemonic representations of Black athletes expose ideological contradictions. For example, a biopic about Black sprinter and long-jumping legend Jessie Owens is called *Race* (Stephen Hopkins, 2016), a title meant to highlight his sport *and* blackness even in a narrative that subsumes the significance of race in favor of celebrating Owens (played by Stephen James) as an apolitical and color-mute national hero.[37] In the tradition of recent biopics about pioneering Black athletes such as *42* (Brian Helgeland, 2013), which recounts when Jackie Robinson broke Major League Baseball's (MLB) color line in 1947, *Race* telescopes in on a few years of Owens's life, peaking at his moment of Olympic glory at the age of twenty-two. The film details little of Owens's tumultuous life after this point, including the racism he faced upon returning to the United States and his struggles to find employment. At one point in his later life, despite being a beloved national hero, Owens raced against horses to make money to support himself. While Owens's personal life and motivations hazily make up the film's subplot, *Race* revels in the sprinter's record-breaking days at Ohio State and exalts his athletic feats at the 1936 Summer Olympic Games in Berlin, Germany, including his victorious long jump and 100-meter, 200-meter, and 4×100-meter relay races. The film shows that, while his record-breaking four gold medals decimated Nazi ideals of white superiority, his sporting successes did not isolate him from racism back home. As the film ends, it briefly mentions that President Franklin D. Roosevelt refused to invite Owens to the White House to honor his accomplishments.

While trafficking in racial narratives, *Race* suggests that skin color does not matter and undermines the importance of Owens, as a Black American man, competing in Germany during Hitler's reign. The film attempts to nullify this significance by pushing forth a competing ideological narrative that suggests that sports are apolitical even when they are being used as international metonyms for the mediation of supremacy. For example, in his decision to run in Berlin after being pressured to boycott the Olympics by the Black community, Owens expresses to his coach Larry Snyder (Jason Sudeikis)—the film's requisite white, paternalistic sports sage—the idea that race matters socially but not in sports. When running, he explains: "In those ten seconds, there is no black or white. There is only fast or slow." The track, in this sense, is an arena for the physical transcendence of race, wherein the only measure of a man's worth is his sporting ability. In *Race*, the cultural fiction and lived dimensionality of race is expunged; winning is self-defining because, in sports, winning is everything. In this view (and counter to the film's title and telos), only the result—not race—matters. In the end, *Race* frames sporting blackness as an obstacle (like the hurdles Owens jumps in the film) to be overcome in order to truly succeed in sports and American society.

Race is not much different from the conventional, "feel good" sports cinema that populates the contemporary media landscape, including acclaimed films like *The Blind Side* (John Lee Hancock, 2009), which lobotomizes the life story of left tackle Michael Oher into a "Black Frankenstein"/ white savior narrative, or fan favorites such as *Remember the Titans*, the interracial football fantasy based on the real T.C. Williams's Titans that showed "how the goal line came to replace the color line."[38] In fact, *Race's* trite conventions are in keeping with many films I examine or reference in this book such as *Friday Night Lights* (Peter Berg, 2004) and *Juwanna Mann* (Jesse Vaughan, 2002), which, despite their respective twists on the genre, operate in typical sports film fashion. However, I am insisting that Black sporting bodies can representationally and formally disrupt and protest their stereotypical depictions and conservative generic scripts. An analysis of sporting blackness, then, becomes a way to get at the explicit and implicit work going on in these texts as well as the work we can do with these representations. This is an improvised labor that operates against sports films' entrenched position in the flow of capital as lucrative entertainment with formulaic modes of ideological storytelling: white saviors, individual achievement through gradualism, Black straight romance, poverty as moral depravity, and so on. *Sporting Blackness* demonstrates how the Black sporting body functions as an unruly historical force that exceeds the generic constraints within sports films' idealized worlds to challenge not only the construction of social identities but also the historical narratives attached to those identities and the formal ways in which they are enacted on screen.

To properly situate the mythos of race as a cultural fiction endemic to sports films, it is necessary to understand the protocols and investments in the representation of blackness in American cinema. Blackness has always been a mutable subjectivity on screen. Its representational fluidity is devised from the ways in which "Black skin on screen became a complex code for various things."[39] Even when there are no Black bodies represented, as James Snead describes, Black racial imagery codes Hollywood films, making legible the devices of mythification, marking, and omission that shape the capacious meanings attached to blackness on screen. As evidenced from the ubiquitous blackface and minstrelsy images in US film history and visual culture, the cinematic Black body is a commodified and overdetermined figure with surplus value and expressivity.[40] However, the overdetermined cinematic Black body is not just a repository of symbolic excess but also a floating signifier, shifting meaning and enunciative functions depending on the sociohistorical context.

The Black filmic image, and specifically the Black sporting filmic image, has been a subject of concern and control throughout cinema's history. For example, this fear of Black representation, identification, and visual/symbolic excess is acutely personified in the fight pictures of John Arthur "Jack" Johnson during American cinema's silent era. Johnson, who was the first Black boxing heavyweight champion, shaped in defining ways early cinema, censorship laws, and the representation of sporting blackness in the public imagination. As Dan Streible recounts:

> During his reign as heavyweight boxing champion from 1908 to 1918 a radically new African American representation forced its way onto the screen. Motion pictures of his daunting knockouts of white champions Tommy Burns (1908), Stanley Ketchel (1909), and—especially—Jim Jeffries (1910) helped break other racial barriers imposed in the age of Jim Crow. Highly publicized feature-film presentations showing Johnson pummeling "white hopes" offered a potent challenge to the social conceptions of race upon which segregation was built. The African American community used these films as occasions for celebration and affirmation when they played on the emerging black theater circuit. White reception of Johnson's image, after some initial curiosity and tolerance, however, was marked by alarm over this icon of black power.[41]

Johnson's screen presence made him the "first black movie star."[42] The racial spectacle of Johnson defeating Jeffries, in particular, for the heavyweight title—a spectacle that shattered the myth of Black athletic inferiority and white supremacy—not only affected the circulation and later censorship of fight pictures but also brokered the larger debates around the medium of film and its place in American culture. "Part of what troubled white commentators so much," sports sociologist Ben Carrington explains, "was not just Johnson's disruption of past racial logics, important as they were in sustaining the present, but what he portended about *future* racial conflicts in which the future suddenly began to look black."[43] As Johnson's cinematic sporting blackness evidences, *looking* Black as embodied and projected states of being and becoming, underscores how the Black athletic body in American cinema has historically performed in excess of itself, containing surplus meanings that always position it both inside and outside a film's singular narrative and representation.[44] In considering both sports films' historicity and the cinematic Black body's surplus expressivity, *Sporting Blackness* addresses how sports cinema shapes Black sporting bodies into what Stuart Hall calls "canvases of representation," whereby the Black sporting body is a creative and mutable corpus, a text made of texts, able to mean and mean again on screen and across media ecologies.[45]

Throughout the book, I focus on the cultural signifiers of US blackness, which are contingent on the historical specificities, social engagement, and cultures and economies of production, distribution, and reception. To "sport blackness" is to challenge film and sports culture, especially for the fact that Black surplus expressivity and projectability is largely fashioned around Black excellence in athletic worlds. Sports films largely absorb, ignore, or disavow the challenging concepts that the films analyzed in this book bring to the screen via historical framing, contestations of Black iconicity, athletic genders in absurd and feminist registers, and revolt (of the Black athlete and the Black filmmaker). I query here race's both flattened and overdetermined functionality within the sports cinema genre, wherein reliance on stereotyping and the received racist notions of Black players and Black communities constrict the narrative to the national telos of race. Blackness here is less a stable racial category and more precisely a theoretical motor, a moving and contested discourse and performance by, of, and between Black sporting subjects. If "race is a story about power that is written onto the body," as Carrington explains, "then sport is a powerful, and perhaps at certain moments even a pivotal, narrator in that story."[46] Sports, therefore, becomes an important armature, medium, and modality for studying the rendering of the Black body in American cinema. An understanding of sporting blackness and its attendant critical muscle memories demonstrates how race, sport, and cinema tell "a *moving, visual, and contemporary* story that [is] not relegated to describing the past but [reveals] the flow of history into the present and even into the future."[47]

CRITICAL MUSCLE MEMORY

I coined and deploy the phrase *critical muscle memory* to articulate the material and tangled histories of Black athleticism in sports films. The phrase and its meanings come from human kinetics, which studies "the motions of bodies and the forces acting upon them."[48] Thus, I use the phrase to characterize the inherent property of muscles as well as engage the interdisciplinary work on corporeality and memory in Black literature and cultural studies. In human kinetics, muscle memory is the process by which motor skills are remembered in the brain and enacted through the body. A form of motor learning, muscle memory is mimetic and procedural, whereby the muscles of a given body consolidate, encode, and come to habituate or memorize specific tasks through the repetition of physical action and long-lasting changes in muscle tissue.

Muscle memory is not just physiological. While it manifests through movement and ritualistic exercise, this form of long-term memory is also a cognitive process, with motor and brain systems working in tandem. In neuroscience, the term is something of a misnomer, as it suggests that muscles make and or store their own memories. Instead, "they respond to signals from the brain, where the actual memories of any particular movement are formed and filed away."[49] While there is some debate about whether locomotory behavior and responses can be driven by independent muscle contractions, the notion that the body remembers repeated action propels many movement-based arts and exercises, including acting, dance, music, and athletics.[50] In this sense, choreographed and improvisational movements enact routine and trained skills and behaviors across time and space. A form of "kinesthetic intelligence," the body has a "kind of spatial intelligence that operates through the muscles and includes muscle memory."[51] For athletes, this combined kinesthesia and proprioception allows them, through the rigors and discipline of training, to actively reproduce past movements seemingly without conscious effort. In sports, reinforced physical learning comes from belabored practices and repeated exercises such as drills, moves, and practice scenarios. Not only a form of mental priming, muscle memory as bodily instruction and mechanics likewise allows for efficiency, endurance, and perceived effortlessness, even if one does not reach hypertrophy. Often the effect of countless hours of training, athletic muscle memory is a ritualistic neural process that manifests through the sporting body in terms of skills and registers as fluidity on the field of play.

The kinesthetic metaphor of muscle memory has been used to theorize Black corporeality, individuality, and sociality in a range of disciplinary settings, including sports literature and philosophy. For example, C.L.R. James's seminal book *Beyond a Boundary* employs the concept in its description of cricket as a "dramatic spectacle" and "visual art."[52] James explains that cricket athletes have muscular memory, one that activates the spectator's embodied memory of their own movement to produce a kind of intra-corporeal and inter-corporeal sensibility. He describes cricket athletes' actions in terms of tactile values that accumulate, explaining: "In our world human beings are on view for artistic enjoyment only on the field of sport or on the entertainment stage [but] what is not visible is received in the tactile consciousness of thousands who have themselves for years practiced the same motion and know each muscle that is involved in each stroke."[53] Following James's critical link between athletes and entertainers, Michelle Ann Stephens extends his theory to an analysis of actor, athlete, and activist Paul Robeson's physique and presence, using the metaphor and poetics of his bodyline to concatenate sites of relationality and performative contexts.[54] Both James and Stephens underscore how Black athletes/actors' individuated movements and gestures (meaning distinct style) engender muscular reflexes that are at once corporeal and incorporeal, subjective and intersubjective. In other words, sporting bodies' individual styles operate within dramatic playing fields of shared physical histories and popular consciousness.

With such contingency, bodily symptoms—particularly muscle tension—are used as metaphors to describe a kind of quotidian muscle memory for Black people, athletes or otherwise. Darieck Scott, for instance, reads Frantz Fanon's notion of muscle tension—a psychic and bodily reaction to colonialism at once mental and physical—as a diagnostic "response to racial and colonial domination, as a kind of bodily knowledge."[55] Communal Black memory, a bodily knowledge, bearing, and conditioning for being in the world, then, repeats itself in and through individual encounters. For example, drawing on the history of the image of Emmett Till's mutilated body, Elizabeth Alexander explains that "the corporeal images of terror suggest that 'experience' can be taken into the body via witnessing and recorded in muscle memory as knowledge. This knowledge is necessary to one who believes 'it would be my turn next.'"[56] Black memory, then, becomes a muscle trained, flexed, and disciplined by colonialism, enslavement, and racial terror, as well as collective Black struggle, achievement, and cultural engagement.

Harvey Young's study of Black boxers Tom Molineaux, Jack Johnson, Joe Louis, and Muhammad Ali's similar and repeated embodied experiences of captivity provides an instructive template for reading athletic Black memory, in my terms, as critical muscle memory. For Young, Houston Baker's term *critical memory* gets at the notion of phenomenological blackness, or how collectivized Black experiences "invite a consideration of history, habit, memory and the process of racial mythmaking."[57] Chronicling performances of stillness and resistance in athletics, among other arenas, Young relates "how similar experiences of the body repeat within the lives of black folk and how select individuals have employed expressive forms to relay their stories and life lessons to largely unimagined future audiences."[58] He focuses on the stilled Black sporting body as a target of violent racial projections in order to "[spotlight] the ways in which *an* idea of the black body has been and continues to be projected across actual physical bodies."[59] In doing so, he "chronicles how the misrecognition of individuated bodies as 'the black body' creates similar experiences."[60] Young mobilizes this notion of the misrecognition of Black bodies by others and oneself as a type of embodied double consciousness that unites and structures the shared experiences of Black people in society as individuated multiplicities.

Muscle memory as a kind of critical analysis/analytic method works to formally disrupt the rehearsed meanings and monological citations that, through their representational iterations, collapse Black athletes, media makers, and critics, as well as everyday people into having the same dim memories. Rather, critical muscle memory as a Black film scholarly tool and technique asserts how, to mobilize Young, "related histories of discrimination, violence, and migration result in similar experiences. Critical [muscle] memory invites consideration of past practices that have affected the lives and shaped the experiences of black folk."[61] In this book's capacity to unpack the dense fibers—textuality, framing, and projection—of Black representation in sports films, critical muscle memory examines the dimensionality of the Black body and the density of blackness. It articulates the historical depth of sporting blackness's (s)well(s) of allusive resonance; asking and answering the question: how deep is the color?[62]

What is "critical" in my elaboration of Black bodies' intra- and intertextuality as muscle memory is the corporeal and epistemic possibilities of the Black sporting body. Critical muscle memory projects Black historiography as an exhibitive mode of seeing and knowing the filmic Black sporting body that exceeds a static frame/framing on screen. The concept is grounded in and through morphological (re)compositions of the body. The Black athlete performs an urgency to read history as racialized corporeality via prosthetic metaphors and bodily mechanisms—joints, attachments, connective tissues, appendages, fractures, appendices, and so on. This corporeality is lived, shared, and constructed in relation to cinema's representational schema. To this point, I draw here on Grant Farred's understanding of the cinematic

Black sporting bodies' representational power and excess. He explains that "the black athlete, in contradistinction to her or his white counterpart, is never permitted the historical luxury of only 'personal' representation."[63] Without such allowance, "the black athlete always speaks, because of the history of violence done to the black body, both in history itself and in the history of the cinema for more than that particular black Self" and thus is "always simultaneously in excess of itself and less than itself: it speaks for its broader community, which means that the single, exceptional individual is always less than the totality of that community."[64] Farred articulates a shared speculation of the signifying power and accretive properties of the Black sporting body, one that I refine through the specific modalities of kinesis, cinema's capacities, and the notion of critical muscle memory. In doing so, I am able to explore representationally and formally what it means to embody, perform, play out, and contest race and the histories associated with sporting blackness on screen.

Throughout *Sporting Blackness*, I use the concept of critical muscle memory as both a descriptive term (and thus sometimes refer to it syntactically as "muscle memory") and an analytical tool to examine filmic representations of Black sporting bodies characterized by this physiological force and phenomenological process. As descriptor, it connotes the acting out and contestations of dominant regimes and codes that treat Black sporting bodies as ahistoric or exceptional. Since most sports films are about real sports figures/history, many of these cinematic bodies already have a known and often acritical source, a shared national history with a usually recorded and/or televised sporting past that can be easily recalled and referenced. As an analytical tool, critical muscle memory disrupts these factitious conventions of the sports film to focus on film content and form, performances and processes of cinematic representation, and the projection of racial differences and subjectivities. In the end, as descriptor and analytics, critical muscle memory provides the necessary dexterity to read these narratives of sporting blackness and study each film's formal capacities that represent and ideologically construct how meaning is made and remade through spectacles of the raced and gendered body in sports and cinema.

GOING INTO *OVERTIME*

Many contemporary artists have taken what Jennifer Doyle terms the "athletic turn," a maneuver that has reoriented our understanding of sporting spectacles, visual culture, and social practices.[65] Conceptual artist Hank

Willis Thomas's video *Overtime* (2011), for example, lucidly demonstrates how sporting blackness is a critical site for Black history's most troubling muscle memories on screen. *Overtime* is similar to Thomas's sports-related photographs *The Cotton Bowl* (2011), *And One* (2011), *Basketball and Chain* (2011), and *Strange Fruit* (2011) (figure 2). Blending trans-historical moments into the same photographic mise-en-scène, imagery of Black sharecroppers, shackle and chain, and lynching, respectively, share visual and discursive space with images of football and basketball players. Thomas's work is about framing in and as context, and these striking images reflect on the Black male sporting body as a site of consumption, violence, spectacle, exploitation, profit, and pleasure.[66] In a manner similar to his photographic oeuvre, most specifically *Strange Fruit*—which depicts a shirtless, Black basketball player, arms extended as if he is dunking; though, here, the basketball is caught in a hangman's noose—*Overtime* explores the legacies of lynching and the slam dunk, making explicit the implicit connections between racial terror and Black sportsmanship, the intertwined historical and economic forces whose confluence is an integral part of race, sports, capital, and Black sociality in the United States.

Overtime begins with a black screen. The image of a hangman's noose slowly appears in the tightly cropped, vertical frame. Swaying against this dark backdrop, the noose symbolizes racial terror as the instrument and emblem of lynching. The video's conceptual mise-en-scène is punctuated by a "haunting chorus that is a combination of a spiritual and a work song."[67] Oral percussionist Ditto shaped the soundscape, using voice and breath tones to auditorily convoke sensational bodily affects, attaching the real Black historical terror, labor, and violence to the reel of physical and meta-physical callisthenic activities. Fading to black, the image shifts to that of a white basketball court. Slipping out of the darkness, a Black basketball player enters the frame, dribbling in slow motion. He makes his way to center court where the noose, standing in for a basketball rim, hangs ominously. The player jumps to dunk the ball through the noose; his body twists, spinning 180-degrees in the air. His moment of "hang time" is fleeting—happening and unhappening—as he is both suspended in air and unable to fully dunk the ball.[68] The player and the noose disappear. The image fades to black as we are left reconsidering the spatial and temporal bounds of the court. Who, what, and when is being played here?

Overtime continues with more images of individual ballers and teams pitted against each other as they attempt to dunk in the noose, giving the viewer a sense that "history—not just a game—seems to hang in the balance."[69] As the title suggests, *Overtime*'s temporality mobilizes the idea of

FIGURE 2.   Hank Willis Thomas, *Strange Fruit*, 2011 © Hank Willis
Thomas. Courtesy of the artist and Jack Shainman Gallery, New York.

"extra time" in sports as an additive labor of "spook" bodies connected to the present and past game unfolding. The video uses slow motion and dissolves to position and remove the body within the video's frame, distilling the vestiges of lynching as a meta/physical presence and absence, what Tisa Bryant's writing on blackness within/without cinema histories describes as an unexplained present absence.[70] On occasion, Thomas elongates the visual symbolism of the court. The tightly framed video stretches the scene vertically, producing a paralleled and symmetrical mirror image of the noose and the basketball players that trouble our understanding of the progressive follow of history: which way is up? The geometrical extension of the rope operates as a tether that coordinates the timelines of history on an axis of terrorizing real and symbolic racial violence. The Black male basketball player is a relational spectacle and specter in and exceeding the game on screen. While some players do dunk through the noose, others hang from the rope, dangling within the frame, visually evoking the lyrics to the haunting song "Strange Fruit" sung by Billie Holiday: "Black bodies swinging in the southern breeze. Strange fruit hanging from the poplar trees"[71] The image is an extraordinarily ordinary violent sports and social spectacle. Black male sporting prowess is constructed as something to be revered and feared, a tortuous body hung and hinged to a history of sensational, performative, and ritualized acts of condemnation and consumption.

As a self-described "visual culture archeologist," Thomas engages forcefully in *Overtime* with histories of Black representation.[72] His archeological field and visual work here is the history not only of slavery and Jim Crow but also of capitalism—the commodification, mass production, and commercialization in advertising and marketing of the Black sporting body. Alongside the video's athletic iconography, the noose and the body are picked up as icons of history that are weighted by contemporary sports commercial overdeterminations and cultural referents. Most notably, the video is reminiscent of Nike's 2001 hit basketball commercial "Freestyle" (directed by Paul Hunter), where professional basketball players and street ballers freestyled moves with a basketball syncopated to the Afrika Bambaataa and Soulsonic Force hip hop classic "Planet Rock." Sporting blackness in both the Nike commercial and Thomas's *Overtime* becomes an acoustic technology of kinetic movement, a rhythm of choreographed Black athletic bodies laboring on the court as performative sporting spectacles.

In its five minute running time, *Overtime* evinces the ways in which sporting blackness and critical muscle memory operates and is rendered throughout this book. The video formally portrays the Black sporting body as both a dynamic current event and a historical situation. In doing so, it casts the body within multiple spectacular entanglements; or what Young calls "charged racialized and racializing scenarios in which [Black-skinned] experiences assume a more active and, indeed, determining role in a person's lived experience."[73] Through its focus on the Black body, Thomas's *Overtime* sutures and enmeshes disparate time periods, revealing structuring absences foundational to spectacles of sport along color (base)lines: black courts, white arenas. As an art gallery video installation, it stages historical crises of racial violence as a conceptual game played by Black men that tightly knots this nation's historical racial terror with basketball as a lucrative and popular form of entertainment.

Overtime is a counter-representation of blackness on screen. Blackness in sports culture and its plethora of media is a visual marker, cipher, and dark-skinned container for assigned and accrued meanings that embody Black histories and communities, deviance and excellence, discipline, and instinct. The video aesthetics mine these representational excesses. As exhibition director Richard Klein notes, *Overtime*'s visual power comes from Thomas's formal choices, particularly his dramatic manipulation of light and darkness.[74] The video's digital effects conjure the Black sporting body but also remind us of the functioning of Black bodies as illusory—there and not there—in American cinema, society, culture, and historical record. Thomas, to borrow a phrase from Toni Morrison, renders a kind of athletic "playing in the dark" on screen via a Black presence coming out of the dark shadows as a spectacular attraction to make us confront Black matters, memory, and history within and beyond the parameters of the court.[75] By playing in the dark and bringing history to the light, the video diffracts "a black refusal to be separate from blackness, from the unknown and the unknowable."[76] The visual effects exhibit this unconceivable process as evocative and expressionistic basketball play—of dunks, dribbles, crossovers, and going hard in the paint—and the editing operates in a manner similar to documentary and televisual sports footage. The video includes "repetition of a performance, often from a different angle; isolation in slow motion or image magnification; and multiple image contrasts that demonstrate how the featured athlete performs differently [or similarly] from his or her peers," which in this case are lynched Black bodies.[77] These formal choices make explicit Black athletic spectacularism and critical muscle memory as emphatically embodied and performed. In doing so, Thomas repeatedly stages scenes with the question: "What happens when the visual legacy of American lynching collides with the visual legacy of the slam dunk?"[78] With *Sporting Blackness*, I ask and answer a similar provocative query: What happens when the visual legacy of blackness in American cinema collides with the visual legacies of Black sporting bodies? In this book, I argue that the expressive historicity of the Black sporting body can be understood in terms of and is represented cinematically as critical muscle memory, a shared conduit to imagine, define, accrete, succumb to, or critically oppose embodied sporting and non-sporting histories now formalized within sport cinema's regimes of representation.

THE GAME PLAN

In my engagement with Black sports films, the case studies analyzed within this book are for the most part contemporary feature films, ranging from 1971 to 2019. The earliest film considered, the experimental short *Hour Glass* (1971), was made by Haile Gerima as a graduate student assignment during his first year in the film school at UCLA (within the nascent and as yet unnamed "LA Rebellion") but was not widely viewable until its release on DVD and made available for digital streaming in 2013. *Hour Glass* is thus not a "new" sports film, but it has resurfaced outside of its circumscribed exhibition context and curricular intent. The contemporary bent (films from the 2000s and on) of my study reflects a specific moment in Black and commercial filmmaking as well as a series of historical shifts in American cinema, sports, and society in terms of Black visibility.

Black representation in early sports films is largely marginal, and, more often than not, Black athletes are omitted in classic sports stories. "With the exception of a few race films," Aaron Baker explains, "African Americans appear only as minor characters (if at all) in feature-length movies about sports, from the coming of sound through the beginning of the civil rights movement."[79] In the 1930s, Black boxers appeared mostly in prizefighting films, including Joe Louis in *Spirit of Youth* (Harry L. Fraser, 1938) and Henry Armstrong in *Keep Punching* (John Clein, 1939). Black characters gained more substantial, albeit often supporting roles in sports films post World War II. During this period, Black athletes were employed on screen to define and edify their white protagonists as supporters of or obstacles to white athletes' advancements, evinced in narratives such as the boxing noir dramas *Body and Soul* (Robert Rossen, 1947) and *The Harder They Fall* (Mark Robson, 1956). In the 1950s, Black protagonists were given their own sporting narratives in *The Jackie Robinson Story* (Alfred E. Green, 1950) and *The Joe Louis Story* (Robert Gordon, 1953). While they privileged accounts of real-life Black athletic heroics, these films sanitize the social realities facing these sportsmen and filter their lives through the paternalistic lens of whiteness.[80] Concurrently, Black athletes such as Paul

Robeson, Woody Strode, Al Duval, Joe Lillard, and Kenny Washington were being marketed on screen in non-sports-related roles because of their exquisite physiques and popular appeal. As Charlene Regester clarifies in her vital study of football players and boxers turned actors in pre-1950s American cinema, Black athletes "were transformed into objects of both danger and desire because of their blackness and their sexuality, becoming symbols of masculinity for both black and white spectators."[81]

Because of this segregationist, sanitizing, and circumscribed history, sports films featuring Black characters in non-supporting roles are a relatively recent phenomenon, with films like *The Great White Hope* (Martin Ritt, 1970), *Brian's Song* (Buzz Kulik, 1971), *Cornbread, Earl and Me* (Joseph Manduke, 1975), and *The Bingo Long Traveling All-Stars & Motor Kings* (John Badham, 1976) forming a sports film canon about post-integration Black life: largely urban, often Northern, naturalistic in aesthetic, and pro–civil rights and Black Power in political stance. These films are linked to the larger corpus of Black action films of the 1970s, including B-films and Blaxploitation releases, and interracialist commercial studio fare. *Bingo Long* came out the same year as *Rocky* (John G. Avildsen, 1976), which starred former professional football player Carl Weathers and won the Academy Award for Best Picture, Best Director, and Best Film Editing, reigniting audiences and critics' interest in sports films more broadly. However, it is not until the late 1980s, 1990s, and principally the 2000s that we experience a well-financed and distributed glut of popular and, in some cases, prestigious fictional and nonfictional sports films about Black athletes and their sporting history, ranging from the mixed animation and live-action commercial fare of *Space Jam* (Joe Pytka, 1996) to the acclaimed two-part PBS documentary *Unforgivable Blackness: The Rise and Fall of Jack Johnson* (Ken Burns, 2004) to the sports industrial complex drama *He Got Game* (Spike Lee, 1998) to the *Rocky* franchise reboot with *Creed* (Ryan Coogler, 2015) and *Creed II* (Steven Caple Jr., 2018). Since the late twentieth/early twenty-first century, the number of films about Black athletes has grown exponentially, paralleling the greater visibility, acclaim, wealth, and significance of US Black athletes in the globalized arena of late capital and competitive sports, cable sports programming, merchandising and branding, and race and the (in)famous sports star. Finally, Black actors (and a few actresses) have found opportunities to flex their talents within the genre, with some actors such as Derek Luke, Omar Epps, Alphonso McAuley, and Rob Brown starring in multiple films about a variety of sports and sports figures. Their recurrent casting (often in biopics) attests to a surplus of athletic types in place of individuated characters, specificity, or nuance.[82] Such hyper-stereotyping or predetermined iconicity underscores not only sport cinema actor déjà vu, but also sports culture's "syncopation with a racialist logic that presents the black body especially as vitality, as raw force, as athleticism."[83] In this book, I interrogate the changing same of this representational fix and fixation through the concepts of sporting blackness and critical muscle memory and the insights they purvey.

While I engage with the history of race in the genre and refer to a compendium of cinematic examples, this book is neither a genealogy nor a complete survey of Black representation in sports films. *Sporting Blackness* studies distinct representational tropes and their formal consequences within and through broader cinematic, sporting, and social traditions, paradigms, practices, and histories. The book is organized into four chapters exploring filmic Black sporting bodies as historical contestants, racial icons, athletic genders, and rebellious athletes. These tropes provide a schema in which to evaluate sporting blackness in terms of a mode of production, transmedia figures and formats, gender performativity, and the upending of genre conventions. In the end, *Sporting Blackness* theorizes race and embodiment in terms of the sports film genre to understand blackness in motion and competition that applies in and outside of the delimiting boundaries and restrictions of the sports film genre.

The first chapter, "Historical Contestants in Black Sports Documentaries," develops my theses on sporting blackness and critical muscle memory within a grounded analysis of documentaries focused on Black historical and contemporary sports, and here I highlight how even within nonfictional modes, representations of race and history on screen are still preoccupied with spectacles of Black pathos and innovation. Given this emphasis on Black spectacularism, I argue that Black athletes, the central focus of these documentaries, are made not only sporting but historical contestants, figures and figurations that challenge and redress prevailing past, present, and future discourses on sports, history, and Black experiences in American society. Questioning, in Stuart Hall's terms, what is this "Black" in Black sports documentaries, I survey both Black documentary film and video and sports documentary traditions in order to examine the fundamental intersections between documentary theory and cinematic race and representation in nonfiction sports films. Unlike fictional sports films that draw on real sports history to tell conservative tales of Black heroics, Black sports documentaries delve into the archive and repertoire of Black athleticism to present the force of Black history and culture, as well as Black athletic and social feats when challenging Hollywood's simplistic and flattened sporting histories. I work with four sports documentaries: *On the Shoulders of Giants: The Story of the Greatest Team You've Never Heard Of* (Deborah

Morales, 2011); *This Is a Game, Ladies* (Peter Schnall, 2004); *Hoop Dreams* (Steve James, 1994); and *Hoop Reality* (Lee Davis, 2007). All four films attend distinctly to the power and structural limitations placed on Black athletic agency in the players' contested, negotiated and (dis)embodied acts of self-canvassing as/in cinematic sporting history. In the end, I make the case that Black sports documentaries are a discourse of and about critical muscle memory.

The second chapter, "Racial Iconicity and the Transmedia Black Athlete," further elucidates the book's thematics on the metaphorical iterability of Black embodiment, the constancy with which Black bodies are made to mean and mean again on screen. Instead of considering a subgenre of sports films, as I do in the first chapter, I telescope in on one "iconic" real-life figure whose sporting blackness travels across different media texts. I focus on the former football player James "Boobie" Miles, whose defeat on the gridiron is initially chronicled in H.G. Bissinger's bestselling nonfiction book *Friday Night Lights: A Town, A Team, A Dream* (1990), which morphed into NBC's short-lived *Against the Grain* (1993), Peter Berg's film *Friday Night Lights* (2004), the critically acclaimed NBC (2006–2008)/The 101 Network (2008–2011) drama *Friday Night Lights*, and rapper Big K.R.I.T's lyrics and videos for "Hometown Hero" and "Boobie Miles." Bissinger's book inaugurates the *Friday Night Lights* multimedia franchise, and Boobie, a transmedia character, travels across time and space to these affiliated and unaffiliated media texts. I read these transmedia representations of a poor southern Black football player's epic persona and tragic legend within the conceptual possibilities and limitations of racial iconicity as articulated by Nicole Fleetwood. In detailing how sporting blackness schematizes racial achievements and stigmas in these ever-shifting media contexts, I examine their attendant formulas and respective publics, which in many ways determine and condition each iteration's content and positionality. Boobie, as exemplar of transmedia sporting blackness, provides the critical complexity to analyze both a body within a text and also follow a body across texts to understand how each site necessitates a formal reengagement with Boobie's tangle of narratives. These representational reworkings of Boobie's subjectivity and his lasting cultural aftereffect form the changing same of his racial iconicity. Critical muscle memory constitutes both the situation and the structure of Boobie as icon within the cinematic apparatus and other performative locales.

The third chapter, "Black Female Incommensurability and Athletic Genders," addresses the critical absences of Black women on screen as well as the measure of gender in sporting blackness. If sporting blackness can affirm or deflate racial iconicity, this chapter troubles how, in both Black filmic culture and life, authority, legibility, and lionization are by default the purview of conventional Black masculine ideals: athletes, fathers, sons, strivers. There are very few sports films about Black women athletes, and women are usually regulated to subordinate roles as wives, mothers, and cheerleaders within the genre's staid gender codes. I enact a Black feminist analysis drawing on Michele Wallace's theorization of Black female negation and incommensurability in an analysis of Penny Marshall's *A League of Their Own* (1992) to explain how Black women's visible sporting bodies on screen are a formal challenge to a genre predicated on their invisibility. I then turn to two very different films about Black women in sports, Gina Prince-Bythewood's *Love and Basketball* (2000) and Jesse Vaughan's *Juwanna Mann* (2002), and scrutinize the representations in both surrounding performances of Black femininity and masculinity. Black women in sports worlds and Black heterosexual romance and misalliance result in sexual and gender panic around Black women's athleticism and inability to coherently signify as athlete and woman simultaneously. I, therefore, consider how the two films representationally explore critical muscle memory through athletic genders—a kind of sporting and social performativity—to examine comedic and romantic narratives of Black basketball along the gender binary. Ultimately, these films conform to dominant film codes via narrative suture. The endings, which disappear each film's more risk-taking and dangerous athletic genders to return to the social order, negate Black women's athletic viability.

The final chapter, "The Revolt of the Cinematic Black Athlete," begins with an opening description of Harry Edwards's call for the revolt of the Black athlete and Tommie Smith and John Carlos's 1968 Olympic protest. This world historical mediatic moment provides a grounding and critical entryway into analyzing how Haile Gerima's 1971 experimental film *Hour Glass* (made at UCLA during the "L.A. Rebellion") pictorializes a revolt of the Black athlete, international in scope and anticolonial in politics. Drawing on Trinh T. Minh-ha's notion of "bold omissions and minute depictions," I argue that Gerima's insurgent Black basketballer is sourced to and citational of Smith and Carlos's originary founding of a politics of liberation that synced the American Black athlete with worldwide struggles against racism, colonialism, and imperial domination. In imbuing imagery and sounds that coded Smith and Carlos's silence and fixed stance as alignment with international revolutionary foment, Gerima takes a standard film school assignment and relocates *Hour Glass* within the protocols of Third Cinema and Third World Liberation struggles and philosophies. *Hour Glass* achieves its intertextual and globalized resonance in ways both oblique and direct in keeping with experimental and Leftist film modes. The dialogue-less film coils its soundscape, emplotment, and dense symbolic and sonic registers around the nascent revolutionary consciousness of its central subject, a UCLA basketball player. The revolt of the Black cinematic athlete in *Hour Glass* is first signaled by his refusal to play, which is conceptually linked to Gerima's refusal of sports film contrivances and graduate school requirements that would have undone the film's avowed radical politics. Drawing on George Lipsitz's work on race as disruptive of genre categories such that racial discourses erupt on screen, I use the film's strategic redoubling and intertwining of Africanist philosophy and an individual act of Black refusal to "play the game" to think through the formal capacities of sporting blackness to undo ideological structures contained within sports films and film criticism.

In "The Fitness of Sporting Blackness," I conclude with an appraisal of the capacity, utility, and endurance of sporting blackness as a hermeneutic to understanding race, sports, and regimes of representation. I draw together my observations on "skin in the game" and "skin in the genre" discussed throughout the book, using my insights on the representational and formal consequences of blackness in sports cinema to both think specifically through Steven Soderbergh's *High Flying Bird* (2019) and broadly consider the current landscape of Black sports films. Finally, I gesture toward critical muscle memory's multivalent interpretive possibilities, specifically in terms of spectatorial affects and Black collective experiences.

Overall, *Sporting Blackness* registers the capacities of the Black cinematic sporting body as a historical force that circulates through, within, and beyond overlapping and interlocking racial discourses, regimes of representation, and generic and aesthetic practices. I theorize race variously as a mode and format, performance and performativity, and code and decoding device. The concepts of sporting blackness and critical muscle memory elucidate the entangling matrices of identity, sports, embodiment, and history. In doing so, Black bodies animate and activate sports films in ways that do and do not play by the rules of the game.

1. Historical Contestants in Black Sports Documentaries

Filmmakers have used nonfiction modes to historicize, entextualize, and recontextualize African Americans' participation in sports. They have embraced and exploited the visual medium's historiographic possibilities and formal strategies to interrelate sports and social issues, probing the impact and implications of sports on Black individuals and collectives' sense of progress on and off the playing field. These works often depict how "sports have historically provided an opportunity for blacks throughout the African diaspora to gain recognition through *physical struggle* not just for their sporting achievement in the narrow and obvious sense but more significantly and fundamentally for their humanity."[1] Framing Black athletes' physical struggles for recognition alongside their accomplishments and defeats within this sports and racial humanist paradigm, sports documentaries often use narratives about athleticism to chart historical shifts and address cultural and political issues specific to Black life while celebrating the spectacle and virtuosity of Black athletes in sporting worlds competitions. These emblematic televisual and theatrical nonfiction stories of racial achievement, "where individual acts and successes become symbolic of collective progress," often function as popular dramas, shaping the public imaginary of, for, and by Black people in American society.[2]

A study of sporting blackness on screen must consider documentary films for they are, by far, the dominant mode of production of sports cinema. At the same time, documentary films are important because they constellate key questions on race and generic forms, historiographic and representational practices, and the cinematic Black sporting body's capacity and utility as an image bank for race relations in the US. In this chapter, I examine the form and traditions of Black sports documentaries. Questioning, in Stuart Hall's provocative terms, what is this "Black" in

Black sports documentaries, I ground my analysis of this subgenre of nonfiction films within both Black documentary film and video traditions and sports documentary traditions. While bearing in mind the distinct strategies and practices of the Black sports documentary, I engage fundamental questions about the intersection of documentary theory and blackness in order to advance the idea that documentaries about Black sporting bodies constitute a genre of and about critical muscle memory.

As sports documentaries attempt to index sporting moments, thus developing our critical muscle memory of Black athleticism, they become an important form and forum to consider Black film and sporting historiography. Joshua Malitsky argues that sports documentaries typically assemble found footage from sporting events as their primary documents, thus indexing "the historical experience of our own mediated histories. [. . .] They offer evidentiary traces of the past, reworking them and signaling their articulation in the process."[3] Examining sports documentaries, I extend Malitsky's thinking in order to situate this formal process in terms of sporting blackness and the production of critical muscle memory as a subjugated form of knowledge and historiographic redress. If "historiography is about arranging and telling stories, not about delivering objective truth," then narratives constructed in this nonfiction production mode can be understood as producing, in Malitsky's estimation, "aesthetic memories," representational "referents with reference" that "[drench] us in the past" of our individual and collective mediated sporting experiences.[4] As I argue throughout this book, the Black sporting body is an expressive body, semiotically understood as a referent with references (a text made of texts) that contains and projects critical muscle memory. In this case, critical muscle memory is the ability for the documentary Black sporting body to echo history, exceed its iconography, and concatenate narratives of Black sporting and non-sporting experiences across spatial and temporal contexts within and beyond the body in and of the film.

Black athletes in sports documentaries are historical contestants, meaning figures and figurations that participate in and challenge prevailing discourses on sports, history, and Black experiences in American society. While I argue more broadly that this contested armature and trope can be read across film forms, here I examine the Black sporting body in four basketball documentaries: Deborah Morales's *On the Shoulders of Giants: The Story of the Greatest Team You've Never Heard Of* (2011), Peter Schnall's *This Is a Game, Ladies* (2004), Steve James's *Hoop Dreams* (1994), and Lee Davis's *Hoop Reality* (2007). The final two examples are studied in relationship to each other. All four examples attend to how sporting blackness becomes a historiographic force for the rendering and redressing of athletes' embodied sporting and non-sporting experiences.

On the Shoulders of Giants; This Is a Game, Ladies; Hoop Dreams; and *Hoop Reality* compel us to think about sporting blackness in terms of the documentary mode and the stylization of aesthetic memories "to critique the artistic, political, and ideological ends this stylization serves."[5] Therefore, I consider authorial voices and representational practices in these films, analyzing how Black players function as historical contestants on screen. For *On the Shoulders of Giants*, I examine the documentary's source material, Kareem Abdul-Jabbar's autoethnographic cultural history *On the Shoulders of Giants: My Journey through the Harlem Renaissance* and the film's use of digital animation to reanimate suppressed pasts. With *This Is a Game, Ladies*, I address how Rutgers University's women's basketball head coach C. Vivian Stringer and her players represent and articulate Black female athleticism in tension with respectability politics as a redress against past, present, and futured racial and gender antagonisms and within the constraints of the documentary's PBS format and other generic conventions. My interest in *Hoop Dreams*, however, is less direct, in part because of the wealth of rigorous critiques and compelling scholarship on race, representation, and realism in the documentary. Instead, I attend primarily to *Hoop Reality* in its citational and diacritical relation to *Hoop Dreams*. As an unofficial sequel of sorts, *Hoop Reality*'s documentary corpora inculcates the canonical *Hoop Dreams* into its diegesis as a metatextual dispute; thus, to talk about aesthetic and embodied histories in *Hoop Reality* is to do the selfsame vis-à-vis *Hoop Dreams*. *Hoop Reality*'s recursivity, then, is a cinematic example of what I am theorizing about Black sports documentary as a formal genre of critical muscle memory. All four examples turn our attention to how the Black sporting body, situated in the impulses, styles, and strategies of documentary production, becomes a contested canvas of representation whereby athletes' incarnate sporting histories that structure and suture discourses about sporting blackness and critical muscle memory. Analyzing the representations of Black athletes in these documentaries as historical contestants invites us to consider how the Black sporting body is framed in and can possibly reframe history and historiographic narratives.

WHAT IS THIS "BLACK" IN BLACK SPORTS DOCUMENTARIES?

In "What Is This 'Black' in Black Popular Culture," Stuart Hall encourages us to reflect on the representational modes, expressive traditions, diasporic communities, and resonant memories that speak to the diversity, complexity, contradictions, and mythic aspects of Black popular culture.[6] A focus on the signifier of "Black," in his contention, is not meant to be "lodged in a biologically constituted racial category" but should be attached to "its historical, cultural and political embedding."[7] I want to extend Hall's suggestion to my understanding of the intersections of race and the sports documentary to question what is the "Black" in Black sports documentaries. My query requires a study of the formal modes, cultural politics, and racial discourses that distinguish documentary and its subcategories. I argue that nonfiction sports films and their attendant histories, features, and narratives broaden and nuance the case studies, and, by extension, the strategies, practices, and typologies associated with the Black documentary tradition and vice versa. This chiasmic configuration amplifies the conjuncture of "sports" with blackness in my reformulation of Hall's animating question. As sociologist Ben Carrington argues of the racial signification of sports in popular culture and Black cultural politics, "a reading of the race and sport conjuncture can produce important insights into both the (changing) meaning and structure of 'race' as well as the importance and place of sport within western societies."[8] My accounting, then, for what is the "Black" in Black sports documentaries is a twofold project that simultaneously regards the "Black" *and* "sport" in Black sports documentaries as "a contested terrain wherein competing ideologies of domination and resistance can be traced" and "[thinks] *of sport as a racial project that both changes and is changed by political struggles in and through race.*"[9] Both configurations require attention to representational systems; social, institutional, and industrial structures; and, in this case, the generic conventions of nonfiction filmmaking.

Broadly speaking, documentary films record, engage, instruct, give perspectives on, and educate us about people and occurrences in the world. They "show us situations and events that are recognizably part of a realm of shared experience: the historical world as we know and encounter it."[10] They provide knowledge, information, and awareness that shape, question, and challenge the formation of popular memory.[11] Bill Nichols aligns documentary to other "discourses of sobriety," or nonfictional systems that can be instrumental in altering perceptions of the world and motivating people to action.[12] As an industry that traditionally relies on securing funding from nonprofit, foundation, and federal institutions, documentary is often a less costly but still a competitive filmmaking endeavor, as the landscape and avenues for funding of nonfiction work have narrowed in scope.[13] While distribution struggles have in the past pushed the form into marginal venues such as film festivals and public television, in the contemporary media landscape, streaming platforms have widened many documentary films' audience reach.

Documentary has been a critical form for the excavation, exploration, and experimentation of and with blackness on screen. In the introduction to their seminal collection *Struggles for Representation: African American Documentary Film and Video*, Phyllis R. Klotman and Janet K. Cutler distinguish Black nonfiction texts (in contradistinction to classic and dominant ideas about documentary filmmaking) as those works committed to "make black life visible; to define black personal and collective identity in ways that counter mass media representation; to find appropriate, expressive film/video language; to gain access to and control of the means of production; to reach an audience; to create effective social and political works."[14] They locate the African American documentary tradition, an extension of Black orature and literature practices, in a variety of mediums and formats, including television, and explain how more recent documentaries have diverged from and extended the kinds of practices associated with the past, particularly the blurred boundaries and aesthetic hybrids between nonfiction and fiction via digital effects. Klotman and Cutler argue that modern-day African American documentary film and video continues a tradition of documenting and authenticating a spectrum of alternative, undervalued, and unrecorded Black experiences "from inside the culture" through a range of narrative and cinematic strategies.[15]

Black documentaries often challenge distorted representations of Black people in mainstream media, particularly those found in fiction film and television. In this regard, many Black cultural producers turn to documentary as a narrative means to assert control and intervene on the images that define Black people and blackness in solely negative terms within popular culture. For documentarians, Clyde Taylor explains, "it [has] always been a struggle to say something real about black life, against the fictions, myths, stereotypes, misconceptions, and lies magnified in the fantasy factory" of Hollywood and even independent Black cinema.[16] Categorized outside of the capital drive of much Black commercial spectacle and entertainment, this has meant that nonfiction filmmaking is usually a less lucrative avenue and receives limited distribution outside of educational television and film festival programming. And yet these films' "ability to portray searing, indelible impressions of black life, including concrete views of significant events and moving portraits of charismatic individuals" makes them compelling social documents.[17] As mediatic objects, Black documentaries do not replace lost or missing Black history but, importantly, signify on gaps in recorded history even as they can be constricted by various production forces.[18]

As a subgenre, documentaries make up an exponentially large amount of sports films, and the popularity of the form lies, partly, in the appeal of sports as a mass cultural phenomenon in our everyday "quest for excitement."[19] With theatrical and televisual traditions, institutional practices, and industrial contexts, this dominant nonfiction mode of sports cinema production arranges and interprets sports history into compelling and coherent naturalist (or realist), spectacular narratives. The lineage of sports documentaries includes, among many others, early Eadweard Muybridge actualities, propogandist films such as Leni Riefenstahl's *Olympia* (1938), bodybuilding docudramas such as *Pumping Iron* (George Butler and Robert Fiore, 1977) and *Pumping Iron II: The Women* (George Butler, 1985), Ken Burns's epic PBS miniseries *Baseball* (1994), and the most recent spate of critically acclaimed *30 for 30* (2009–present) films produced by the sports media empire ESPN. In the last ten years, many contemporary sports documentary feature films have won Academy Awards, including *Free Solo* (Elisabeth Chai Vasarhelyi and Jimmy Chin, 2018), *Icarus* (Bryan Fogel, 2017), *O.J.: Made in America* (Ezra Edeleman, 2016), and *Undefeated* (Daniel Lindsay and T.J. Martin, 2011), or been nominated for an Oscar in the nonfiction category, including *Hale County This Morning, This Evening* (RaMell Ross, 2018) and *Minding the Gap* (Bing Liu, 2018). Currently, made-for-television and streaming/on-demand sports documentaries are the most commonly produced works in the genre. These films are extremely popular with audiences (more so than other kinds of documentaries on television), and all the major networks, including ESPN, Fox, and NBC Sports Group, have production units for this kind of filmmaking. Relatively inexpensive to make in comparison to the rights cost for live games, Travis Vogan argues that "these television productions, for instance, are influenced by media organizations' efforts to build recognizable and respectable brands, vie for market share, promote other programming, and create a supply of content that can be efficiently and economically recycled."[20] As a result, many media corporations have shown more openness to diverse subjects and voices in sports documentaries, including films about and by women and people of color.[21]

Sports documentaries capture sporting worlds, events, and figures in ways that are banal, gripping, evocative, expressionistic, and informative, mapping onto Michael Renov's poetics of documentary typology and Nichols's classification of documentary modes of representation in compatible ways.[22] Sport documentarians are aided by the fact that "sport, a rich source of 'mythologies, allegories and narratives' provides fertile terrain for the filmmaker" because of sports' propensity for drama, suspense, pathos, and even comedy.[23] However, sports docs, like all documentaries, "do not simply display reality but build histories that arrange indexical images into ideologically loaded narratives with the potential to resist and perpetuate the conditions they showcase."[24] The form can be best be understood as not reflecting reality but producing, shaping, and critiquing interpretations of histories, regimes of truth, and systems of beliefs and values about sports and its place in society and popular memory. While there are many distinctions within the subgenre, as Malitsky describes, "the confluence of sports and documentary" reveals "that sport is imbricated with capital, that it is visually spectacular, that it celebrates individual expression, that it is always already narrativized, and that thinking about sport always entails thinking about and through media."[25]

The sports documentary's ontological status, historiographic practices, and ideological processes invite us to consider how nonfiction modes and specific traditions render race, history, and the Black sporting body on screen. Black sports films like *On the Shoulders of Giants*; *This Is a Game, Ladies*; *Hoop Dreams*; and *Hoop Reality* are a growing, yet, critically neglected nonfiction subcategory of both Black and sports documentary traditions. Placing sports films within Black documentary traditions, as I do, not only emphasizes the fact that "sports documentaries constitute a significant part of the documentary tradition" but also underscores how discourses of and about race shape modes of representation and methodological approaches.[26] I read the four documentaries through this raced interpretive lens and within the lineage of sport and Black documentary traditions, framing culturally how sports, sports figures, and the (real and imagined) sporting worlds represented have significance and signify beyond the games, people, and places themselves. Black sports documentaries athletically negotiate "film blackness," showing how sports cinema "is imbricated in a vital expanse of renderings, practices, and critical traditions devoted to blackness."[27] Therefore, the "Black" in Black sports documentaries is the mutable expressivity of sporting blackness, a mode of producing nonfiction tales of Black sporting bodies and critical muscle memory. However, such expressivity is not meant to be solely aesthetic or iconic, and these Black documentaries are not always progressive or subversive in their formal and representational politics. Rather, the critical strategies of both Black players and documentaries of sporting blackness are meant to convey Black interiority with regard to athletic achievement and failure within a capitalist and racist culture. Black sports documentaries, then, are cinematic works that employ the constitutive elements of race and athletics as historically grounded discourses that are embodied, imagined, and projected history and critical muscle memory.

HISTORICAL CONTESTANTS IN *ON THE SHOULDERS OF GIANTS*

Providing a genealogy of Black exclusion and participation in professional basketball, Deborah Morales's 2011 documentary *On the Shoulders of Giants: The Story of the Greatest Team You've Never Heard Of* contests dominant sports history. Adapted from athlete-actor-writer-activist Kareem Abdul-Jabbar's 2007 book *On the Shoulders of Giants: My Journey through the Harlem Renaissance*, the documentary chronicles the experiences and impact of the "Rens," the first all-Black professional basketball team in America. The film creatively challenges the contemporary image of the National Basketball Association (NBA) as a Black-dominated professional league by examining the performances of the "original ballers" who were barred from entering the all-white pro-leagues at the time. The documentary introduces the Rens' coach Robert "Bob" Douglas, who in 1910, at the age of nineteen, emigrated from the West Indies to New York City and is known as the "father of Black basketball." In a deal worked out with William "Hal" Roach and the Sarco Realty Company, Douglas charged patrons for a night of watching basketball and dancing to a live orchestra at the Renaissance Casino and Ballroom on 138th Street and Seventh Avenue in Harlem. In doing so, he put together the New York Renaissance Big Five (also known as the "Rens," the "Harlem Rens," and the "Big R Five"), naming the basketball team after the building and, concomitantly, the social and cultural milieu of the time. The documentary relays the history and contributions of these pioneering Black basketball players and their coach, connecting them and their sporting performance to the arts, music, and culture of the Harlem Renaissance.

On the Shoulders of Giants is a historiography of absences, with a recuperative narrative that historicizes Black athletes' experiences to inform, shape, and challenge popular history and cultural memory related to and exceeding the world of sports. Significantly, by highlighting the history of segregation in professional basketball, the documentary critiques the contemporary politics surrounding the NBA's ironic anti-Black racism—specifically criticism that the league is "too Black" in terms of demographics, aesthetics, and style—in the post-Jordan/after Artest moment.[28] Released in February 2011 during Black History Month, *On the Shoulders of Giants*, alternatively, celebrates blackness and the Black bodies currently in the pros through its account of the Rens' exclusion from such leagues at the time. By challenging dominant ideologies that frame race relations within athletics and stereotype Black people's past and present participation in the league, *On the Shoulders of Giants* contests hegemonic discourses about race, masculinity, policy, and governance in professional basketball for contemporary audiences.

In telling the "never heard of" story of the Rens, the documentary examines sporting culture in the 1920s and 1930s, fills gaps in Black sports history, and links basketball to Black sociality. It foregrounds Harlem as both the cultural epicenter for Black modernity in the early twentieth century and the site for African Americans' cultural influence on basketball in the modern era. The Harlem Renaissance, as Cornel West explains in the film, was a burgeoning period of intellectual and artistic breakthrough. It was also a period in which sport was central to redefinitions of blackness and racial pride. Drawing on archival images and artistic renderings of Harlem in the 1920s and 1930s, *On the Shoulders of Giants* highlights the Rens' grueling schedules barnstorming across racially tumultuous regions; the racism they encountered from opposing white fans and the whites-only professional basketball league; the competition between them and the white-owned Harlem Globetrotters based out of Chicago; and their attempts to play for and win the world championship.

Led by basketball legend and interlocutor Kareem Abdul-Jabbar and narrated by Jamie Foxx, interviewees—including athletes, activists, historians, and artists—contextualize the impact of the Rens' fluid, "up in the air," passing-style of play on the modern game of basketball seen today. Detailing how the Rens embodied Harlem's sound in this style of play, *On the Shoulders of Giants* links their improvisational athletic performance to the liveliness of jazz during this period of Black sonic innovation. The documentary's tale culminates in a recap of the Rens' 1939 championship-run season, where they defeated the all-white Oshkosh All-Stars in the World Professional Basketball Tournament. Having previously been denied entrance into the segregated American Basketball League and the National Basketball League in 1926 and 1937, respectively, the Rens went down in history as world champions, playing and defeating teams from both leagues. By besting the top Black *and* white teams to win the championship, the Rens—similar to other Black athletes before them, including heavyweight boxing champion Jack Johnson and athlete-activist-singer-actor Paul Robeson—helped to shatter racist myths of Black inferiority on and off the court. Despite these sporting and social achievements, the Rens are largely forgotten figures within sports and Black history. *On the Shoulders of Giants* combats this erasure by providing context on this neglected athletic history of Black self-determination, entrepreneurship, and creativity.

As co-screenwriter, producer, and star of *On the Shoulders of Giants* and author of the documentary's source material, Kareem Abdul-Jabbar's intimate and historical account of the Rens and the Harlem Renaissance is characteristic of authorial tendencies in Black documentary.[29] Detailing his personal connection to the Rens, Abdul-Jabbar, like many Black documentarians, stresses his relationship to and identification with the film's subjects while framing the broader historical stakes and meanings of the subject matter. A former Los Angeles Lakers center and the NBA's all-time leading scorer, Abdul-Jabbar is a basketball legend commonly known for his signature "skyhook" shot and quiet demeanor. However, in recent years, Abdul-Jabbar has emerged as an actor; a sports commentator and political pundit; and a columnist, screenwriter, and author of ten books including two memoirs. Examining the autoethnographic elements in *My Journey through the Harlem Renaissance* and its adaptation, *On the Shoulders of Giants* demonstrates how personal and historical lessons Abdul-Jabbar gleaned from the Rens are shaped by his embodied presence and critical muscle memory in both book and film.

My Journey through the Harlem Renaissance is a cultural history about exceptional and inspiring Black figures, an homage to African American history, and a memoir detailing Abdul-Jabbar's passions: Harlem, basketball, jazz, and education. Balancing autobiography and historical nonfiction, the memoir examines how Harlem became a Black Mecca in the 1920s, drawing attention to artistic figures including Alain Locke, Zora Neale Hurston, Countee Cullen, Duke Ellington, and Thomas "Fats" Waller. Tracing the historical strands of the artists, places, and forces behind the Harlem Renaissance, Abdul-Jabbar shines a light on the cultural shadows of the movement.[30] The chapters in the book are structured as a call-and-response, which, as Abdul-Jabbar notes, allows him to discuss particular aspects of the Harlem Renaissance and then respond with his own personal narrative about their influence on him.[31] This first-person history reflects an autoethnographic impulse in the book; one that I argue extends to the documentary's adaption, placing it firmly within Black literary autobiographical traditions that entwine the historical record and the memoir.

The story of the Rens and how Abdul-Jabbar came to learn about the team features prominently in the book. Going from the chapter "Basketball Comes to Harlem" to "How the Rens Basketball Team Influenced My Life," Abdul-Jabbar provides a contextual history and personal reflection on the

Rens by tracing the team's origin and legacy in the former chapter and reflecting on this history personally in the latter chapter. Abdul-Jabbar remembers, while born and raised in Harlem, that he did not learn about the Rens until he was seventeen. Despite not knowing about the team, he explains that he "had connections to them [he] wasn't even aware of."[32] Unwittingly absorbing the Rens' style of play from watching basketball tapes at camp and playing against older players coached by former Rens player William "Pop" Gates, Abdul-Jabbar recalls "undoubtedly learning Rens plays and moves without ever having heard of them."[33] He locates the Ren's playing history within his own critical muscle memory, embodying and reproducing their past movements without being fully conscious of their history. Going through various degrees of separation with the Rens, Abdul-Jabbar writes that their "history was brushing against me all the time, like strangers bumping while passing on a crowded street. Historical connections and influences were all around me, but I hadn't noticed."[34] Abdul-Jabbar's intracorporeal recognition of a shared, intercorporeal sporting experience is punctuated by the fact that he sees his own basketball career as an extension of the Rens' courageous actions on-and-off the court. For him, "there is no doubt that they made it possible for [him] to be as successful as [he] was."[35] Arguably one of the best basketball players to ever play the game, he sees himself as connected to and an inheritor of the Rens' legacy, one in which the Rens "[endured] racist threats and abuse, so [he] could step out on the court as a black man and no one would question it."[36] Abdul-Jabbar's embodied knowledge of the Rens engenders an experience of his own body's muscle memory as connected to past Black sporting and social experiences; and these related and shared embodied experiences inform his knowledge of himself, Black cultural history, and his place within it.

My Journey through the Harlem Renaissance transmutes its basketball history pedagogy into the documentary *On the Shoulders of Giants*. The film uses educational, autobiographical, and performative modes of address to depict the story of the Rens and the history of the Harlem Renaissance. As a cultural historian turned documentary producer, Abdul-Jabbar's starring role is centralized in the diegesis. While Jamie Foxx's voiceover narration provides context for *On the Shoulders of Giants*, Abdul-Jabbar embodies the role of a griot in the documentary. As storytellers, poets, musicians, and historians that can be traced back to West Africa, griots are "elders in the community who mentally record, then verbally recount, local and familial tales."[37] For example, *On the Shoulders of Giants* opens with Abdul-Jabbar "schooling" prominent basketball figures associated with winning professional teams on the historical erasure of, arguably, "the best team you've never heard of."

As on-screen interviewer and tour-guide through Harlem, Abdul-Jabbar is both a "race man" interested in consciousness raising as much as the documentary's "color man," a sports commentator "who reminds the viewer of the statistics, past achievements, and world records, while placing current events into historical perspective."[38] Illuminating facts about the Rens and Harlem in the early twentieth century, Abdul-Jabbar uses his own history on-and-off the court to engage interviewees about the Rens, jazz, and the Harlem Renaissance. Alongside athletes, artists, historians, and activists, Abdul-Jabbar creatively intertwines and interrelates personal and collective expression on sports history and social realities within a broader cultural context. From print to screen, Abdul-Jabbar's fundamental roles in creating both texts are significant. He does more than celebrate the achievements of the Rens and Black culture in the 1920s and 1930s. As an athlete, turning to cultural production as means of expression, he extends the ways in which we can consider Black athletes, whose spectacular virtuosity in the arena of athletics are well known, as creative agents of and within popular culture.[39] His embodied knowledge contests history on and off the court by creatively reimagining in print and on screen the all-but-forgotten Black pioneers of American basketball.

Documentarians use various aesthetic strategies and formal modes of address to examine Black history, culture, and experiences. Non-prescriptive strategies reoccur in many Black documentaries, and Klotman and Cutler describe these features as "an emphasis on performance as a mode of expression and opposition, an interest in exploiting the possibilities of first-person narration, a creative insistence on capturing the speech/voice of documentary subjects, the significant role of music as an agent for change."[40] *On the Shoulders of Giants* mobilizes many of these features to not only narrativize the Rens' absent history but also to frame the cultural movement of the time period. The documentary emphasizes embodied performance with real and animated footage of the Rens. It uses first-person narration with Abdul-Jabbar acting as a historical guide and cultural commentator. The film creatively renders the Rens' style of play through digital animation, while the work of artist Justin Bua imbues the documentary with the look and feel of Harlem in the art direction (figure 3). Nonvisual elements like Bill Cunliffe's score and the sounds of Herbie Hancock, will.i.am, Wynton Marsalis, and Chuck D & Johnny Juice are used to connect basketball's creativity with the artistry and improvisation of jazz and hip-hop expression. Black sonic citations thus play a critical role in this film's development of critical muscle memory.

FIGURE 3.   Justin Bua's art direction creatively renders the play of the Harlem Rens in *On the Shoulders of Giants* (Deborah Morales, 2011).

Merging these animated and sonic features at the documentary's outset, these elements work together to shape the visual economy of the Rens' place within history. In the opening credit sequence, digitally animated silhouettes of contemporary Black basketball superstars are layered on top of vibrant, color-saturated images of Harlem. The first animated figure shown is Abdul-Jabbar doing his signature skyhook. Framed by the architecture of the city, the urban landscape is a luminous mix of animated brick buildings. Viewable through the windows, shifting black and white footage of couples dancing and footage of basketball games are superimposed, representing the confluence of sports and dance at the Renaissance Casino and Ballroom. With a lively jazz and hip hop soundscape, silhouetted contemporary basketball players pass basketballs to the silhouetted figures of the legendary Rens players. In doing so, Rens players Charles "Tarzan" Cooper, John Isaacs, William "Wee Willy" Smith, Clarence "Puggy" Bell, and Clarence "Fat" Jenkins are formally animated, "brought to life," as they move the ball through space and time to modern day players Kobe Bryant, Kevin Garnett, Carmelo Anthony, and LeBron James.

In this stylized scene, the digitally animated actions of the players and the jazz score do more than shape the design and performance of the bodies on screen. The scene depicts how the Black body can function as a looking-glass and repository of critical muscle memory, mirroring and reflecting on shared Black histories of *and* at play. Suturing the flow between past and present Black sporting bodies, the "give and go" movement structures the documentary's narrative. This strategy links the passing and receiving concept to not only the literal interpretation—the ball moving from one teammate to another—but also to its implied metaphor of historical exchange between past histories and present realities. This exchange visually connects the athletic performances of Black basketball players while also projecting and reimagining the missing Black historical bodies for contemporary audiences. The use of digital animation in this moment and throughout the documentary not only blurs nonfictive and fictive elements, it also engenders a process in which counternarratives on Black male basketball players' embodied experiences can be explored. This process inflects, as Valerie Smith suggests, how some Black documentaries "gesture toward the fictional or the artificial in an attempt to enter suppressed narratives into public discourses."[41] Operating within this aesthetic tradition and cinematic practice, *On the Shoulders of Giants* experiments with digital animation in order to defamiliarize audiences' cursory knowledge of Black participation in professional basketball. Showing that well-known, contemporary Black basketball players are indebted to the unknown Rens, the documentary narrativizes a "truer-truth" about race and fair play in sports.

The film's opening scene is just one example of many in which the Rens players are animated in the documentary. Because of the lack of archival footage and coverage of the Rens in popular print and visual media, production studio Calabash Animation created digitally animated figures and tableaus to illustrate the Rens' style of play and reenact championship game sequences.[42] The lack of Rens playing footage is a consequence of fragmented and absent Black sports archives, a concern for documentarians that shapes "the relationship between available technology and historical representation."[43] In *On the Shoulder of Giants*, fictive techniques and digital technologies help to fill gaps in Black sports history. In doing so, this film, like many contemporary avant-garde Black documentaries, eschews conventional modes of realism to assert an imaginative reality. Michael Renov characterizes technical mediation as always already present in all documentaries, and the use of digital animation to connect past and present Black basketball players together cites the performative and improvisational elements aligned with Black culture and cultural production.[44] By animating the Rens games and play, *On the Shoulders of Giants* enters into the mainstream the obscured true story of these Black ballers and their experiences. By reimagining the Rens on screen, the documentary shows how "reinvention is a political act," one that is able to remember and redress the Rens' impact and import on basketball and Black history.[45]

Looking closely at the spectacle of the Black sporting body, *On the Shoulders of Giants* constructs Black bodies on screen as historical contestants beyond the athletic context that is its purported subject and focus. The embodied histories that resonate out from the Rens and the histories attached to them not only relay the story of segregation in professional sports but also narrate the spectacle of racial terror in American society at the time. Individual as well as communal bodies and experiences resonate in and project out of representations of Black sporting bodies. The "give and go" of past and present Black athletes evokes muscle memory, showing how larger arenas of meaning and related signage are produced by choreographed bodies moving alongside each other.[46]

For example, an early sequence of images in *On the Shoulders of Giants* connects the history of sporting spectacles of the Rens' play to the spectacular racial terror of lynching. The sequence begins with photographic images portraying the agrarian-based labor of Black people after the turn of the century. As narrator Jamie Foxx details African Americans' struggles and their social and political isolation at the time, the screen goes black. Against a white backdrop, the all-black silhouetted image of a man standing near a lynched body appears on screen. As the camera zooms in, the image is filled in with its indexical referent, an actual photograph of a lynching victim hanging from a tree with a crowd of white people staring on (figure 4). The use of the silhouette against a blank canvas onto which any body *and* anybody can be physically and psychologically projected is reminiscent of the work of artist Kara Walker. Walker, who uses cut paper silhouettes in her provocative and graphic art, which often depicts scenes of racial and sexual violence in diorama installations, recognizes how the form "produces an extraordinary space of psychological projection."[47] This highlights how the Black body, particularly Black men's bodies, "represents an amalgam of fears and projections in the American psyche which rarely conveys or contains the trope of truth about the black male's existence."[48] Linking to and going beyond sports history, *On the Shoulders of Giants* uses the Black masculine body as a mutable image and repository of critical muscle memory, an individuated multiplicity that opens up to represent and project Black sporting and non-sporting experiences. I define this resonant documentary figure of the Black athletic body as a historical contestant, a figure and figuration able to challenge the elisions in representational regimes of Black athletes.

Over the aforementioned hanging images, Foxx narrates that "lynching was still a popular method of stopping any notion of integration. Over

FIGURE 4.   The lynching silhouette becomes a repository of critical muscle memory in *On the Shoulders of Giants* (Deborah Morales, 2011).

200,500 Blacks had been lynched, mostly in southern communities." The digitally animated silhouette activates this history, moving beyond the photographic in an effort to reveal a cohort of Black bodies that have been the target of violent state terror and racism. As the image of the Black hanging body gains dimensionality, the photo shifts four times to reveal similar images of lynched Black bodies. The final lynched figure is William Brown, who was kidnapped by a lynch mob after being accused of molesting a white girl, hung from a lamppost, mutilated, riddled with bullets, and then burned in Omaha, Nebraska, on September 28, 1919.[49] As the film blends images of lynched Black bodies and white onlookers with the voiceover tale of vigilante racism that dominated the Jim Crow era, the documentary explicitly links the embodied presence of the Rens to this larger social world of racialized terror.

These still-life images of lynchings are punctuated within the film's spectacular contexts of Black sporting history; and their display literally resonates and projects images of other Black bodies and historical experiences of racial terror. In this sense, the Black body implicitly and the documentary explicitly construct muscle memory via a critical examination of white spectators looking on at lynched and sporting Black bodies as entertainment. As Amy Louise Wood describes, lynching was popular, performative, ritualized and "frequently made public—even spectacular—through displays of lynched bodies, as well as through representations of violence that circulated long after the lynching themselves were over: photographs and other visual

imagery, ballads and songs, news accounts and lurid narratives."[50] By including the visual history of lynching in a manner reminiscent of Hank Willis
Thomas's *Overtime* discussed in the introduction, *On the Shoulders of
Giants* links the Rens' professional basketball history to the collective vulnerability of Black communities to terror, violence, and death in the postbel-
lum United States. In doing so, the film shows how "professional sports and
their commoditization of the black athletic body also bring us face-to-face
with the psychic and physical violence of the racial state that continually
attempts to dominate and manipulate black bodies."[51] Thus, the documentary's use of the animated lynching silhouette is a reminder of the historical
simultaneity of unparalleled collective achievement by Black athletes and
writers within the Harlem Renaissance and the genocidal campaign of terror
that was the lynch mob in the Jim Crow era.

PAST, PRESENT, AND FUTURED ANTAGONISMS IN *THIS IS A GAME, LADIES*

Peter Schnall's *This Is a Game, Ladies* chronicles the 2000–2001 season of
Rutgers's women's basketball team, the Scarlet Knights, capturing the
sporting and social forces that influence the team on and off the court.
Produced by Partisan Pictures, this feature-length documentary circulated
at several film festivals before being aired nationally by the Public
Broadcasting Service (PBS) in 2004, earning an Emmy nomination for its
cinematography. Shot on 16 mm, the film's verité style captivates and provides an eye-opening look at women's collegiate sports and Black female
athleticism. Like many sports documentaries, *This Is a Game, Ladies*
includes archetypal filmic elements, including game and practice scenes;
coaches and players in one-on-one interviews, talking heads, and archival
footage. The film registers most acutely its positivist PBS format and tone
via its emphasis on imaging "girl power." The documentary's adherence to
a PBS style and politics makes for a simplified narrative that mutes racial
history and Black agency, particularly Black women's historical treatment
in sports and society, to educate without alienating white viewers, restrict-
ing the film's depth and scope to reinforce liberal ideologies of Black female
respectability.[52] Despite the film's tepid engagement of the racial and gender antagonisms faced by the Black Rutgers basketball players, the film's
athletic stars function as historical contestants in and in excess of the documentary itself. Specifically, the racial and gender attacks by Don Imus on
the Scarlet Knights reinvigorates the documentary's critical muscle memory of similar sporting and social experiences.

Hilary Sio, head of Story Development for Partisan Pictures, conceived of *This Is a Game, Ladies* after being captivated by the 1998 National Collegiate Athletics Association's (NCAA) women's college basketball finals. Researching colleges and universities close to Partisan Pictures' headquarters, Sio and the film's director, Peter Schnall, decided on Rutgers University. While proximity played a significant role in the school selection, Sio and Schnall chose the public institution and its Division-1 team because it, according to them, also had "one of the most dynamic and successful coaches in basketball—C. Vivian Stringer."[53] While *This Is a Game, Ladies* examines Rutgers's 2000–2001 basketball season, Schnall and his team spent the year prior prepping for the film, getting to know Stringer and the team and making them comfortable with being filmed. The 1999–2000 season ended in a spectacular fashion. Stringer coached the Scarlet Knights to their first-ever appearance in the NCAA final four. The documentary's producers recall that "the stakes suddenly got much higher—and Partisan knew they really had a film on their hands. The team knew they had to return for the next season to follow the rise or fall of a championship team."[54] This sporting quest for championship glory functions as the film's central arc, while the documentary's tone oscillates between the generic tone and tenor of fictional sports films and the maternal melodrama.[55]

This Is a Game, Ladies provides an uncommon filmic treatment on women's collegiate athletics as site of competition, competence, pleasure, empowerment, and drama. Schnall's documentary redresses the neglect of and ignorance about women's sports in general and women's college basketball specifically in popular culture.[56] As sports historian Susan K. Cahn explains, "Since its invention in 1891, basketball has been the most consistently popular sport among schoolgirls and young women."[57] This popularity, however, magnifies and intensifies the sport as a site of racial and gender surveillance, cultural conflict, and institutional control, with the women's game being modified and marginalized to appease shifting and constricting norms and expectations placed on female athletes, young Black women, coaches, and players. With so little television coverage of women's sports by mainstream media outlets, *This Is a Game, Ladies* contests an aporia in cultural production about female athleticism, positioning women's sporting blackness as a central remedy to women's overall invisibility in popular culture.[58] The film, like other Black documentaries, is linked with "struggles for social and political empowerment," and in this case for Black women's autonomy and self-determination in particular.[59] In consenting to participate in the documentary, Stringer explains: "I agreed to let the cameras into

FIGURE 5. Dynamic cinematography captures the intensities of women's basketball in *This Is a Game, Ladies* (Peter Schnall, 2004).

the gym and the locker rooms because I wanted to bring attention to the women's game, even if it meant losing some of our privacy. It was important to me to show the world how hard these young women worked."[60] In an engaging and sophisticated manner typical of PBS documentaries, Schnall dutifully renders the athletic ability, aptitude, aggression, and camaraderie in women's collegiate basketball on screen (figure 5).

This Is a Game, Ladies fuses elements of the fictional sports film into its documentary mode. This includes an inspiring chronological sports journey celebrating determination and discipline over personal and sporting obstacles. The documentary uses stylized game footage as action sequences (including the requisite sports film training montage), interpersonal conflicts that advance plot, and a lively soundtrack to inform the film's emotional beats.[61] Beginning with footage from the Scarlet Knights' loss in the 2000 NCAA Final Four, *This Is a Game, Ladies* fast-forwards six months to the preseason, introducing the audience to returning as well as new players during the first official practice of the year. While the players stretch, Stringer explains to them that they are title contenders who can shape their own destiny through their work ethic. Visually confirming the principle that effort begets reward, the audience witnesses the team's rigorous training and conditioning before and during the season. While the Scarlet Knights win their first game, beating California by 19 points, Stringer calls their performance "unacceptable," explaining that the team needs to play better to beat tougher opponents. Her shocking reaction to Rutgers winning play encourages the audience to expect more from women's basketball than a positive result—that is, a win. Instead, heightened discipline, dominance, virtuosity, and consistency are her exacting criteria for evaluation.

While the team is nationally ranked in the top 10 and later the top 20 for most of the season, Stringer struggles to get her team to play up to their potential, losing to many ranked opponents before finally taking down the number-1-ranked team, Notre Dame, handing the Fighting Irish their first loss of the season. Surveying the ups and downs, wins and losses, and strife (two players quit) that the team faces, Schnall captures the fluid, gritty, spectacular, and, sometimes, heartbreaking play of these student athletes. Following the team into the postseason, the Scarlet Knights lose to Missouri State University in the second round of the NCAA tournament. After this devastating loss, the documentary employs sports films' tried and true redemptive third act. We witness two players drafted to the Women's National Basketball Association's (WNBA), Rutgers's senior commencement ceremony, and a "where are they now" update on the players spotlighted in the film, all of whom have gone on to seemingly successful basketball and non-sporting careers since the production wrapped. *This Is a Game, Ladies* concludes having gone narratively full circle, with the start of preseason for the 2001–2002 playing year, showing Stringer preparing her players for what lies ahead on their journey to win a collegiate national championship.

While principally about Rutgers's women's basketball season, the documentary is also a profile of Stringer, one of the Black foremothers among the coaches of collegiate women's basketball. While not explicitly a biographical documentary, Stringer is given a hagiographic treatment typical of PBS documentaries about great Black leaders.[62] Stringer began her coaching career at Cheney University, a historically Black university, then was the head coach at Iowa, where she led them to an NCAA final four in 1993. Arriving at Rutgers in 1995, she remains the head coach as of 2019. While the documentary captures Stringer's exemplary athletic acumen and coaching abilities, the film's tone is steeped in pathos, delving into her personal tragedies and psychic traumas including her husband's death years prior, her daughter's spinal meningitis, and her sixteen-year old son's nearly fatal car accident the summer before the 2000–2001 basketball season. While Stringer discusses these events on camera, Schnall also filters this story into the documentary through intertextual mediation, aestheticizing the memories of her misfortunes and heartbreaks for melodramatic effect.

This sensibility is rendered on screen in a way that feels both intimate and distant. During an away game, Stringer sits on a couch in her hotel room watching herself on an episode of HBO's *Real Sports*, where she discusses the tragedies that have befallen her and her family. The documentary enmeshes the footage of the spectating Stringer to the *Real Sports* interview with Stringer, which becomes the documentary's main, full screen footage. This intertextual merge of frames—televisual and filmic documentary productions—becomes a mediated mirror able to reflect and magnify the melodramatic televisual moment for representational purposes. This collapsed and collaged mediatic moment heightens the audience's awareness of Stinger's intrapersonal identification with herself and her history of tragedy. As tears stream down Stringer's face on the television program, the camera cuts back to her in the hotel room as tears roll down her cheeks. No longer the tightly cropped close-up footage from *Real Sports*, Stringer sits far removed from the frame as the director asks her about watching the interview and the difficulty with publicly discussing her life (figure 6). The repetition with a difference fuses aesthetic and embodied memories, the documentary with the melodrama, the women's film and the sports film. The television show and the documentary's dual surveillance and rendering of a double Black embodied experience—the camera watching Stringer and Stringer watching herself—constructs her critical muscle memory as the reliving of past personal traumas in the present moment via television's domestic and domesticating function.[63] Melodramatic moments of excess such as this rehearse a sentimentality meant to intensify audience identification with her struggles and reinforce her role as a maternal figure to those on and off the court. Stringer self-identifies as a mom figure to her team, and the players reinforce this familial designation, melding the private and public spheres into the same arena. As such, *This Is a Game, Ladies* operates within familiar registers of the maternal melodrama, where Stringer's sacrifices on behalf of her home and the home team cast her as both the self-less victim and sporting heroine in the film.

In addition to profiling Stringer, the documentary provides coverage of the Rutgers women's team players on and off the court, showing the diverse athleticism of Black female sporting bodies. While not an all-Black squad, the Scarlet Knights are a predominately Black team.[64] While highlighting their skills on the court, the players also discuss their adversities on and off the hardwood, some coming from rural and inner-city environments and often having to prove themselves on the court against boys and men before they were taken seriously as women athletes. Schnall principally

Coach watches herself on HBO's "Real Sports"

FIGURE 6. Coach C. Vivian Stringer's personal tragedies steep *This Is a Game, Ladies* (Peter Schnall, 2004) in melodramatic pathos.

follows two groups of players: seniors and freshman. The seniors include Tasha Pointer, the tenacious and driven five-foot-six point guard who goes on to make Big East history as the first player, male or female, to accumulate over 10,000 points, 7,000 assists, 500 rebounds, and 250 steals in her collegiate career. Pointer is shown as the heart and soul of team. Alongside Pointer is senior Linda Miles, a gifted athlete who is one of the best defensive players in the Big East. Miles, who is suspended from the team multiple times due to her attitude, comes off, nonetheless, as likeable and self-assured. In one scene, she marvels at herself while preening in the mirror, explaining that she enjoys being a Black woman who can be/look feminine and sweet as well as perform on the court as a strong and confident baller. Alongside Pointer and Miles, the documentary highlights the prowess of Olympian and future WNBA star Tasha Sutton-Brown, though she does not participate in many on-camera interviews. Contrasting these senior players, Schnall turns his attention to the incoming elite freshman recruits, principally Nikki Jett and Mandy Clark, who both struggle with Stringer's demanding practices and high expectations as well as the rigors of college academics. During the season, Clark and Jett are suspended from the team but are allowed to rejoin after demonstrating contrition for their lackluster effort and attitude. Never fully able to adhere to Stringer's expectations, Clark ends up quitting the program and transfers at the end of the year to a new university and different women's basketball program.

By focusing on these players and engaging occasionally with other Scarlet Knights, *This Is a Game, Ladies* presents sporting blackness as a forum for dynamically skilled female players and engaging young personalities. Overall, Black women athletes are shown as polymorphous in look, attitude, and style of play; and the team represent a range of expressions of femininity and female masculinity on and off the court. Their sporting desire is never linked to relationships with men or male approval. While the documentary does not comment on the players' sexuality (only Linda Miles mentions her looks in terms of male desire), Clark, Jett, and others' Black AG (butch aggressive) aesthetic implicitly articulates against a presumed heterosexual homogeneity and normatively gendered femininity.

While *This Is a Game, Ladies* provides a fuller rendering of women's athletics on screen through its focus on Stringer and her players, the documentary embraces the rhetoric of the "lady" in ways that both affirm and challenge the comportment of Black female sporting blackness. The aphorismic title, which is derived from a comment Stringer makes in the locker room after a loss, reflects the overarching representational politics of the film's portrayal of the team, specifically the Black players, within codes of respectability that PBS documentaries centered on Black experiences such as these encourage.[65] In the film's basketball terms, "lady" is not meant to convey the derogatory idea of "playing like a girl."[66] For Stringer, the apothegm's use of "ladies" is meant to teach the players about how to translate their athletic skills into their everyday lives as a kind of sports-themed dictum on social decorum. The title's preceding clause—"this is a game"— connotes the idea of sporting and social worlds as a competitive field of play. As such, Stringer wants her players to be successful, confident, responsible, and accountable athletes and adults (as defined, refined, and embodied in the ideal of the "lady") in their future activities.

Stringer's idealistic rhetorical framing and the team's acquiescence not only propagates gendered patterns into sports/social logic but also exposes the tensions and fears around Black female sporting blackness. Stringer's insistence on her team embodying a "lady-ness" can be understood as a strategic maneuver, one that pushes back against the ways in which, historically, Black women in general and Black women athletes specifically are always already narrativized outside of idealized womanhood. As Cahn explains, "the long exclusion of both African American women and female athletes from categories of acceptable femininity encouraged the development of analogous mythologies."[67] Black women are often represented as and thought to be animalistic and sexually deviant. "The charge that sport masculinized women physically and sexually resonated with scientific and popular portrayals of mannishness and sexual pathology among black women. The assertion that sport made women physically unattractive and sexually unappealing," Cahn continues, "found its corollary in views of black women as less attractive and desirable than white women. The correspondence between stereotyped depictions of black womanhood and athletic females was nearly exact, and this doubly resonant in the case of African American women athletes."[68] While the documentary does not detail this history explicitly, the critical muscle memory of the racialized standards of femininity that affect Black female athletes on and off the playing field manifest in Stringers' sporting rhetoric and the players sporting and social lives.

For Stringer, being a "lady" operates as a kind of embodied resistance to this history in a manner similar to past Black sportswomen who "did not tie femininity to a specific, limited set of activities and attributes defined as separate and opposite from masculinity. Rather, they created an ideal of womanhood rooted in the positive qualities they cultivated under adverse conditions: strength, family commitment, community involvement, and moral integrity."[69] Being a "lady" is a contesting force against the racism Black female athletes face, a counter-muscle memory of Black female dignity in the historical face, flex, and flux of prejudice and discrimination in sports and society. In the documentary, Stringer explains: "As a Black female, I want to personify that [a strong lady] because it means everything in the world to me and I want my players—any woman—to be able to feel good and feel proud about who we are and what I represent. And with that I feel that we do not need anyone else to define us." Stringer's "uplift politics" reify within her team's deportment the ways in which respectability as ideology and strategy becomes an embodied defense/offense, wherein individual behavior challenges social values and perceptions attached to Black women/womanhood. The problem with respectability politics, however, is that they are steeped in bourgeois values that recognize inequities but also blame Black people who transgress white and Black middle-class propriety.[70] The documentary's lack of historical perspectives about Black female athleticism reflects its institutionally add hyphen oriented sensitivities. The PBS-ification of Black women athletes' ambitions is meant to "[expand] the knowledge base of white audiences" through the "acceptance of simple-minded ideology of racial assimilation."[71] There is no larger context presented for the possibility of deeper analysis; instead *This Is a Game, Ladies'* engagement with Black female athleticism and respectability plays out most "politically correct" in the documentary's recounting of a journalistic racist and sexist attack on the team's players. The film thus reinforces liberal and humanist racial ideologies, using this gendered uplift strategy to pacify racial tensions that erupt after an incident and name-calling.

The documentary captures the incident when the Scarlet Knights were verbally attacked by local sports journalist Chris Elsberry. In his column for the Connecticut Post titled "Rutgers Team Have Yet to Earn Huskies Respect," Elsberry targeted Stringer and her players in a brazenly disparaging fashion with remarks on their bodies and style of play. Superimposing an image of the column onto the screen, the documentary narrates excerpts from Elsberry's article: "All the tattoos, all the black uniforms, and the headbands and the bravado don't mean a thing when you do not have the talent. . . . When is Vivian Stringer going to get that into her team's head? . . . That street style has never meshed well against the Huskies poise and depth."

Elsberry's references to the Rutgers' women's bodies conjures stereotypes about blackness and is meant to script them as an urban masculine menace. The racially loaded language evinces how, despite Stringer's insistence on "lady-ness," the Black Scarlet Knight players are read through the racist and sexist scripts of racial tropes, idealized (white) femininity and (Black) bodily comportment. The documentary presents three representative reactions to Elsberry's abhorrent attack on the team's sporting blackness. First, in Stringer's response, she admonishes the columnist, stating in a one-on-one interview with the filmmakers: "I think that all too often people who are not the sports people involved for whatever reason stand to the outside, and they want to demean young people who deserve so much more, so much respect, and so much appreciation for the efforts they all give." Her restrained reaction is in keeping with her exercises in dignity and respectability shown throughout the film. Her strategy befits the PBS frame of the post-Reaganite era to be "ideological in the widest sense: they hope to influence how people think" without causing too much offense.[72] The second response comes from one of the players. Schnall asks freshman Mandy Clark about Elsberry's statements. She tells the camera that Stringer has told the team that they are being called thugs in the media. Clark, who seems unsure of what is going on exactly and uneasy to form an opinion, is the only player approached (at least on camera) about the incident. Her apprehension, if not confusion, shows that she and other players may not have been instructed to speak on the matter publicly.

Instead of engaging with the players about their experiences of the intersections of race, gender, and sports in a direct or even roundabout way, Schnall contrives an expository scene without them to unpack Elsberry's comments. He sits down Kate Smith and Greg Tufaro, two white local sports journalists who are reoccurring figures in the documentary as talk-ing heads and sports color commentators. In the staged scene, Smith and Tufaro sit next to each other facing the camera as they discuss whether Elsberry's comments contained racial undertones, as well as the merits of Stringer's call of bias. Smith tries to mitigate the idea of race being a factor in Elsberry's words, reminding the audience that Elsberry did not explicitly call the players thugs. Instead, it was Stringer who inferred that connota-tion. Stuttering, Smith continues to explain that Elsberry's statements could have been misinterpreted "by a Rutgers fan" as implying thuggish behavior, but that after having spoken with Elsberry she believes that it was not his intention to paint the team in a racially derisive way. As a counter-argument to Elsberry's comments as nonracial, Tufaro forcefully dismisses that suggestion, claiming that the Rutgers players have never conducted themselves in the manner Elsberry portrayed in his column. Defending Stringer's inference of Elsberry's racially derogatory intention with her use of the word *thug*, Tufaro rejects the issue of semantics and states that while Elsberry did not write the word, that was still the subtext of his comments. Tufaro ends his explanation saying he, like Stringer, was offended.

The lack of first-person address by the players and the staging of this politely numb white-on-white dialogue about race underscores what Clyde Taylor calls "PBS's Novocain anesthesia" about racial issues, where jour-nalistic even-handedness is meant "to shield the defensive sensibilities of white viewers, the majority public whose response can make or break a successful public television reception."[73] Tufaro's wholesale rejection of Elsberry's description of the players' behavior frames the idea of Black urban identity ("street style") as opposite that of the embodied rhetoric of the lady, a respectability maneuver against the racial antagonisms of Elsberry's racism. The fact that he gets the last word on the matter conveys that his point of view is the larger takeaway. At the same time, Smith's intentionality narrative destabilizes the idea that a racial offense was even made at all. Both sides of the argument are shared in a (white) liberal humanist way that affirms each point of view and cancels out any critical stance the documentary could take on the gendered and class aspects of sporting blackness. In other words, issues of race appear in the documentary as current "news" largely because of the deracinated framework and a lack of explicit historical contextualization about Black women's sporting and non-sporting experiences.

While at first Stringer defends her players' right to look how they want (in an expansion of and contradistinction to the idealized "lady"), she later capitulates, policing their bodies and making them cover their tattoos during the postseason playoffs. Senior player Karlita Washington is shown putting bandages over tattoos that represent her love for her mother. In her act of compliance to the revised decorum of acceptable female embodiment, Washington reveals how Stringer's "lady" is emptied of Black female genealogy, agency, and history. When asked point-blank by Schnall if she is making the players hide their tattoos because the media is judging her and the team, Stringer emphatically and defensively denies his inquiry, stating: "It has nothing to do with the media, and I resent that thought. It has much more to do with my own thought. It is my job to protect my young ladies from perception and give them as much as an equal opportunity for this world because I want them to have everything." The ideology of ladylike comportment becomes for these young Black women confinement and protection, diminishing their individuated subjectivity in an effort to render them palatable and non-threatening. Thus, via effacement, the thug becomes a lady, and hopefully a winner.

This Is a Game, Ladies deals with racial antagonisms as a contemporary issue despite the muscle memory of past Black women's athletes struggles in sports and American society. These experiences create a Black female sporting habitus, or what Harvey Young describes as the ways in which "experiences and memories structure our behavior. The past, memories and previously learned lessons, 'survives in the present and tends to perpetuate itself in the future.'"[74] For the players in *This Is a Game, Ladies*, the respectability politics and the racist and sexist attacks on Black women's athleticism in the film replay past histories of defensive and offensive posturing. The past and present filmic critical muscle memories are futured as a new team of Scarlet Knights experience similar events as those captured by Schnall.

During the 2006–2007 NCAA women's basketball season, Stringer led the Scarlet Knights to their first NCAA championship game, losing in the finals against Pat Summitt and the Tennessee Vols. While disappointed by the loss, Rutgers' celebration of their amazing run to the title game was undercut by the infamous shock jock Don Imus. On his nationally syndicated and simulcast radio talk show, Imus ridiculed the Scarlet Knights, mocking their tattoos and calling them "rough girls" and "nappy headed ho's." The show's producer, Bernard McGurik, called the players "hard-core hoes," saying the game looked like Spike Lee's *School Daze* (1988) with the Scarlet Knights as the "jigaboos." While Imus would first defend his comment as his usual racist and sexist schlock (which he has aimed at other Black female sports stars such as Serena and Venus Williams), going so far to blame hip hop music, the controversy caused a national uproar with critics, pundits, and activists calling for Imus to be fired and leading him to formally apologize to the Rutgers team. In the end, MSNBC canceled the televised simulcast of *Imus in the Morning* and the CBS company canceled his radio show, though he would of course go back on the air a short time later. Stringer and the nearly all-Black Scarlet Knights were cast into the public and media spotlight after the attack, holding a nationally televised press conference where they expressed their hurt, anger, and pride while defending their womanhood.[75] The players' dignified responses highlighted not only their athletic abilities but also who they were outside of basketball: future doctors, valedictorians, dedicated and humorous friends, musical prodigies, and so on. This eruption of young women's sporting blackness into national scandal across media (newspaper, radio, television and the internet) signals how even strict adherence to ideologies of the "lady" can be disrupted by racism and phobic projections onto the Black female sporting body.

The events and media spectacle of 2007 around Black women's sporting bodies are striking when compared to the issues that come to bear in *This Is a Game, Ladies*, demonstrating how "the experience of the black body becomes *futured*, the present and future understood from a past perspective."[76] This past perspective is that of the history of Black women and Black women athletes' inequitable treatment, which becomes present in the documentary and futured in the 2007 media controversy to create—in Young's terms—a "closed loop" of sporting blackness.[77] Sporting blackness, here, operates as transhistorical corporeal entanglement and contingency with gendered and racial scripts. Read in this temporally fluid and yet fixed context, the documentary, as a discourse of and about critical muscle memory, meta-textually responds to recurring racial and gender antagonisms against the team and Black women in general.[78] The re-collection of misogynoir, or "the anti-Black racist misogyny that Black women experience," in *This Is a Game, Ladies* replays the game, placing these ladies on a historical continuum that, although often occluded from Black and sporting histories by networks, sportscasters, and scholars, is as urgent and engaging as that recorded in Black male sporting documentaries.[79] In this sense, the Black female sporting bodies in *This Is a Game, Ladies* operate as historical contestants against past, present, and futured racial and gender antagonisms within and beyond the bodies in and body of the film.

CONTESTING *HOOP DREAMS* IN *HOOP REALITY*

Steve James's 1994 documentary *Hoop Dreams* and Lee Davis's 2009 follow-up documentary *Hoop Reality* examine the world of basketball prospects.

James's film ushered in a subgenre of sports documentaries: the "prospect doc," or, films that follow young athletic hopefuls as they vie for exclusive spots in collegiate and/or professional sports.[80] An independent feature film, *Hoop Dreams* is one of the most acclaimed sports films of contemporary times. The canonical cautionary tale about the singularity of professional basketball as *the* Black male future is played out as a family, sporting, and national drama of epic proportion, clocking in a run time of three hours that spans years in the protagonists' lives. Filmmakers Steve James, Peter Gilbert, and Fredrick Marx first set out to make a half-hour short film for PBS with funding from Kartemquin Educational films. The short documentary was supposed to be about street-basketball culture in Black urban areas in Chicago. Instead of making the thirty-minute educational film, James, Gilbert, and Marx intermittently shot *Hoop Dreams* over four years, amassing a staggering 250 hours of footage.[81]

The commercially successful and Oscar-nominated documentary focused on William Gates and Arthur Agee, two talented teenaged African American males who have the possibility of going from Chicago's Cabrini-Green housing projects to a top-college program and then, hopefully on to professional basketball in the NBA.[82] Shot in a cinema verité style, this epic melodrama about basketball as means for class ascension chronicles these teenaged boys' high school years and their life and ball struggles, telescoping in and out of familial, scholastic, and game scenes to holistically portray their individual pressures, family dynamics, and sporting futures. While critical of the sports industrial complex, Cheryl L. Cole and Samantha King argue that "there are a number of ways in which *Hoop Dreams* indicts and fails to indict the economies of sports" and that the "criticism [of the film] is ultimately directed to and displaced on to the bodies of a particular social agents who are visualized as virtuous or vicious."[83] The film's sparse voiceover narration, lack of contextual framing, and its opaque and unquestioned narrative telos create a film fascinated with "the dream" of ghetto escape, money beyond measure, and the meritocracy of sporting ability. These ideological undercurrents ultimately work in the tired register of Black familial pathology/Black families as a pathology that has been central to US policy and rhetoric from slavery to the Moynihan report. The major act of displacement, King and Cole argue, occurs in the film's vilification of St. Joseph's white high school basketball coach, Gene Pingatore, who is represented—not unfairly—as someone who exploits and discards Black talent from the inner city in the pursuit of a state championship.

While Gates and Agee both have the opportunity to play for the predominantly white private school St. Joseph's, their paths and plots quickly diverge. After being "recruited" by local Black talent scout Earl Smith, who lives in their neighborhood, Agee is kicked out of the school in his sophomore year because his family cannot afford the tuition. Gates, who is also of the working poor, is given a scholarship to cover the costs. This white institutional exclusion of Agee and the charitable largesse shown to Gates are predicated on notions of athletic exceptionalism and racial stereotyping. Pingatore considers Agee to be less focused, playing a more "street ball" idiom of the game, thus less disciplined and more of a risk, and he is forced to return to his local public institution, Marshall High. Obsessed with having coached NBA star Isiah Thomas, Pingatore sees Thomas's abilities in Gates, describing him as having "a combination of personality, confidence, talent, [and] intelligence." Gates, who is more reserved and withholding than the boisterous and expressive Agee, is denied his own interiority by Pingatore; instead, he becomes a vessel and a vehicle for whatever his coach and others can project onto, invest in, and use for their own gains.

As their basketball careers diverge, *Hoop Dreams* follows both Gates and Agee, separately, as they play for their respective high school teams and attempt to gain collegiate recruiters' interests. For Gates, this is a period of injuries, the birth of his first child with longtime girlfriend Catherine, the signing a letter of intent to play at Marquette University, and a growing disillusionment with the game of basketball. For Agee, this is a time of familial discord, as his father, Bo, battles a crack addiction and leaves the family, forcing Agee's mother, Sheila, to go on welfare. Later, Sheila becomes a nurse's assistant and a newly sober Bo returns to the family. In their senior year, Gates and Agee hope to send their respective basketball teams "up state" to play for a championship. While Gates and St. Joseph's fall short with a loss that ends their season, Agee's team has a thrilling run for a state championship, taking third place in the playoff tournament. Despite Agee's breakout senior season, he is unable to meet the SAT requirements needed to attend a Division-1 school and ends up receiving an athletic scholarship to Mineral Area Junior College.

While neither Gates nor Agee make it to the NBA, the documentary sparked celebratory acclaim as well as scathing condemnation.[84] For some critics *Hoop Dreams* is "an exemplar of realism, social advocacy, and media activism," and "was revered and imbued with the status of a vanguard film" that "drew attention to the good intentions and personal virtues of its three white filmmakers."[85] On the contrary, the good intentions and personal virtues of the filmmakers were criticized forcefully by others, most notable being bell hooks. In a blistering review, she condemned the film's "voyeuristic pleasure at being able to observe from a distance the lives of two black boys from working class and poor inner city backgrounds."[86] Situating the film within "the continuum of traditional anthropological and/or ethnographic documentary," hooks describes *Hoop Dreams* as formally unremarkable and narratively dependent on classic Hollywood tropes, explicitly critiquing how the poverty and struggle of both Agee and Gates become "cheap entertainment."[87] Whether one sees it as vanguard film or cheap entertainment, *Hoop Dreams* has had a profound impact on popular culture, sports, and the sports film in its evocation of basketball, competition, ambition, class, race, success, and failure. The narrative and production history of *Hoop Dreams* has shaped the media environment of not only nonfiction films but also the social and sporting discourses embedded in contemporaneous and subsequent fictional basketball films such as *Above the Rim* (Jeff Pollack, 1994), *Blue Chips* (William Friedkin, 1994), and *He Got Game* (Spike Lee, 1998) that attempt to capture the dramatic momentum and urban ecosphere aestheticized in the documentary. Additionally, *Hoop Dreams* inspired its "sequel" *Hoop Reality*. In its citational and diacritical relationship, *Hoop Dreams* becomes inculcated discursively as critical muscle memory in *Hoop Reality*'s replay of the basketball fantasy.

Hoop Reality is an unofficial continuation of the *Hoop Dreams* story, and its non-idealistic title is meant as oppositional addendum and anecdote to the original documentary, one that captures the sobering "keep it real" sporting and societal outcome of such ambitions. The director and screenwriter Lee Davis is an apprentice of Spike Lee, who has a cameo in *Hoop Dreams* where he warns a group of young Black ballers at an elite basketball camp about universities' exploitative practices toward athletes like them. Davis's documentary, released fifteen years after *Hoop Dreams*, is relatively unknown and often goes unacknowledged in relation to the original film. While the documentary is described as a "sequel" to *Hoop Dreams* in its production material (and the very few reviews that exist on the film), the film has no direct production ties to the original. Neither James, Gilbert, nor Marx had any role in Davis's continuance of the film's storyline. In an oral history completed in 2014 to honor the twentieth-anniversary of the film and its restoration, James announced that the filmmakers swore they would never do a *Hoop Dreams* sequel.[88] They were, however, filming updates and interviews in 2005 for the Criterion digital rerelease of the film. James explains: "We did a lot of interviews with all of the principals, we started getting great stuff, and we thought, 'Why waste it on just a Criterion extra?' We were convincing Criterion to go along with something when Bo [Arthur's father] died."[89] While Bo's death foreclosed the idea of a sequel for James, Gilbert, and Marx, the effects of this tragedy on Agee are of principal interest to Davis in *Hoop Reality*. In the oral history about *Hoop Dreams* for *The Dissolve*, no one, including Agee, mentions *Hoop Reality*, despite the fact that *Hoop Reality* was released years prior to their interview with the online magazine and the documentary stars Agee. It is therefore important to think about the intertextual links between *Hoop Dreams* and *Hoop Reality* as well as the intentional production and narrative disjuncture between the two. These links and contradictions become embodied in Agee's reappearance in *Hoop Reality*'s familiar tale as a historical contestant, shaping the documentary as a meta-textual dispute about and with *Hoop Dreams*. Agee participates in a revised and updated version of the story that made him famous, surfacing anew within a familiar narrative and mise-en-scène of "hoop dreams."

Hoop Reality turns its documentary lens on Arthur Agee, now an adult coming to terms with his post–*Hoop Dreams* fame, as he mentors a promising young high school player, Patrick Beverly, who plays for Agee's old basketball team, the Marshall Commandos. William Gates is notably absent from the documentary, which centers Agee's "where are they now" story alongside Beverly's prospect narrative.[90] Sans Gates, *Hoop Reality*, in some ways, confirms hooks's critique of the film's seductive diegetic rivalry between Agee and Gates. Despite the protagonists' camaraderie throughout *Hoop Dreams*, hooks charges that "by constant comparing and contrasting their fate, the film creates a symbolic competition" where Agee is celebrated for his unrelenting obsession with basketball and Gates is marginalized for his critique of competition.[91] *Hoop Reality* cements even as it critically assesses the idea that Agee is *Hoop Dreams*' triumphant individual, the one "who remains obsessed with the game."[92] For Agee, hooks declares that "there is no escape. He has to keep playing the game. To escape is to fail."[93] Consequentially, *Hoop Reality*'s emplotted circularity elevates Agee as a cinematic character and star, one that is bound to and unable to been seen outside of the narrative that has bracketed his place in sporting history and the public imaginary.

Hoop Reality feels both more and less intentional than *Hoop Dreams*. Unlike *Hoop Dreams*, which used voice-over narration by filmmaker Steve James sparingly for exposition and in interviews, *Hoop Reality* employs robust voiceover narration, on-screen interviews, talking heads, and an overbearing amount of screen text that mimics the typography of a scoreboard. All of these expository elements cohere to demystify the idea of a "hoop dream" through epistemic docu-knowledge that gives "the impression of objectivity and of well-substantiated judgement" about the sports industrial complex.[94] At the same time, *Hoop Reality* feels narratively rushed and is choppily thrown together. While Agee's hoop dream narrative inaugurates the documentary, the relationship between him and Beverly seems almost accidental even if serendipitous. The film narrates Agee's interest in Beverly as a conditional response brought about by the filmmakers' interest in Beverly's rise on Agee's old high school basketball team, the Marshall Commandos. The film's focus remains on Agee's post–*Hoop Dreams* life, principally his newfound career as a motivational speaker, his father's death, and his desire to start his own Hoop Dreams clothing line with the slogan "control your destiny." Davis's documentary has both thematic and visual similarities to *Hoop Dreams*, including an interest in player, coach, and family dynamics; class mobility; as well as an attention to game and behind-the-scenes basketball footage that place it well within the genealogy of Black male sports documentaries.

Hoop Reality, however, does not have the narrative scope or cinematic pacing of *Hoop Dreams*. Instead, the documentary mostly chronicles Beverly's final, senior season of basketball and his hopes to attract a scholarship offer from a Division-1 collegiate program after spurning an offer from Toledo University's lower-tier basketball program. Previously living in the suburbs, the Beverly family moves back to the West Side of Chicago to allow Patrick the chance to play at Marshall and test if his skills are good enough to compete against the likes of teenage stars Sherron Collins and Derrick Rose. While we learn of Beverly's upbringing, particularly his being raised by a single mother, and witness the father-son dynamic with Marshall coach Lamont Bryant, the main focus of the film is whether Beverly has what it takes to play at a top college and then for the NBA.

The specter of the NBA as the ultimate basketball goal looms heavy in *Hoop Reality* as much as it did in *Hoop Dreams*. However, the fantasy of basketball as a ticket out and up is also narratively demystified through talking heads and on-screen text that continuously reminds the viewer that the odds are almost insurmountable if not impossible. Some interviewees remind the audience how difficult it is to stand out to top basketball programs without attending one of the sneaker-affiliated basketball camps that serve as markets for college recruiters. On-screen text provides various facts about the limited number of Division-1 athletic scholarships available and the even smaller number of those drafted to the NBA. Alongside these sobering statistics, Beverly, who has not gone to the necessary camps, has a compelling senior season and is positioned in the story as an individual who can beat the odds. In a remarkably similar fashion to *Hoop Dreams*, Beverly leads the Marshall Commandos "up state" and, like Agee's 1991 team, to a third-place finish at the state tournament.

Despite the basketball déjà vu, *Hoop Reality*'s conclusion offers what *Hoop Dreams* could not: a success story that affirms the basketball dream of making it out the hood on talent (and luck) alone. Beverly did gain prominence his senior year, attracting and accepting an athletic scholarship to the University of Arkansas where he played for two seasons before being deemed ineligible to play due to academic fraud. Beverly later went to play professional basketball overseas in Ukraine before entering the 2009 NBA draft, where he was selected with the forty-second overall pick by the Los Angeles Lakers before being traded to the Miami Heat. The Heat waived Beverly from the roster and, thus at the time of the documentary's completion, he was not playing in the NBA. The film includes this information as a kind of postscript, tacking it to the end of the documentary. However, it does not capture Beverly's current participation and praiseworthy play in the NBA after signing with the Houston Rockets in 2013 and being traded to the Los Angeles Clippers in 2017, where he currently plays point guard.[95]

The aesthetic memories in *Hoop Reality* come from many elements, including the parallel settings of Lee's film with its *Hoop Dreams* precursor. *Hoop Dreams* opens with a shot of the Chicago skyline, establishing the city as its sporting milieu. An elevated train barrels across the screen alongside a freeway taking passengers, including the viewing audience, into the cityscape and the world of the film. The camera cuts to an image of an inner-city basketball court cramped into the urban geography. There is a group of young Black men playing on the court, including one we will later recognize as William Gates. The soundscape echoes the commissioned hip hop track "Hoop Dreams," whose repeated titular refrain punctuates the (false) promise of sports for Black male athletes. The train's on-screen movement suggests the film's narrative trajectory as the camera cuts from the court to the housing projects populating the city to the "Chicago Stadium" where the Thirty-Eighth Annual NBA All-Star game is being held. Footage of the pro-game shows Michael Jordan, who plays for the "East" team, stealing the ball and doing a spectacular dunk as the crowd goes crazy. Returning to the image of the moving train, the camera cuts to the Cabrini Green Housing Project. Inside one apartment sits Gates, watching the All-Star Game before he tells the camera: "I want, you know, to play in the NBA like anybody else would want to. That's who, that's something I dream-think about all the time, you know playing in the NBA." The camera then cuts to a highly stylized scene of Gates on an outdoor basketball court. As he goes up to dunk the ball, his body is depicted in slow motion. The sound of the cheers from the Chicago stadium are supplanted onto Gates's sporting image. Interviews with Gates's mother and brother about their hopes for his professional prospects follow before the film shifts to the West Garfield Neighborhood, introducing Arthur Agee and his family.

This opening sequence is meant to propagate the Horatio Alger sports fantasy of basketball stardom, "[highlighting] an issue Americans of all races, but particularly white Americans, can easily identify with—the longing of Black males to become great basketball players."[96] It represents Gates's existing form as a futured body—being and becoming—potentially similar to that of Michael Jordan or, as Coach Pingatore hopes, Isiah Thomas. The film's crosscutting and sonic interlay of the All-Star game and Gates on the courts produces dialogic and experiential overlap between Gates and Jordan where being and becoming are cinematic and sporting projections. *Hoop Dreams* renders critical muscle memory as a possible shared and near utopic sporting future. In doing so, the documentary contains several of these kinds of moments where Agee's and Gates's sporting and non-sporting experiences are enveloped in the embodied histories of Black superstar figures that ultimately function in the narrative as cautionary tales.

Like many Black documentaries that intervene on reoccurring and pervasive images of Black people, *Hoop Reality* signifies on *Hoop Dreams*'s opening sequence, reproducing while demystifying the allure of "making it" from the hood to the NBA. Davis's film begins with a black screen. On-screen text appears as scoreboard typography that reads: "Only 0.03% of high school basketball players will one day play in the NBA." From this opening, the reality and not the dream of professional basketball aspirations is centered in and through the text. *Hoop Reality*'s first images include that of its Chicago Westside environment, mirroring that of *Hoop Dreams*. The mise-en-scène of a train above the urban basketball court cites and parallels the earlier documentary. As young Black men play on the court, a shaky hand-held camera captures their competition. The film cuts from close-range shots to long ones of the court as the camera is placed outside the fenced area of the outdoor playground. Removed from the action, the camera peers through the fence. The distanced look is reminiscent of the ethnographic aspects of *Hoop Dreams*'s filmmakers' scouting for Black talent on the playground. While *Hoop Dreams* idealizes this introduction as a sporting fantasy (Gates *could*, as the 1992 Gatorade ad suggests, "Be Like Mike" according to the cross-cutting at the documentary's outset), *Hoop Reality* uses facts about the NBA to provide sobering statistics as well as the (melo) dramatic stakes for Beverly's attempt to make it to the league.

While *Hoop Dreams* eschews a consistent voice-over to orient the viewer through direct address, *Hoop Reality* relies on Agee as its narrator throughout the film. Providing Black athletes the opportunity to voice their own histories, this first-person narration strategy is endemic of Black documentary aesthetic practices. In the beginning of *Hoop Reality*, Agee explains that many inner-city youth still believe that the NBA is their ticket out of their impoverished environment. Intercutting shots of players at the Adidas sponsored Phenom Academy and players at Marshall High School, Agee explains that the days of going straight to the NBA directly from high school are over. With that path to basketball glory gone, he clarifies that, now, a high school baller's best bet is to be recruited by a Division-1 college team first if they want a chance to make it to the professional league. Since *Hoop Dreams* premiered, the eligibility rules of the NBA draft have changed and no player can sign with the league until they are nineteen years old, a controversial decision that produced a host of "one-and-done" college players. While detailing this important eligibility distinction, *Hoop Reality* visually punctuates this point through references to *Hoop Dreams*. The documentary cuts to footage of Agee during his college years playing for Arkansas State University before switching to a black screen where text reads: "Only 1.5% of high school graduates will get into a Divison-1 college." Agee reiterates this fact, detailing that the odds are extremely unfavorable that an athlete can make it to the NBA. As he explains, the image of a sweat drenched Beverly sitting on the sidelines with current Marshall High School varsity basketball coach, Lamont Bryant, is shown. These shots underscore *Hoop Reality*'s recursivity and the changing same of Black male hoop dreams. Beverly stands in as a contemporary Agee even as the younger baller hopes to not repeat Agee's fate. The two players' similar and repeating experiences are visually framed within the long-shot narrative that both documentaries employ. In contradistinction to *Hoop Dreams*, *Hoop Reality* states the near impossibility in plain terms. On-screen text explicitly states that: "Only 1.2% of college players will be drafted by the NBA each year." A meta-textual dispute with *Hoop Dreams*'s false promise (even as it repeatedly engages with and is predicated on such wishful thinking), *Hoop Reality*'s opening works as a cautionary tale by relying on harsh truths and statistics about professional basketball aspirations and realities. Using the now canonical iconography of its predecessor, Davis imbricates a cinematic pattern of aesthetic memories into his film that connects the unofficial "sequel" to *Hoop Dreams*. These memories are captured not only through an analogous mise-en-scène but also through the embodied presence and critical muscle memory of Agee's sporting experience in the original documentary. In doing so, *Hoop Reality* rescripts the past in terms of the present with the intent to revise and revive our critical muscle memory about basketball hopes.

FIGURE 7.   Shots of newspaper clippings featuring *Hoop Dreams* (Steve James, 1994) ephemera function as intertextual citations in *Hoop Reality* (Lee Davis, 2007).

Early in *Hoop Reality*, Agee introduces himself in voice-over, saying: "My name is Arthur Agee. I am one of those that did not make it." Newspaper clippings of Agee in college are held before the camera before being placed on a table that also includes his 1991 senior yearbook from Marshall High School. Agee explains that he was in the film *Hoop Dreams*, and *Hoop Reality*'s camera cuts to newspaper clippings documenting that basketball period of his life (figure 7). In one image, there is a large photo of Agee signing a *Hoop Dreams* poster alongside his father and another of him hugging President Bill Clinton with the headline: "Hoops with the Chief." Giving a bit of biographical data, Agee reminds the viewer of his high school glory days, particularly Marshall's 1991 run down state for a third-place finish. The lack of footage from *Hoop Dreams* is most likely an issue of rights and licensing, another reason why *Hoop Reality* is not really an official sequel to the 1994 film. However, Agee's body does bridge the cinematic gap between the *Hoop Dreams* past and the *Hoop Reality* present, acting as an authorial and authenticating figure that works across temporal and social structures to shape how we understand the dream and reality of sports.

While in *Hoop Dreams*, Agee's and Gates's bodies are connected to those of future NBA stars, *Hoop Reality*'s rendering of critical muscle memory emanates from a more dialectical representation of Agee and Patrick

FIGURE 8. Arthur Agee and Patrick Beverly in *Hoop Reality* (Lee Davis, 2007).

Beverly (figure 8). Agee's mediated, aspirational basketball history becomes grafted onto Beverly. In this documentary, Agee explains that he had been told that there is a player that reminds everyone of him. Once he sees Beverly play, Agee agrees with the similarity and begins to mentor him. This evocative confluence enfolds the two because to see one's self in another's story can be, as Jared Sexton describes, "another way of saying, 'I did not see you,' even if the resultant connection is heartfelt. I did not see you, only the availability of your story, your image, your name. Or your body, its shape, its movement."[97] However, Black athletes' seeing themselves in others is also a way to recognize critical muscle memory as individual and collective experience, a familiar connection between two bodies and two stories. *Hoop Reality* constructs critical muscle memory as acts of reflection on and shared recollection of embodied Black sporting and nonsporting experiences. As Beverly comes into his own as a player, he remediates and re-embodies Agee's sporting history with a twist: he makes it to the NBA. Beverly and Agee are cinematically structured and sutured as a temporal binary, singularity, and futurity. From the present-day perspective of Agee and Beverly, *Hoop Reality* acts recursively as a meta-history of and a meta-textual dispute with *Hoop Dreams* that, to borrow and inflect Harvey Young's words, "accounts for the evolution in [basketball] culture but also enables an imagining of what life would be like had things been different."[98] In the formal sense, *Hoop Reality* (along with the other films examined here) is a documentary of and about critical muscle memory.

GENRE OF/ABOUT CRITICAL MUSCLE MEMORY

On the Shoulders of Giants; This Is a Game, Ladies; Hoop Dreams; and *Hoop Reality* exemplify both sports and Black documentary traditions. As a dominant mode of sports cinema production, Black sports documentaries are a robust subgenre dedicated to the rendering of critical muscle memory. Like Black documentaries, these sports-mediated histories engage blackness and Black people as viable subjects, using documentary/cultural production as a historiographic and investigative tool to produce subjectivities, provide counternarratives, contextualize social and political forces, and visualize connections to Black people and experiences across space and time. In the end, these documentaries archive, interrogate, and reinvent lost Black sports histories; fill gaps; and expose and correct errors and misrepresentations on Black life and culture.[99]

Since *Hoop Dreams*, there has been a compelling compendium of sports documentaries produced that evidence these practices. These works range from the coming-of-draft-age story *Through the Fire* (Alistair Christopher and Johnathan Hock, 2005); the athlete-activist-actor biography *Jim Brown: All-American* (Spike Lee, 2002); the fall-from-grace profile *Marion Jones: Press Pause* (John Singleton, 2010); the tennis wage gap tale *Venus Vs.* (Ava DuVernay, 2013); the legendary WNBA baller profile *Swoopes* (Hannah Storm, 2013); the race, fame, and sports in Los Angeles miniseries *OJ: Made in America* (Ezra Edelman, 2016); and the tightly crafted docuseries on Serena Williams's return to tennis after motherhood *Being Serena* (HBO, 2018). Directed by filmmakers who work sometimes in both fiction and nonfiction, these texts demonstrate the importance of nonfictional imaginative processes to cultural producers who are invested in shaping Black images on screen. Ranging in sport subjects, these films visually register sports' spectacular qualities, using footage and interviews to approach athletes' bodies as "articulate matter" in order to "demonstrate the central role that physicality plays in constructing both individual agency and sociality" for Black people.[100]

Unlike most fictional sports films that draw on real sports history to tell conservative tales of Black heroics, Black sports documentaries archive Black history, culture, and athletic and social feats to challenge Hollywood's reductionist narratives and blunted sporting histories even as they, too, sometimes are seduced by sanitized stories of sporting greatness. They use sports figures, worlds, cultures, and events to celebrate Black achievement, examine (subversively or not) the commodification of Black bodies, and provide a forum for Black athletes to not only talk about themselves but also talk back to and sometimes against their own placement within history. In doing so, they show how documenting the Black athlete and his/her/ their sporting performance can, as Cutler writes of Black documentaries, "express the richness and multiplicity of black experience" and locate these experiences in larger conversations about sports, culture, and the social world.[101]

Invested in remembering and recording the Black sporting body through archival footage/images, reenactments, and personal testimony, Black sports documentaries reflect upon and recall Black athletic experiences, visually archiving the embodied social and athletic actions of Black sporting figures and tying them to movements, cultures, and worlds. Indexing Black athletes' embodied passions, they show how "black bodies carry within themselves a history, a memory" and, in turn, are repositories of these histories and memories via sports footage, interviews, and reenactments.[102] Representing and reproducing this embodied knowledge, Black sports documentaries such as *On the Shoulders of Giants*; *This Is a Game, Ladies*; *Hoop Dreams*; and *Hoop Reality* are films of and about critical muscle memory. They exist, in performance studies scholar Diane Negra's terms, as both the archive and the repertoire, mediated through documentary's representational systems.[103] As a mutually constructed and enacted semiosis of and about critical muscle memory, Black sports documentaries "configure a tradition of codes and conventions of bodily signification that allows bodies to represent and communicate with other bodies," both on screen and for their viewer.[104] The codes and conventions of the sports documentary and Black documentary traditions shape the Black athlete as a mutable subject and object of study able to generate, record, and transmit muscle memories.[105] As such, Black sports documentaries are formally expressive, communicative bodies of work that highlight, document, investigate, and historicize Black sporting bodies "doin' work" as historical contestants.[106]

2. Racial Iconicity and the Transmedia Black Athlete

You know God made Black beautiful.
God made Boobie beautiful, Black and strong.
And when Boobie knocks some fools out,
Boobie gonna knock 'em out with black Nikes on his feet.
Ain't that right?
And I'ma smile when I do.
Yeah. Yeah. I'm distinguished now.

—BIG K.R.I.T.'S "Hometown Hero"

In 2010, critically acclaimed rapper Big K.R.I.T. released the single "Hometown Hero" from his mixtape *K.R.I.T. Wuz Here.*[1] The track explicitly samples and remixes the cinematic football player, James "Boobie" Miles. Boobie's life on and off the gridiron was initially chronicled in *Friday Night Lights: A Town, A Team, A Dream*, H.G. Bissinger's best-selling nonfiction book about the intense and grim effects of high school sporting culture on the small town of Odessa, Texas.[2] Recounting the 1988 football season of the Permian High School Panthers, Bissinger provides a thick description of the school's sporting ecology. In the book, football functions as a communal epicenter, a tangled knot of social and racial tensions exacerbated by the competitive stakes attached to the game itself. The "Friday night lights" illuminate the historical forces splintering the segregated West Texas community, while their "Friday night politics" are put into play on and off the field. Permian High School's spatial, racial, and intergenerational dynamics narrate a complex tale of sports, race, class, mobility, and stasis. As the book details, the Panthers are the winningest team in Texas history. Their drive to the 1988 State Championship is largely set against the backdrop of the economic crises that have beleaguered the town since its charter. The yearlong investigation is principally refracted through Bissinger's lens—his point of view on the game's spectacle; the head coach, Gary Gaines; and a small cadre of players on the team. Bissinger's unflinching account provides a celebratory and consequential examination of the allure of sports and the danger of weighted expectations. The book is an evocative and blistering saga of how hope comes alive on Friday nights, one that soberly dismantles the intoxicating thrill of victory and discloses the devastating agony of defeat.

Boobie's significance to the book is evident in the text's prologue, which begins in media res, midway through the Panther's season. Permian is playing against archrival Midland Lee. Boobie, the former standout running back who tore his anterior cruciate ligament (ACL), is trying to regain his prominence on the field since being replaced by Chris Comer, Permian's new "great Black hope." Bissinger explains that Boobie, realizing that he is never going to play as well as he once did, "sat on the bench and felt a coldness swirl through him, as if something sacred inside him was dying, as if every dream in his life was fleeing from him and all he could do was sit there and watch it disappear amid all those roars that had once been for him."[3] Boobie quit the team two days later. The pathos of Bissinger's account, a projected interiority, and Boobie's fated tragedy, a literary mythos, register the false promise of sports for Black athletes who seek fame and acclaim in this unforgiving public arena. Despite his sidelining, Boobie is central and of critical significance to Bissinger's story about Permian and Odessa, a school and a town that "had once anointed him the chosen son but now mostly thought of him as just another nigger."[4] The book details how "the sports field is often the space where we are most likely to find forms of fanatical hyper-identification and even idolized devotion towards black athletic bodies *and* some of the most violent expressions of anti-black racism, sometimes occurring within the *same* sporting locations and directed towards the *very same* athletes."[5] Once adored and then discarded, Boobie is the Black body at the pivotal fulcrum of this acclaimed American sports and cautionary tale.

In his afterword, *After Friday Night Lights: When the Games Ended, Real Life Began. An Unlikely Love Story*, released over two decades after his bestseller, Bissinger affirms that Boobie's narrative indelibly shapes the impact and legacy of his book.[6] Describing Boobie's iconicity in sports and the public imaginary, Bissinger declares: "He was the book's most talked-about character and a symbol of everything wrong with high school football because of the tragedy that befell him as a rising senior and the virulent racism directed against him afterwards. He became the country's ultimate cautionary tale of what happens when a young athlete puts all his hopes in the false god of football."[7] Boobie embodies the emblematic and vexed meanings and corollaries associated with being what Nicole Fleetwood describes as a "racial icon," though certainly distinct in magnitude from the iconicity of sensational athletes like LeBron James and Serena Williams examined in her work on Black sports stars in visual culture.[8] As Fleetwood emphasizes:

The racial icon is both an exceptional and common figure. She or he is exceptional as a symbol of overcoming racial inequality and perceived inferiority; she or he is common, given the American public's familiarity and investment in exhausted notions of race, nation, and (under)achievement. Whether a self-conscious and deliberate construction or a product of circumstance, the racial icon—as image, political figure, celebrity, or sports hero—conveys the weight of history and the power of the present moment. *To stand apart* and *to stand for* are the jobs of the racial icon.[9]

As a deified high school football player, Boobie was worshipped in the small town of Odessa and looked up to as a sports role model. His physicality and athletic prowess and promise marked his body as extraordinary, a spectacular blackness predicated on his embodied exceptionality. Punished on the field, however, his leg injury proves the rule about professional sporting aspirations—failure is the most common of fates for those who seek fame under the stadium lights.

Bissinger's *Friday Night Lights: A Town, A Team, A Dream* provides Boobie's initial subject formation and framing, a starting point to consider how his mythos and signification is made and made sense of through a transmedia sporting performance that recycles, recirculates, and revises discourses about his sporting blackness. Bissinger's book inaugurates the *Friday Night Lights* multimedia franchise, and Boobie is a transmedia character who travels across affiliated and unaffiliated media texts in a manner similar to other representations of transmedia Black athletes such as Jackie Robinson and Muhammad Ali.[10] My use of the term *transmedia* here refers to the flow of similar content across media texts. At the same time, I am also drawing on the paradigmatic formal, industrial, and consumer practices of transmedia storytelling.[11] I read Boobie's transmedia representations within the conceptual possibilities and limitations of racial iconicity, detailing throughout how sporting blackness in this case schematizes racial achievements and stigmas in terms of shifting content, forms, and points of positionality. Boobie, as an example of transmedia sporting blackness, provides the critical entanglements to analyze a body within a text and also follow a body across texts to understand how each re-representation engages, modifies, and reworks his original subjectivity in terms of the changing same of his racial iconicity. While a transmedia figure, Boobie's sporting body, as Hortense Spillers suggests of all bodies, "should be specified as a discursive and particular instance that belongs to a *context*, and we must look for its import there."[12] To be clear, I am not attempting to examine Boobie's real body with its mortal complexities and fleshed dimensionality, though I recognize and often refer to his biographical narrative. I am, instead, interested in the literary, cinematic, and sonic textualization and tropification of his male sporting body as a racial icon, specifically the discursive intratextuality and intertextuality mobilized in and through different representational modalities and respective publics. I argue that Boobie's sporting history has become memorialized as iconic and familiar, a discourse on exceptionality and failure, and a site of cultural (re)production for those who (re)imagine him in popular culture.

In the *Friday Night Lights* multimedia franchise, Boobie's muscle memory—his movement and representation in and across texts—becomes critical to and of his mythologization. Critical muscle memory in transmedia sporting performances evinces a shared and derivative, intratextual and intertextual embodied sporting history. Attention to this measure of critical muscle memory affords a consideration for representations of Black athletes as emblematic and epithetic, abstractions and ideations of blackness and the sporting body that personify, flow, and transform from one medium to another. Boobie's literary figuration, an urtext, becomes an appellation, one that scripts new performative identities, enacting a transmedia critical muscle memory of his familiar textual racial iconicity in new formal contexts.

While Bissinger's book inaugurates Boobie's iconicity, Peter Berg's 2004 film adaptation, *Friday Night Lights*, "metastasized him into a celebrity," and the film is the crux of this chapter's analysis of his sporting blackness on screen.[13] As played by Derek Luke, Boobie's representation in *Friday Night Lights* anchors this study as I drift to and from his cinematic figuration, moving from a focus on the racial politics of *Friday Night Lights* to the film's depiction of Boobie as a (fallen) racial icon outward to his other popular locales. A close textual analysis of Boobie in *Friday Night Lights* confirms the abject ways sporting blackness is rendered throughout the film. This focus on the semiotics, narratology, and subject-positioning of Boobie's body demonstrates the ways in which his cinematic image in particular carries the embodied histories of his and others sporting experiences. The film mobilizes Boobie's "symbolic freight," the surplus meaning and value that resonate beyond him and connects him to other embodied experiences.[14] As an analytic approach to reading moments of shared embodied experiences, critical muscle memory is represented in the film's depiction of Boobie's injury and formalized through cinematic doubling in scenes where the actual Boobie Miles watches the acted Boobie Miles as played by Derek Luke. Critical muscle memory, in this instance, constitutes both the situation and the structure of Boobie within the cinematic apparatus; it is the process of representing and identifying similar athletic embodied experiences.

Throughout this chapter, I trace how Boobie's racial iconicity has been multiplied in popular culture and remediated in and across texts, from the book's original print to the film adaption to televisual abstractions to lyrical citations in rap music. Because of the ways in which he is both recognizable and reenvisioned in different texts, Boobie as a transmedia character exhibits what Robin Bernstein calls the "properties of elasticity and resilience."[15] Boobie, meaning and meaning again, from source to source, demonstrates my argument throughout this book that Black sporting bodies function as canvases of representation, textual corpora that re-signify in new contexts. The notion of racial iconicity, I suggest, travels "across the play of significations" attached to Boobie's body, rearticulating his cinematic embodied defeat and corollary critical muscle memory within new frames and racial logics.[16] Shifting from the silver screen to the small screen, I cull the various televisual exclusion/inclusions of Boobie in NBC's short-lived drama *Against the Grain* (1993) and the critically acclaimed NBC (2006–2008)/ The 101 Network (2008–2011) drama *Friday Night Lights*. Though no character in the latter program is named after the iconic football player, a cohort of Black athletes on the *Friday Night Lights* television series inherits Boobie's characteristics and biographical data. Finally, I turn to rapper Big K.R.I.T., born Justin Scott, whose stage name is an acronym of Big King Remembered in Time, and his lyrics and videos for "Hometown Hero" and "Boobie Miles," both of which sample or cite the cinematic football player. I read the ways in which Big K.R.I.T.'s hip hop spectatorship formally reclaims Boobie's embodied failures on screen as a site of rhetorical agency, adopting prosaic and performative expressions of critical muscle memory. The textual and visual complexity of these hip hop narratives and identity formations articulates a modality of embodied virtuosity. Big K.R.I.T. produces alternative, counter-ideological ways of seeing and remembering the venerated and denigrated athlete as a Black familiar racial icon and folk hero. He gives us a way to sonically imagine and legitimate Boobie's successes and failures as connected to and outside of the transmedia character's dominant narrative, temporal, and visual frames.

THE TEXTS AND TEXTURES OF A RACIAL ICON

H.G. Bissinger's detailed account of Boobie's high school football career provides the initial discursive framing of Boobie as a transmedia racial icon. In *On Racial Icons: Blackness and the Public Imagination*, Nicole Fleetwood outlines the critical capacities of Black iconicity in American culture, consciousness, and public life. Fleetwood convincingly argues that Black icons are public fixations, figures, and figurations that come to represent and negotiate meanings about race, desire, belonging, valuation, degradation, equality, injustice, inclusion, and exclusion in American culture. "The racial icon," Fleetwood posits, "as both a venerated and denigrated figure serves a resonating function as a visual embodiment of American history and as proof of the supremacy of American democracy."[17] The two concepts of veneration and degradation graph the subtle distinction between iconicity and racial iconicity for Black subjects. Extending W. J. T. Mitchell's notion of race as an iconic concept—"the merging of an ideational complex with individual and collective passions, congealed in forms of totemism, fetishism, and idolatry"—Fleetwood suggests that Black racial icons are chimeras, iconized but never fully sainted because of the encumbered historical narratives around blackness in American society and thus become a diagnostic of the embattled racial state.[18] The Black racial icon, then, oscillates between notions of "the singular and the collective, the exceptional and the familiar" that publics and counterpublics embrace, reject, debate, define, and redefine.[19]

Beginning with the funereal iconicity of Trayvon Martin's hoodie, a symbol catalyzed to protest his murder, Fleetwood extends her attention to iconicity through interrogations of different cultural arenas, including politics, celebrity culture, and popular music. Her final study on sports provides the conceptual framework for evaluating how Boobie, first described in Bissinger's bestseller, comes to be understood within the critical measures of racial iconicity.[20] Black athletes as racial icons come from their circulation as superstar players in national and global fields, contexts, and markets. The affective and capital investments in Black athletes shape the fraught politics of their valuation, fetishization, and repudiation. As Kobena Mercer suggests, Black men as sports heroes underscore how sports reproduce the schisms of white ambivalence, a fear and fantasy about Black male prowess. "This schism is played out daily in the popular tabloid press," Mercer explains: "On the front page headlines black males become highly visible as a threat to white society, as muggers, rapists, terrorists and guerrillas: their bodies the imago of a savage and unstoppable capacity for destruction and violence. But turn to the sports pages, and the black man's body is heroized and lionized."[21] This front page–sports page split underscores what Fleetwood describes as visual cultures' "binary modes of rendering black subjects through narratives of exceptionalism or deviance."[22] Embodying ludic appeal, agentive force, creativity, and control, Black athletes are simultaneously celebrated and feared, desired and threatening spectacles.

Because his impact on the world of sports is not of the same magnitude or professional level of achievement as that of icons like Lebron James and Serena Williams that Fleetwood closely examines, the racial iconicity of Boobie Miles offers subtle distinctions to her acute configuration. How can a high school running back who was injured his senior year and never played one second of professional football be a widely-known celebrity, cautionary tale, and, later, folk hero? Scaled-down in proportion to his sporting status and blown-up by his literary, cinematic, and pop culture mythos, Boobie modulates the scales of racial iconicity in the public (literary, cinematic, televisual, and sonic) imagination. The continuing representational currency of his image—where a newspaper will profile a former teammate who blocked for the "famous Boobie Miles"—starts with the discursive framing and mediation of his sporting blackness in Bissinger's *Friday Night Lights: A Town, a Team, a Dream.*[23]

In Bissinger's expository account of high school sports, Boobie operates within the vexed dialectic of the Black athlete as a racial icon, a celebrated and condemned sporting body. Boobie's story activates and animates the racialized sporting dynamics in the book, yet his narrative arc is contained to two chapters explicitly dedicated to him: "Boobie" and "Boobie Who?" The chapter titles—a before and after anecdote—signal the ways "racial iconicity hinges on a relationship between veneration and degradation and this twinning [shapes] the visual production and reception of black American icons."[24] In the chapter "Boobie," Bissinger builds on his introduction of the football player and his failed comeback in the prologue, where the devastating effects of Boobie's injury set the stage for an interrogation into the history, people, and politics that shape the significance of football in Odessa, Texas, and in America more broadly. This titular chapter continues the narrative of Boobie's injury while providing biographical data and historical context. Bissinger depicts Boobie's sporting blackness— his athletic acumen and physical dominance—as a refraction of racial politics in West Texas. Boobie's injury, which is detailed early in the chapter, provides the entryway into Bissinger's account of the town's segregationist politics. Using the story of Boobie's legal guardian, L.V., and his denied opportunities to play football at the all-white high school in town, Bissinger explains how sports shaped the race relations of the neighboring town of Crane, Texas, which the white people called "Niggertown."[25] This shift of focus provides the critical framing of Boobie as hopeful progeny, representative of L.V.'s desires for sports to be what John Hoberman calls "a utopia of equal opportunity where blacks could demonstrate their long-denied 'manhood' and 'fitness' for full citizenship."[26] The chapter ends with a return to Boobie's injury during a scrimmage against the Palo Duro Dons. What is first thought to be merely a sprained ligament turns out to be extensive knee and cartilage damage, a torn ACL in need of arthroscopic surgery.

Bissinger is both fascinated and stupefied by Boobie's physicality and describes it as graceful, powerful, and seemingly indestructible. He considers how others, particularly white coaches and community members, see Boobie as a commodity and their ticket to success. Boobie narratively stands in for magical and historical processes of racialization, thus becoming the text's totemic figure of racial identity politics and abjection. Boobie is described and framed in terms of his chiseled, sinewy, and hard body, an idealized physique of sporting prowess. He is a "blue-chip" recruiting prospect, a prized player for top college football programs in Texas and across the nation. Boobie's value is derived from his bodily utility and how that will serve a team and its associated educational institution and the economic bottom line that connects the two in high school as well as college. His invaluableness is linked to discourses of Black exceptionality; yet, when injured, he becomes attached to racially tinged notions of worthlessness. This economy of sporting racial capital shapes the legibility of Boobie's blackness in the book and its later derivative media texts as well as the broader landscape of contemporary sports popular culture that traffic in representations of exceptional Black male athletic bodies, including films such as *Above The Rim* (Jeff Pollack, 1994), *The Air Up There* (Paul Michael Glaser, 1994), *He Got Game*, (Spike Lee, 1998), and *Any Given Sunday* (Oliver Stone, 1999).[27]

Bissinger explores how race shapes Boobie's commodification on and off the field. Boobie, who has a learning disability and would have been ineligible to play as a college freshman, is only tolerated because of what his body can do on the field. His subjectivity is the fulfillment of purpose sans agency. When his body fails him, he is not a person but an abstraction. This fact is rendered clearly in Bissinger's recalling of a white Permian coach's response about who Boobie would be without football: "A big ol' dumb nigger."[28] This projected epithet demonstrates Harvey Young's description of the *idea* of the Black body: "It is the black body and not a particular, flesh-and-blood body that is the target of a racializing projection."[29] Boobie is transformed in the book to the well-worn racist slur. His body has been constructed and deconstructed by this kind of textual work; he is familiar and unremarkable if always already racially marked and narrativized.

Boobie's reprise in the chapter "Boobie Who?" confirms his fall from grace. Bissinger is critical of the ways in which the white coaches frame

Boobie's bodily injury as a by-product of his mental deficiencies whereby sporting blackness attests to Black inferiority. "Sometimes it sounded as if they were talking about a pro player making a million dollars a year with a contractual obligation to play," he writes, "not an eighteen-year old kid playing for his high school team who, to be here at all, had overcome abandonment by his mother and foster homes and learning disabilities."[30] Detailing how Chris Comer takes his place as starter and star on the team, Bissinger points to the interchangeability of Black athletes, the dehumanizing ways in which those in the spotlight can be moved to the periphery when their utility diminishes or is extinguished. Marginalized, Boobie's failed attempts to make a comeback affirmed the reality of his situation and its affects. As depression sets in, Boobie's life of hardship has only just begun. In the afterward *After Friday Night Lights*, the traffic between affection and guilt drives Bissinger's relationship with Boobie through the intervening years. The short piece of writing is essentially a story of Boobie and Bissinger's points of crossing on the former running back's off-track life. At the same time, the afterward also helps to reconstruct the complexity of Boobie's athletic prowess, injury, and racial iconicity in the present day and from the long-view of Boobie's tumultuous years post football. "His was an all too typical American celebrity," Bissinger explains, "misleading because [the book] didn't move his life forward a single inch, destructive because it only makes it a hundred times harder for Boobie to get a grip on the simple rigors of an ordinary life."[31]

This mix of celebrity and the ordinary modulates the tenor of Boobie's lived racial iconicity in terms of the quotidian. He is an example of racial iconicity in terms of the vernacular, or "Black familiar," a "failed" Black cultural figure reclaimed and valorized by Black people as a football folk hero.[32] Bissinger's analysis of Boobie's sporting blackness serves as a starting point, a means to think through the Black body's narrative textures across media forms and beyond authorial intention.

SPORTING BLACKNESS IN *FRIDAY NIGHT LIGHTS*

In order to understand Boobie's cinematic racial iconicity, it is important to first consider *Friday Night Lights'* broader racial imaginings of venerated and vilified sporting blackness in terms of the film's diegetic sports narrative. Peter Berg's film adaptation, like many based-on-true-events sports films, takes many liberties with its source material. Despite revising the factual history included in Bissinger's text, the film provides a level of verisimilitude to its story about the isolated and insulated town of Odessa and the local politics of high school sports in Texas. As a selective recount of the 1988 football season of the Permian Panthers, the film follows many sports-genre conventions. The narrative eschews historical record, employing both cinematic realism and the melodramatic mode to heighten the identificatory, emotional, and moral registers in the film.[33] With its "feel-good" qualities and, for those unfamiliar with the Panthers' story, surprisingly non-triumphant ending, *Friday Night Lights* operates within these sports film tropes and textual systems while paradoxically maintaining and challenging ideological notions of meritocracy and the American Dream.

While the film adaptation condenses the book's historical, political, economic, and cultural investigation of the sociality of sports, Berg's creative interpretation of Bissinger's text has made it one of the most celebrated sports films. *Friday Night Lights* captures Odessa's obsession with football and how it puts pressure on the coaches and players to be "perfect," the abstract quality defined as the team winning the Texas state championship. Head coach Gary Gaines (Billy Bob Thornton) is under the microscope of parents, community members, and boosters, who expect him to produce a championship team, and likewise the teenage football players also experience the stress and anxiety of others' expectations of and projections on them to be excellent.

To summarize, *Friday Night Lights* begins during preseason and highlights the worlds of a small collection of players on and off the field. They include: the shaky but effective quarterback Mike Winchell (Lucas Black) who wants to find a way out of the small-town that has trapped his family in a state of cyclical depression; athletic but troubled fullback Don Billingsley (Garrett Hedlund), whose abusive father previously won a football state championship for Permian; smart and upwardly mobile safety Brian Chavez (Jay Hernandez), the sole Mexican American player who is also the class valedictorian and on his way to Harvard; quiet and intimidating Ivory "Preacher Man" Christian (Lee Jackson) who is the ambivalent heart and soul of the team; third-string running back Chris Comer (Lee Thompson Young) who is not very good initially but blossoms into a great player; and the gifted and arrogant star running back James "Boobie" Miles who sees football as a way out of the ghetto for him and his family.

In the beginning, the Panthers' success is largely predicated on their star player, Boobie, who is being recruited by top college football programs across the nation. In the season opener, however, Boobie tears his ACL during the blow out game. Despite the pressure on Coach Gaines to exploit Boobie's talent—evidenced in the objectifying and dehumanizing dinner party scene where a white female booster tells Gaines to play Boobie on offense and defense because "that big nigger ain't gonna break"—he is accused of overusing the team's now-fallen star. The loss of Boobie, and ostensibly Coach Gaines's entire offensive strategy, leads many in the town to demand his resignation. However, he does not quit; instead he rallies his team to win despite Boobie's absence. Boobie attempts a premature comeback later in the season despite being warned that his injury is too severe and that he may never play high-level football again. Unfortunately, Boobie exacerbates his injury, sealing his football fate. Dejected, he quits the team. Forced to find a way to win without him, the scrappy Panthers' team play and the out-of-the blue, spectacular performance of Chris Comer makes them postseason contenders. The regular season ends, and the cinematic second-act concludes with the Panthers in a three-way tie for a trip to the playoffs. With their fate decided by a flip of a coin, Permian secures a spot in the playoffs and makes it to the Texas state championship.

In the final game, the Panthers are matched against the undefeated Cowboys from the all-Black Dallas-Carter High School. Playing at the Houston Astrodome, the stakes to win are high for both teams. The Panthers struggle in the first half of the game as they are pounded by the faster, bigger, stronger, and dirtier play of the Cowboys. The physical disparities and racial optics at play on the field signal what James Snead describes as Hollywood's marginalization of Black people on screen through cinematographic contrast, the play between the visual binaries of light and dark. This tactic of the marking of blackness as morally and imagistically overdetermined codes the visual economy throughout the game with the Cowboy's "othering" predicated on Black stereotypes.[34] The Black players from Dallas-Carter are depicted as hyper-aggressive, oversized, and animalistic (they even bark at the Panthers), and their characterization engages the racist connotations of Black people as genetically superior in sports because of their subhuman nature. When both teams run out of their respective tunnels to warm up on the field, the contrast between the Panthers (wearing their white away jerseys) with the Cowboys (in a bold red) cannot be clearer. The Cowboys look like grown Black men next to the mostly white, rugged teenage players of the Panthers. Even the cheerleaders are opposites: the Dallas Carter's all-Black squad saunters out with attitude as Permian's all-white squad stares, blank-faced holding their pompoms. If rule-governed contests rely on competition and regulation, the hierarchies elicited in the scene create a "vertical order of being" that codes these antagonisms as dramatic and racial in the film's narrative.[35]

Eschewing the traditional win incorporated in many sports film's "happy-endings," *Friday Night Lights* concludes in defeat. Similar to contemporary films about defeated Black athletes such as *Cool Runnings* (Jon Turteltaub, 1993), *Sunset Park* (Steve Gomer, 1996), *Coach Carter* (Thomas Carter, 2005), and *Creed* (Ryan Coogler, 2015), Berg's film challenges sports films generic tendency to celebrate winning as sporting excellence.[36] Dramatizing what J. Jack Halberstam calls the "antiglamour of losing," Berg's film attempts to capture the hidden personal, communal, and sociopolitical labor and costs of striving to win in football's gladiatorial contests.[37] However, despite the film's attempt to dignify loss, *Friday Night Lights'* double-movement—its critique and celebration of the sports industrial complex that commodifies and monetizes pain, sweat, and tears (which is just a way to brand and market punishment, exhaustion, and suffering into sports idioms)—signals the contradictory space of sports in popular culture. There is a repulsion and fascination with the physicality, complexity, spectacle, competition, affectivity, and embodied practice of football. *Friday Night Lights* captures much of this fraught sporting dimensionality; however, the film's possible "counterhegemonic discourse of losing" is undone by its conservative racial politics that shape what losing really means in the film.[38]

Failure in *Friday Night Lights*, I contend, is not fully actualized in the narrative's most obvious place—the final game outcome at the film's conclusion—but, instead, is located elsewhere. The team's devastating loss is softened by and through the team's relationship to the film's overdetermined production of sporting blackness as abjection, as a tendency and repudiation of too much embodiment in terms of the Black athletic characters in the film. Darieck Scott contends that "[Black] abjection is a way of describing an experience, an inherited (psychically introjected) historical legacy, a social condition defined and underlined by a defeat."[39] The relevance of Scott's observation resonates when considering the overdetermination of Black people's representations in American cinema, in which they have historically been assaulted. *Friday Night Lights'* representation of defeat and coding of blackness as (always already) defeated signifies what Snead denotes as the mythic conventions of cinematic codes in terms of plot, structure, and stereotypes.[40] This process of mythification in the film, or the interrelationship between Black and white bodies, not only encrypts the final game's imagery in terms of racial hierarchies but also "correlate[s] these images in a larger scheme of semiotic valuation."[41]

Winning in *Friday Night Lights* occurs in a different form—winning for losing. The film exalts the primacy of whiteness though its denunciative and redemptive gestures. Jared Sexton substantiates this observation, noting: "The bad black athletes may win the game, but they are a disgrace to the sport and, moreover, they fail to attain—and are likely even unaware—of the higher rewards it offers to the true believer."[42] The Panthers achieve what Sexton calls a *"moral* victory" though their "valiant and narrow defeat at the hands of their black urban counterparts (whose mythic invincibility is dealt a symbolic blow)."[43] A racial conquest, this blow comes in the form of the film's final moments when on-screen text reveals that the following year Coach Gaines would lead Chris Comer to an undefeated season and a state championship. The epilogue bookends the diegetic loss with a subsequent win. This futured success is underscored by the extradiegetic knowledge that Dallas-Carter's 1988 Texas State Championship win would be vacated soon after due to academic fraud, a detail included in Bissinger's book, ESPN's *30 for 30* documentary *What Carter Lost* (Adam Hootnick, 2017), and Netflix's sports drama *Carter High* (Arthur Muhammad, 2015). If the Panthers have a moral *and* imminent victory in the film, how and where does failure exist? I argue that failure becomes embodied in Boobie— the film's first celebrated, then injured, and later discarded Black player. Boobie's racialized corporeality stages its own complex subjectivity and critique on winning and losing in America's sporting culture.

BOOBIE'S EXCEPTIONALITY AND DEFEAT

In *Friday Night Lights*, Boobie is represented as a Black sports icon, an athlete whose mastery and dominance on the field sets him apart and whose career-ending injury renders him a "commonsense" the harsh reality of sports. With a mercurial and outsized personality, Boobie's braggadocio is stereotypically expected, his showboating, as semic code, is in keeping with his exceptional athleticism, the team's racial objectification, and the film's mythification of his blackness (figure 9). Like many Black characters in sports films, Boobie is defined by his physicality whereby his racial capital and potent performances on the field circulate already existing tropes about Black athletic aptitude. He represents what Hoberman's forceful and controversial criticism of Black people as "Darwin's athletes" posits about the eugenic fantasies of innate toughness, endurance, and "natural" ability.[44] The film revels in and reveals the investments in this kind of historical fantasy in sports culture.

For example, in an early scene in the film, Boobie's uncle and guardian L. V. (Grover Coulson) sits in the stadium filled with college scouts from top football programs, boosters, parents, fans, and press watching the Panthers train during a preseason practice.[45] The scene functions differently than the requisite training montage in sports films; the sequence is not about watch-

FIGURE 9.   "Now hype is something that's not for real. I'm all real." Boobie Miles in *Friday Night Lights* (Peter Berg, 2004).

ing Permian get better but about seeing them already *be* the best, personified by Boobie's outstanding abilities that make him stand out as the best player on the team. L. V. details Boobie's exemplary gridiron skills to college football recruiters, boasting: "He can block, tackle, score the touchdown, snap the ball, hold the snap, and kick the extra point. Hell, the boy will fill up the Gatorade cooler, walk your dog, and paint your back porch. I'm telling you that boy can flat out play football." Collapsing sporting and other labors, L. V.'s pronouncements to the college scouts reify the ways in which modern-day sports create an "auction block" mentality for all those involved, one that bell hooks insists "call[s] to mind the history of slavery and the plantation economy that was built on the exploitation of young strong black male bodies. Just as the bodies of African-American slaves were expendable, the bodies of black male ballplayers cease to matter if they are not able to deliver the described product."[46] This final point rings particularly true in relationship to Boobie in the film. Later injured, Boobie, a former "blue-chip" football prospect, is fated to reprise this common Black sporting scenario.

Friday Night Lights' focus on Boobie's embodied prowess commodifies his bodily utility, concretizing it as his sole source of mobility, social and otherwise. His on-the-field nickname and persona, "Terminator X" codes him as man and machine, Black icon and sporting cyborg. For example, in the opening scenes of the film, Boobie is first seen on screen running amid establishing shots of his impoverished environs. Jogging from "the other side of the tracks" to Permian High School, his morning exercise serves the double function of being both a workout and his means of getting to school before preseason practice. His journey also underscores how, as William C. Rhoden explains "for the past fifty years, the prime raw resource in the sports industry has been black muscle. The work of the industry is to extract those bodies from where they primarily reside—in the black neighborhoods of rural and urban America—and put them to work."[47] Shirtless and sweaty as he listens to music through his Walkman, Boobie's richly dark, muscular physique seems to effortlessly make its way up a hill; with each sway of his arm, his body fills more of the screen's frame. His exposed, glistening torso emphasizes what Mercer refers to in his analysis of the photographs of Robert Mapplethorpe as "the glossy, shining, fetishized surface of black skin [that] thus serves and services a white male desire to look and to enjoy the fantasy of mastery precisely through the scopic intensity that the pictures solicit."[48] The moving image of his surface resplendence is both sporting and fetishized, visual appreciation and objectification all in one. While drawing focus to his bodily form and movement, the film's formal sonic devices negate his subjectivity, foreclosing any possible interiority for the racial sports icon. Instead, diegetic voiceover is that of a radio host and caller discussing the fact that Permian's head coach makes more money than the school's principal. In a town devastated by deindustrialization, the dialogue underscores the broader economy of schools (and by extension state and national governments) that have ample money for stadiums and coaches but none for new textbooks. Despite his amateur status, the film sonically exposes Boobie's personal fitness as a kind of employed professional labor for which he reaps no present salary or monetary reward. The physical work he puts into himself at this stage of his career is for his coach's financial gain, signaling how amateur sports as much as professional ones mix culture and commerce, where "the fundamental roots of racial capital are interwoven into the seemingly meritocratic and voluntary markets of athletics."[49] As the scene continues with Boobie running, a cohort of little Black children wearing his jersey—number forty-five—ride bikes and run alongside, desperately trying to keep pace with him.

The film's opening sequence underscores the visual grammar of critical muscle memory as representational, intratextual content. It attempts to represent collective racial assemblage in the images of the iconicized Black body as projected experiences of shared sporting and non-sporting sociality. As both portrait and proxy, Boobie embodies both forms of representation. These two modes, Gayatri Spivak explains, reinforce each other where the ability to speak on behalf of a community requires that one is also framed within that community.[50] In his diegetic introduction, Boobie represents the lone exemplary Black athlete and the collective Black hope for achievement, an exceptional and yet familiar sporting figure circulated in Black and white communities and the public imaginary as "the signature achievement of black America, the reigning symbol of black 'genius.'"[51] His moving body creates its own wake with the group of little Black boys trailing behind him. Boobie, full bodied and kinesthetic, and his little followers, a collective and kinetically connected body, are visually structured and ideologically sutured within sport training's regime of movement, motioning to a pipeline that connects his curtailed story of mobility through athletics to histories, bodies, and narratives of such flows. An individuated multiplicity, Boobie projects the collective experience of Black boys in the fraught arena of sports. As someone to be imitated, he represents the athletic desires of all the little Black boys who want to literally and figuratively follow in his footsteps.

An exceptional running back, Boobie is shown as a charismatic if arrogant athlete. He basks in his athletic prowess and uses it as an excuse to not worry about his education. As Boobie attests, he gets good grades because he is an athlete and, as a result, football is the only subject necessary to make the grade in school. The film presents this systemic educational problem when Boobie, during a weight room session, struggles to read the letters from college programs interested in recruiting him. As he slowly reads aloud a letter from the University of Southern California, he gets to a word he does not know. His teammate, Brian Chavez, tells him the word is "distinguished." Boobie's inability to pronounce the word is countered with his boastful barb to quarterback Mike Winchell: "You gonna come visit my distinguished ass in California." A distinguished body, Boobie's athletic abilities are used to excuse his academic deficiencies. Able to block, spin, and juke players, his exceptionality structures how the film articulates failure in terms of his embodied performance on the field. Defeat for Boobie is an undoing of his embodied excellence; the breaking of him from the inside out. It is a personal injury—in terms of an ACL tear—with collateral damage—in terms of his future prospects. Defeat is individualized in him and systemic, a dual cautionary tale of personal and collective Black failure to achieve lives and careers through bodily force. The effects and affects of his undoing, as bell hooks writes, render clearly "the spirit of defeat and hopelessness" that informs Boobie's perceived lack of choices and the ways "in which institutionalized racism and white supremacist attitudes in every American life actively prohibit black make participation in diverse cultural arenas and spheres of employment while presenting sports as the 'one' location where recognition, success, and material reward can be attained."[52]

To understand how Boobie's embodied failure comes to be the real "defeat" in the film, it is first important to recognize and textually unpack how his injury shapes and propels *Friday Night Lights'* narrative. A close reading of the film, particularly the scenes of injury, exposes how Boobie's trauma structures the film's story arc and ideological conflicts. Presented as the film's first act's inciting incident, Boobie's injury becomes a plot point, another obstacle for the Panthers to overcome through hard work, self-reliance, and determination. While there are previous glimpses of his exceptional skill and ability during the preseason practice and season opener, his on-the-field play takes up only a small fragment of the film's nearly two-hour run time. Instead, Boobie's life-changing knee injury catalyzes the team to find a new offensive strategy based on teamwork and not just one individual talent, thereby increasing the stakes and potential payoff of the Panthers' hard-fought journey to the state championship game. As Sexton describes: "Boobie was to be a sacrifice for the team, for the school, and for the city in this precise sense: as the team transforms the substance of its internal bonds at his direct expense and in his name—all the better now as a non-competitive mascot—departing from the blind drive to win only to return to it more proficiently, his *subtraction* from the journey to maturity seems both permissible and *preferable*."[53] I want to think with and through Sexton's reading of Boobie as a sacrificial figure to affirm his interpretation as well as extend it for this chapter's critical investments in analyzing Boobie's cinematic embodiment of sporting blackness and critical muscle memory.

Sexton underscores the ways in which race operates within the film's narrative framework to construct Boobie's sporting blackness—his body as hypervisible and overdetermined. Similar to the opening sequence of Boobie's physique on display, *Friday Night Lights* amplifies the masculinity and muscularity of his body through shots of his topless frame. In one scene, as Boobie and his teammates get dressed for preseason practice, Boobie tucks a white towel embossed with "Terminator X" into his waist band, the contrast between the light and darkness of his skin becoming more pronounced. While surrounded by his teammates, he admonishes his other Black teammate Chris Comer for not having a girlfriend because he does not wear black Nike cleats. In this exchange, his exposed body becomes a hyper-reality of signification, masculinization, objectification, and monetization. When he fails to get Ivory, the third and final Black player on the team, to echo his sentiment about wearing black Nikes instead of white Adidas, Boobie calls foul and proudly proclaims that: "You know God made Black beautiful. God made Boobie beautiful. Black and strong. And when

Boobie knocks some fools out, Boobie gonna knock them out with black Nikes on his feet. Ain't that right?"

The film's visualization of Boobie's body and his own divine introjection of the "Black is beautiful" campaign attests to how, as Fleetwood argues, "blackness becomes visually knowable through performance, cultural practices, and psychic manifestations."[54] And yet, in the film, Boobie's speechifying is undercut by his own teammates ridiculing of his "mouth getting bigger and bigger and bigger." Boobie's body's hypervisibility, its meta-mediation of his blackness frames Luke's performance throughout the film. Boobie's blackness becomes visually aligned to and associated with the Panther's Championship game opponents, the Cowboys, the all-Black squad depicted as antagonists of mythic menace. A familiar yet disruptive body, Boobie becomes the team's handicap, an impediment to the team's moral victory over its undeserving Black opponents (a team of Boobies) in the state championship game. In this regard, Boobie represents abject blackness, his troubling presence is exorcised by his injury and failures, to be later recuperated once his career is over and he learns to cheer for others rather than himself. As an act of what Imogen Tyler calls "social abjection," Boobie's "inclusive exclusion" from the team functions here to "not only [describe] the action of casting out or down, but the condition of one cast down—that is, the condition of *being abject*."[55] As the racially and socially abject figure, Boobie is subtracted from the film; however, this subtraction and its ramifications capture only a fraction of his embodied manipulation in the scene where he is injured, a corporeal arithmetic that visualizes critical muscle memory as experiential diegetic and extradiegetic overlap.[56]

Friday Night Lights depicts Boobie's injury as an avoidable, unfortunate twist of fate. In the final minutes of a game the Panthers are decisively winning, third-string running back Chris Comer is summoned from the bench to play his first snap of the game. With Comer unable to find his helmet, Boobie reenters the game. As the on-field play continues, the Panthers quarterback hands the ball off to Boobie who takes off, running to the outside in an attempt to make it down field. As he cuts back in, Boobie is tackled by an opponent, who sends him toppling over another opposing defender stretched out behind him. The camera focuses on Boobie's legs askew at impact; a loud popping sound magnifies the bone-crunching and cartilage-tearing contact. Screaming out and writhing in pain, Boobie's injury freezes all action on the field as players take a knee. The once fast-moving game slows down as reaction shots provide alternating stunned viewpoints on Boobie's injury and subsequent fate.

FIGURE 10. Coach Gaines's perspective on Boobie's injury in *Friday Night Lights* (Peter Berg, 2004).

The moment of Boobie's undoing is visually framed through shot-reverse-shots of his injured body caught up in paroxysms of pain and others' perspectives on his state of undoing. The film's editing in this scene provides a calculated measure of affective reactions, filtering Boobie's personal experience through communal witnessing. The methodical cutting renders cinematically Bissinger's literary description of everyone "looking at [Boobie's] knee as if it were a priceless vase with a suddenly discovered crack that had just made it worthless."[57] From one angle, Boobie's uncle and guardian L. V. sits in the crowded stadium in disbelief, his eyes pleading for Boobie to be okay all the while knowing the potential life-changing stakes at play. From another angle, fans in the stadium stand up, holding their breath in quiet hope that Boobie will be able to walk off the pain and lead them to a championship. Between these shots, the camera cuts to view Boobie on the field, his cries growing in pained intensity (figure 10). As the film score swells, the vantage point shifts to Coach Gaines, reframing Boobie's injury as his own personal traumatic experience. Disoriented by the emotional impact of his star player down, Gaines asks another coach if he thinks Boobie has injured his knee, a joint figuratively holding together the Coach's entire offensive strategy. The film cuts to more shots of the crowd, interspersing their hopeful stares with Boobie's fallen body on the field. Boobie's image goes in and out of focus as the field of vision shifts from L. V. to the silent fans back to Coach Gaines. Boobie's cries pierce the continued montage of reaction shots, including fellow teammates as well as opponents, adding them as stakeholders with vested interest in Boobie's outcome. The most insidious of the group, however, are the two opposing players who give a sly, celebratory slap of hands at Boobie's distress.

One of the final perspectives on this moment comes from the camera cutting to the Panther's sideline, where two assistant coaches look toward the injured star. In a small role, the real-life Boobie Miles plays one of the assistant coordinators, shaking his head in a close-up. The scene cuts back to the fictional Boobie in pain, shots of the crowd, L.V., and the lopsided scoreboard to underscore the dashing of Boobie's professional football dreams, a tragedy made even more heartbreaking by the fact that the Panthers were decidedly winning and did not need him to stay in the game. The film, however, quickly reorients the camera and the narrative, focusing on Coach Gaines (who seemed to never actually make it over to check on Boobie) as the camera orbits around him and he stalks back toward the bench. Staying with Gaines into the next scene, it becomes apparent that Boobie's individuated tragic fate on the field is the starting point for Gaines and his player's collective competitive journey to the top and the film's narrative ascent to its actual climatic moment—the state championship game against Dallas-Carter. As an injured player, it is Boobie who comes to embody failure in the film.

If Boobie's sacrifice subtracts him from Permian's journey, what can be made of the injury scene's corporeal arithmetic; the bodily divisions, additions, and multiplications exhibited? Boobie's knee fractures his once whole, exceptional body into a fraction of himself. Divided, the cameo of the actual Boobie Miles adds an extra-diegetic bodily dimension to the film. One "Boobie" body is multiplied on screen to make two; bodily fiction and facticity occur within the same mise-en-scène. Boobie's real body and reel body are linked and contrasted as past and present, star and cameo. This double-take shows the real Boobie wince at the fiction(s) of himself, evidenced in the acting of Derek Luke as well as the revision of his injurious moment, which actually took place during a preseason scrimmage. Boobie's face provides both an immediate and delayed reaction at the (un)expected (re)enactment of the beginning of the end of his football career. The twin diegetic characters represent Boobie's before and after, the promise of Black exceptionality that the emotional devastation of injury converts to an almost pathological (defined by the real Boobie's troubled post-football life) state of being. Boobie has been damaged beyond repair in this cinematized moment. As the real-life Boobie watches from the sideline, he (re)views what it means to put your body on the line in sports. Unable to use his body to make a future for himself, the actual Boobie's witnessing is embodied testimony to his own undoing on the playing field.

Critical muscle memory as a framework for understanding this scene requires a consideration of the embodied doubling and looking relations crafted on screen. The scene represents the recollection and reflection upon an embodied experience. As the real-life Boobie and his cinematic character are contrasted, they operate as paradigm and metonym. A simulated model of Boobie's past, the fictional character stands in for the real history of the former Permian Panther. At the same time, the cuts to the real-life Boobie reproduce this representational pattern of actuality and fiction. Even as he acts as an assistant coach and not himself, the real-life Boobie *is* the embodied history of the dramatization occurring in front of him. The "troubling vision" of such traumatized sporting blackness signals both the transtemporal looking relations and critical muscle memory as an optical process in the film.[58] The eyes are a scopic muscle of the body, and the real Boobie gazes upon the illusion of his lived experience. His wince, a muscular flinch, announces his looking as twofold: seeing and being seen. This framing of the real-life Boobie looking back at his cinematic body double produces a temporal bridge between the sporting acts of his past and the lived experiences of his present. The twin Boobies render blackness as both seeing double and double trouble, meaning overrepresented, overdetermined, and in need of narrative containment.

The real-life Boobie's cameo echoes a long history of Black athletes like Jackie Robinson, Muhammad Ali, Joe Louis, Michael Jordan, Lawrence Taylor, Kareem Abdul-Jabbar, Charles Barkley, O.J. Simpson, Lisa Leslie, and LeBron James, among others, either playing themselves or versions thereof on the big screen. Most notably, Robinson portrays himself in Alfred E. Green's *The Jackie Robinson Story* (1950), adapted from the book of the same name by Brooklyn Dodgers publicist Arthur Mann. The cinematic Robinson is a transmedia character similar to Boobie, whose real-life story catalyzes his derivative media representations. As the star of his own biopic, Alessandra Raengo describes Robinson's body image as both source material and adaptation.[59] She notes, "unlike other biopics, by having Robinson perform himself, the film conflates the usually visible distinction between the actor and the character in a tightly sutured and suturing text."[60] The real and representative Boobies in *Friday Night Lights* function similarly but with two important differences. First, the real Boobie is not acting as himself but as a fictionalized assistant coach. Second, the real Boobie's authenticating presence requires additional spectatorial knowledge of not just who he was then (the skilled six-foot teenager who could run the 40 in 4.5 seconds) but more about who he is now (the overweight, grown man sidelined by forces in and out of his control). Despite these distinctions, Boobie's visibility and invisibility suture the mechanisms of his identification in the film. The cinematic apparatus structures these looking relations in terms of recognition and voyeurism, a diegetic projection and production of both Boobies' subjectivities for the viewer to witness. The film's intertextual cues negotiate this double-embodiment, providing the real Boobie and the audience diegetic distance to watch his athletic and filmic undoing, his fictional being and later veritable becoming.

The extra-diegetic Boobie appears twice more in the film. First, when his on-screen character tries to play again and further exacerbates his injury, the real Boobie once more watches the moment from the sidelines, instantly replaying a familiar script that has haunted him throughout his life. Second, he appears at the end of the film in an emotionally charged locker room scene during the half-time of the championship game. As Sexton previously described, Boobie becomes a non-competitive mascot for the team, cheering the Panthers on from the sidelines despite having quit the team earlier, a revisionist act of melodramatic redemption since, in actuality, Boobie never rejoined the team. In his half-time speech, Coach Gaines points to Boobie as an example of someone who wishes he could play as a means of inspiring his team. As the two Boobies stand next to each other, the message of being and becoming is twofold (figure 11). This redoubling narrates the physical and emotional consequences of curtailed opportunity and unfulfilled talent, not only for the individual subject but also for the countless others who will suffer the same fate—what Young calls a "remarkable similarity, a repetition with a difference."[61] In this scene and previous scenes, this Black experiential twoness, to follow Scott's reading of Du Boisian double consciousness through Frantz Fanon, "is slightly recast as double-*bodiedness*."[62] Again, critical muscle memory operates as explicit visualization of the Boobies' sporting reality, one that—like Derek Luke's masterful performance as Boobie throughout the film—stands in as a representational metaphor for similar Black sporting-embodied tragedies. The film's double-bodiedness insists we remember the cruel exploitation of athletic professional hopes, the "commonsense" ideology and truth of Black social and economic mobility through athletic achievement in a society where, as Garry Whannel explains, "lived experience constantly tells us that most people do not succeed, that the gap between winning and losing is significant, and that it is not a level playing field."[63] In *Friday Night Lights*, the real Boobie and his cinematic figuration are the lived and imagined experiences that remind us of this sporting reality. As the film's narrative ends, Boobie's on-screen text follow-up explains that he played football in junior college and now lives in Monahans, Texas, with his four-year-old twins. Currently, Boobie is imprisoned.[64]

Through his diegetic injury and the film's racial stereotyping, Boobie is constructed as the victim. This process of racialization within the film's

FIGURE 11. The real-life James "Boobie" Miles stands next to his on-screen character, played by Derek Luke, in *Friday Night Lights* (Peter Berg, 2004).

melodramatic narrative shapes his vulnerability and designation as no lon-ger an exceptional Black body but a pathological, wounded one, a self-destructing body of a "damaged" person/people. A subject of contempt and pity, he is the narrative vessel for defeat, the embodiment of suffering, thereby compelling the film's anxieties about race in terms of injury and melodrama. Linda Williams figures slavery as the original injury in melo-drama, the melodramatic racial fix that replays itself over and over again in popular culture.[65] Boobie becomes both racialized victim and villain, a mor-ally failed character whom the film tries to recoup as a cautionary tale. In this way, he is exemplary of the processes and products emitting from racial iconicity "as a vibrational force—an affective energy—that leads to our valuation of the people we venerate and the devaluation of the lives of many others."[66] Boobie's narrative, across texts and as a lived life for spec-tatorial consumption, rejection, and retrieval is produced in the chasm between veneration and devaluation, what Fleetwood names "racial vulner-ability."[67]

Boobie becomes an abstraction in the text, a critical muscle memory of curtailed Black athletic achievement. Explaining that he "can't do nothing but play football," Boobie narrates the lived and affective experiences of multitudes of Black male athletes in various sports (but particularly foot-ball) whose failure transcends the field of play and incorporates their feel-ings of failure in real life. As previously described, the scenes of Boobie's reckoning detail the fact that his body is now devalued in society. Boobie's realization that his football career is over speaks to the financial complex of sports as an economic enterprise, one that so rarely works in favor of or justly compensates Black athletes. The sports American Dream exploits poor Black males who are willing to risk their bodies and—considering the frequency of Chronic Traumatic Encephalopathy (CTE) in football—their lives in pursuit of success. Boobie thus becomes an embodied memorialization, a way to remember the countless boys who, like Boobie, dreamed that their legs would be their ticket out and up. His story is a reminder, as Bissinger points out in his *Afterward*, that "legs are not a ticket. They're just legs: fragile, exposed, subject at any moment to irreparable hurt."[68]

A NEW SPELLING OF MY NAME

Beyond the book and film, Boobie exists in other forms and by other names.[69] His transmedia character appears as an abstraction on the small screen. His televisual framing builds on a shared identity instantiated by Boobie as a racial icon in the *Friday Night Lights* franchise, constructing a transmedia critical muscle memory—a connected representation and sporting history—of his familiar character that is produced by and through these derivative works. Bissinger's bestseller and Berg's film spawned two television series: NBC's *Against the Grain* (1993) and *Friday Night Lights*, which ran on NBC (2006–2008) and The 101 Network (2008–2011).

Against the Grain is very loosely inspired by Bissinger's book, attempting to capture some of the regional fanaticism of Texas high school football on the small screen. The show follows Ed Clemmons (John Terry), an insurance salesman who returns to Sumpter, Texas, to coach football at his former high school, where he was once a star player. Trying to turn a losing team into state champions, Ed clashes with his team and the town when he replaces the arrogant quarterback Bobby Taylor (Rick Peters) with his son Joe Willie (Ben Affleck). With mixed reviews, *Against the Grain* lasted only one season. The series, while steeped in the saga of high school football, excises the racial politics that shaped Bissinger's book. Cutting out Boobie as a character and representing the town and team's main players (and thus the supporting cast) as all white expunges much of the dramatic tensions and plot possibilities, leaving the show to focus on the struggles of white fathers and sons without any self-critical representational strategies or dramatic flair. Sans Boobie, or a like character of color, whiteness in *Against the Grain* assumes its normative static iconicity in the genre, and narrative monotony ensues.

The television series *Friday Night Lights*, however, mobilizes the complex social dynamics imbricated in Bissinger's book to create a compelling hour-long drama. While the series never had high ratings and was on the fringe of cancellation throughout its run, it garnered widespread critical acclaim. Over its five seasons, *Friday Night Lights* built an ardently loyal fan base; topped many "best-shows" lists; and won numerous awards, including a Peabody, a Humanitas Prize, a Television Critics Association Award, and Emmy Awards for actor Kyle Chandler and writer and executive producer Jason Katims. Peter Berg, who directed the film adaptation, developed the series for NBC Universal, explaining that he believed television is the "perfect medium" to delve into the deeper issues discussed in the original source material.[70] In readapting Bissinger's book and his own cinematic work, Berg took advantage of television's long-form storytelling possibilities to continue the transmediation of Boobie's character. Boobie is not directly named in this representation; instead his characteristics and biographical data are filtered across different characters: Smash, Voodoo, and Vince. Their sporting blackness produces a repetition with a difference and scripts new dimensions into Boobie's embodied narrative in each iteration.

Friday Night Lights' televisual sports drama is set in the fictional rural, small-town of Dillon, Texas. Like the townspeople in the book and film, the Dillon residents are deeply invested in the success of the Panthers, Dillon High School's football team. The television series conveys a level of verisimilitude through its docufictional shooting style. The show's verité elements cohere to produce an expressionistic drama, driven by subjective perspectives and emotional experiences.[71] At the center of the series' ensemble cast are the two lead characters: Eric Taylor (Kyle Chandler), the head football coach of the Dillion High School Panthers, and his wife Tami Taylor (Connie Britton), the guidance counselor turned principal at Dillon High School. Connie Britton reprises and revises her role as the head coach's spouse from the 2004 film into a more fleshed-out character in the series. Over the course of five seasons, the Taylors and a group of high school players, parents, community members, and boosters interact on and off the field in this swirling social drama about sports, education, class, family, religion, race, gender, and ability.

Unlike *Against the Grain*, the series *Friday Night Lights* has integral Black players on the team and in the storyline, figures who are meant to be Boobie-inspired characters. During the first season of the show, the character Brian "Smash" Williams (Gaius Charles) is a representational nod to the cinematic, literary, and actual football player (figure 12). A redemptive character, he embodies the idea of what might have been if Boobie could have been saved from himself/his cinematic fate. Like Boobie, Williams goes by an alias, "Smash," a nickname given to him by his father to refer to the sound he made when he ran into a water heater as a child. This nom de guerre carries over to his brash personality and dynamic style of play. As

FIGURE 12. NBC's acclaimed television series *Friday Night Lights* reimagines the character of Boobie as Brian "Smash" Williams.

the star running back for the Panthers, Smash inherits many of Boobie's personality characteristics, including his grandstanding and referring to himself in the third person; his impoverished background and looking to football as the means for him, his two sisters, and his widowed mother to escape their economic entrapment; and his narrative obstacles, specifically an on-the-field injury that puts his football career in jeopardy. Even with these similarities, however, the series significantly deviates from Boobie's literary and cinematic character and the corollary meanings associated with his sporting blackness. Unlike Boobie, who has no maternal figure in his life, Smash is being raised by his mother, Corina Williams (Liz Mikel), a nurse, who provides him with moral grounding and guidance throughout the series. Instead of thinking he "can't do nothing but play football," Corina steadily reminds Smash of his opportunities on and off the field. Playing football becomes a means, not the *only* means, for Smash to advance his life, even if it is his dream to make it to the pros. Beginning as a junior in the series, Smash's high school playing career extends over the first two seasons, going from a main character to a recurring one in the third season to being absent for the show's final two seasons. This dwindling televisual presence and later narrative absence is a common fate for the show's players as their character arcs are often defined by their high school sporting years. Smash is unique, as his third season presence extends beyond high school and the Panthers.

Smash's variance with and adherence to Boobie's narrative throughout his three-season run reflects the series' redemptive gestures and complicated racial storytelling. Unlike Boobie, Smash is shown as both an individual and in solidarity with other Black characters. For example, Smash leads a boycott of the Black players after an assistant coach makes racist comments to the local press about the prowess of Black players. The series fails to take this opportunity to explore racial solidarity and the racial differences that structure and fracture the team, however, and instead devolves into liberal racial reconciliation. The racist coach helps to save Smash from the hands of the law, and the show's earlier gesture of Black athletic radical noncompliance is defused and supplanted by a liberal-humanist rendering of masculinist allegiance and belonging between young Black athletes and their white racist coaches.

While both cinematic and televisual characters share the narrative obstacle of physical injury, Smash's embodied undoing during the second season is neither instantaneous nor absolute. In fact, the show, unlike its cinematic referent, does not depict the visceral act of injury on screen. This narrative choice was not a creative decision but an industrial default. The series' production was halted during the 2007–2008 Writers Guild of America strike, which lasted for one hundred days, stunting or ceasing productions on many scripted series. Season two was slated to have twenty-two episodes, but, due to the strike, the show did not film the final seven episodes, ending the season prematurely without finishing the story arc of the Panthers' attempt for a repeat state championship. At the beginning of the third season, the viewers are told that the Panthers made it to the playoffs but lost, in part, because Smash hurt his knee. Injured, Smash's scholarship to Whitmore, a college he had decided to attend after losing all previous athletic scholarships, is rescinded. A high school graduate now working at the local fast food chain, Smash spends the entirety of the third season trying to make it back onto the playing field, rehabbing his body (strengthening his leg and increasing his speed) and mind (learning humility and fortitude) with Coach Taylor.

Smash's narrative of sporting redemption is markedly different from Boobie's cinematic end, an outcome that turned him into a sacrificial mascot for the team. Translating his injury as a setback and not a life sentence, Smash's season-three arc narrates a more typical comeback sports story, where hard work, gradualism, and self-determination are necessary for sporting success. Instead of suffering Boobie's fate, the show attempts to "save" Smash, a televisual labor employed, in part, because his narrative was cut short by industrial forces outside the showrunner's control. His comeback is executed with the help and guidance of Coach Taylor, whom he more deeply bonds with in the third season. While there is an obvious element of a "white savior" narrative here, typical of many sports narratives, Coach Taylor's actions are not solely inflected on a racial divide, as the dynamic between him and the white poor and working-class players on the team take a similar form. A class issue as much as a racial one, Coach Taylor's saviorism is emphatically stressed throughout the series such that salvation and parental surrogacy are sutured into his job description as coach. Willing to work hard under Taylor's advisement, Smash is further differentiated from the ways in which Boobie has been narrativized and cinematized as "naturally" talented and, thus, "uncoachable," a racially coded designation. While a gifted player, Smash's sporting blackness inverses the notion of innate talent. For example, after having a bad game in front of college recruiters, Smash turns to performance-enhancing drugs to help give him an edge but is accidentally outed by his mother to Coach Taylor; she had angrily assumed that the Coach or another Panther had forced the drugs on her son. Smash's moral and physical dilemmas play out across racial, kin, and educational polarities, all of which his mother and Coach Taylor often rhetorically inhabit. In the end, Smash's hard work earns him a walk-on tryout and, later, a roster spot on Texas A&M's football team, thus affirming the traditional ideals of meritocracy in sporting discourses.

While Smash is the character imagined as Boobie, the series also more broadly distributes aspects of Boobie's abject sporting blackness across Black characters throughout the series run. During the first season, Smash is joined by Ray "Voodoo" Tatum (Aldis Hodge), a Hurricane Katrina evacuee who moves to Dillon. A quarterback, Voodoo's stay with the Panthers is short, as he clashes with teammates and Coach Taylor before being expelled from the team. Later in the season, Voodoo and Smash go head-to-head in the state championship game, but not before Voodoo attempts to get Smash to leave Dillon High School and play for his team, West Cambria. Unlike in the film, where the Cowboys win the championship, the television series provides a heroic home-team climax with the Panthers winning, making Smash's personal triumph belong to the mostly white Panthers and not to the collective Black sporting body. Voodoo's loss is meant to be a literal and moral defeat. Throughout his time on the show, Voodoo is painted as a duplicitous figure on and off the field. He is vilified as a violent, selfish player who refuses to follow Coach Taylor's game plan. With the nickname of "Voodoo," his sporting blackness in the series operates in a similar manner to the film version's marking and mythification of its Black athletes, particularly the all-Black Dallas-Carter Cowboys with whom Boobie is aligned in the film.

As Smash's character exits after the third season, Vince Howard (Michael B. Jordan) enters as another (re)iteration of the f(l)ailings of Black male athleticism attached to Boobie's persona. His character is riddled with racial tropes and stereotypes, habituated through white projection, narratological control, and implied viewership. Vince is first introduced running from the cops, and he moves between the two stereotypical poles that structure Black masculinity—criminal or athlete—throughout the show's run. Vince's background, including having a drug-addicted mother and an ex-con violent father (played by Cress Williams), reverberates with Boobie's biographical history, but does so in a way to suggest the necessity of white intervention in his life. Coach Taylor, again, functions as a father figure who must teach him not only how to win but also how to be a model son, player, and citizen. In fact, all three Boobie-esque characters on the show reify notions of Black criminality. Smash buys and uses steroids, breaking doping rules; takes meetings with recruiters in breach of NCAA protocols; and fights a group of racists attacking his little sister, violating rules of Black comportment (e.g., "turn the other cheek" in response to racism), all of which result in his loss of scholarship offers. Voodoo defies eligibility and housing requirements (costing the Panthers a game) and is always framed as gaming the system for his own economic and egocentric benefit. Vince is the most at odds with his criminality (his ability to run on the football field is figured as emanating from his vice-ridden life running from the cops). Of the three, he lacks Boobie's prima donna antics, and in a critical juncture for his character, he must decide between violent retribution—killing someone who killed his criminal friend—or moving on with his life. While Vince relies almost completely on other Black characters during this arc, he turns his gun over to Coach Taylor, demonstrating his character's distancing from violence and vice—a significant scene in his character development.

All three Boobie stand-ins—Smash, Voodoo, and Vince—filter elements of the literary and cinematic character into the televisual realm. Their characters and narratives expose the inequities of the sports industrial complex for young poor Black men of athletic means while the televisual apparatus and overall telos suture these narratives not to a critique of the raced athletic system but, more often, to the moral and material deficiencies projected onto Black manhood. Boobie's televisual representations underscore the different and differentiating processes of rapper Big K.R.I.T.'s reclamation of his story. As unofficial sonic and media narratives, Big K.R.I.T.'s "Hometown Hero" and "Boobie Miles," are subversive tracks and videos that resound rap music's critical capacities to "[prioritize] black voices from the margins of urban America."[72]

THE HOMETOWN HERO

Historically, Black male athletes on screen have been visually and ideologically reduced to their bodies, commodities of danger and desire shaped by the intersections of race and masculinity.[73] The Black sporting body, as I argue throughout this book, is a canvas of representation, a mutable form and fluid subjectivity creatively mobilized to mean different things in new contexts. Boobie's cinematic body operates within this framework of surplus of expressivity. His transmedia shapeshifting continues and amplifies the signifying processes of his body, re-addressing and redressing his relationship to the notions of iconicity and failure in and through popular culture. Specifically, Boobie's textual reappearance in hip hop culture engages in the kinds of rhetorical signifying practices that Henry Louis Gates Jr. denotes of black vernacular traditions.[74] In this context, hip hop spectatorship shapes the formal specificity of Black intertextuality.[75]

Hip hop "underground" artist Big K.R.I.T.'s songs and videos for "Hometown Hero" and "Boobie Miles" signify upon the cinematic Boobie in *Friday Night Lights*, reclaiming the fallen racial icon into the "Black familiar." The territory of the Black familiar, as Lisa Kennedy explains, is the representational space "to be black without trying to explain blackness (to whites)."[76] Big K.R.I.T.'s songs are richly symbolic, and the imagined community he speaks to is fluent in the Black familiar, a mode of literacy across a myriad of sources that marks and makes legible specific cultural codes and modes of being and blackness.[77] The southern rapper imports and inverts the cinematic portrait of Boobie and his fate for his own invention and intervention. In both "Hometown Hero" and "Boobie Miles," Big K.R.I.T. demonstrates how "the quotidian becomes adventurous" in Black familiar cultural productions by turning the everyday story of the fallen racial icon into an audacious exaltation of a Black football folk hero.[78] I am suggesting, here, that there is a relationship and distinction between being a racial icon and a Black folk hero. The former is distinguished by Fleetwood's accounting of the exceptional/common figure while the latter pivots to consider the distinct demographics (the "folk" being Black people) of those who appreciate the hero and circulate tales and songs about their heroics. The Black folk hero is the hometown hero (i.e., street legend) of Black communities.

Friday Night Lights is one of the rapper's favorite films, and the fact that Boobie's character is cited in both songs denotes the former football player's import to the lyricist.[79] Big K.R.I.T.'s then record label, Cinematic Music Group, further underscores the relationship between iconic Black images in visual culture, hip hop spectatorship, and sonic modes of cultural production and creative expression. To be clear, *Friday Night Lights* is meaningful to Big K.R.I.T. despite the film's ideological contradictions and representations of blackness as abject. That is, the rapper's liking for the film derives from his affective investment in Boobie's story, which is negotiated through those very contradictions and representations. Big K.R.I.T. explains that he pens his impressive rhymes "based off the emotion and just understanding what it's like to feel like you're following your dreams and everything is going good, and something happens that makes you have to start over."[80] He and other hip hop artists use the film's symbology and Black athlete iconography as fungible commodities for self-expression.[81] Big K.R.I.T's references to Boobie in *Friday Night Lights'* fraught cinematic depiction and commoditization calls attention to the critical and formal capacities of and creative consumption by Black youth in contemporary culture industries. As Ben Carrington considers:

> It is important to remember that, especially within the black diaspora, the processes of cultural consumption and identification cannot simply be reduced to the circuits and flows of commodity spectacle. There is always an element of creative consumption and reworking of cultural texts that need to be acknowledged if we are to avoid a "top-down" ideological account of how cultural meanings are produced, decoded, and then used. Indeed, the play of desire and fantasy always works to both reproduce and challenge dominant ideologies.[82]

Carrington's insistence on avoiding a top-down ideological account echoes J. Jack Halberstam's ideation of low theory and Henry Jenkins's work on participatory collective knowledge/intelligence, operating from different levels at once, as a methodology for examining popular culture and discourse.[83] Big K.R.I.T.'s importing of *Friday Night Lights* and his identification with Boobie evinces the formal creative consumption and skilled reworking of the football player as a transmedia figure and figuration. Boobie, for Big K.R.I.T., becomes (re)textualized in the Black familiar as a football folk hero that Black people specifically can fixate on, attach themselves to, and signify upon.

Boobie is first referenced in Big K.R.I.T.'s song and music video for "Hometown Hero," a track from his 2010 mixtape *K.R.I.T. Wuz Here*. The song samples both Adele's single "Hometown Glory" and snippets of dialogue from *Friday Night Lights*. "Hometown Hero's" lyrics self-consciously reflect on Big K.R.I.T.'s southern roots and newfound fame. In her seminal

FIGURE 13.   Shot in his hometown of Meridian, Mississippi, Big K. R. I. T.'s music video for "Hometown Hero" constructs the cultural geography of the south as a Black lived and sonic space.

hip hop studies text *Black Noise*, Tricia Rose suggests that rap video "conventions visualize hip hop style and usually affirm rap's primary thematic concerns: identity and location."[84] Fixating on these bimodal interests, Big K.R.I.T.'s music video was shot at night in the rapper's hometown of Meridian, Mississippi, setting the landscape and stylistic context for the video's reception (figure 13). With much of the city shut down, Big K.R.I.T. travels freely about the streets in King City, crossing railroad tracks, posted up in front of a local house, standing on empty bridges, and parked in desolate lots. The music video and the lyrics provide a visual and sonic cultural geography of the rapper's hometown.

Big K.R.I.T.'s visual and sonic rendering of lived space operates in stark contrast to the opening sequence in Berg's Friday Night Lights, one that juxtaposes the landscape of Odessa and Boobie running with white male narration about the economy of sports in the small town. In an attempt to locate him and rap in the South, Big K.R.I.T. alternatively claims and situates the audiovisual cultural terrain as a Black lived *and* sonic space. His local Black neighborhood becomes an entryway into regional discourses and styles of rap (e.g., East Coast, West Coast, Dirty South, etc.) and social identity. As he raps near a fuel station plastered with the word "Dixie," the spatial politics also render the vestiges of the American south and the "afterlife of slavery" into a new hip hop context.[85] A "we buy gold" sign in the video's mise-en-scène aligns Big K.R.I.T. with the notion of value while also signaling the deindustrialization of the southern urban land-scape, where pawn shops and advance-checking chains structure the preda-tory transactional economies in urban ecosystems against their inhabitants. As a solitary journey through Big K.R.I.T.'s familiar stomping grounds, the video's low-budget production value enhances the intimate mode of visual storytelling depicted on screen. The parking lot lights, similar to the fluorescent beams of sports stadiums, shine down on him. Many shots are somewhat out of focus, and part of the rapper's face is often obscured in darkness. The hand-held camera, however, provides the close-up, visual intimacy emoted in this deeply personal and meditative track.

"Hometown Hero" begins with edited dialogue from Berg's football drama, using the braggadocio of Boobie's character as both a prelude and proclamation for the confident, yet contemplative track. With narration lifted from two different scenes in *Friday Night Lights*, Big K.R.I.T. sam-ples and remixes the film, turning Boobie into his own hype man. The song begins with cut-and-spliced quotations from the film:

> You know God made Black beautiful.
> God made Boobie beautiful, Black and strong.
> And when Boobie knocks some fools out,
> Boobie gonna knock 'em out with black Nikes on his feet.   '
> Ain't that right?
> And I'ma smile when I do.
> Yeah. Yeah. I'm distinguished now.

As the edited snippet continues, quarterback Mike Winchell's voice enters the soundscape, reminding Boobie that he did not lift any weights during the training session. The next line, Boobie's response to Winchell, pride-fully rings out:

> Come on man, this is God given.
> Only thing I got to do is just show up.

Responding to this call to "show up" on the track, Big K.R.I.T. takes over the beat with his southern lyrical flow. Boobie is mentioned one more time in the song at the end of the first verse. Lamenting what will happen to hip hop after him if he left the rap game, Big K.R.I.T. flows:

> That's like a torn ACL to an athlete
> Boobie Miles, Friday Lights, capture me.

The cinematic Boobie sampled on this track is used as a point of identifica-tion, self-expression, and recognition. Big K.R.I.T.'s identity as a rapper from the "Third Coast" mobilizes the character of Boobie to situate his own artistic persona and pivots the perspective on both figures toward local heroism and iconoclasm.[86] In doing so, the song and video, as examples of hip hop spectatorship, demonstrate what Stuart Hall meant about "identity as constituted, not outside but within representation, and hence, of cinema not as second-order mirror held up to reflect what already exists but as that form of representation which is also able to constitute us as new kinds of subjects and thereby enable us to discover who we are."[87] Boobie's sporting blackness becomes both an embodied performance and a persona, a put-on character that Big K.R.I.T. uses to "flex," that is show-off, on the track.

The track's beat and "the wonders of this world" riff from Adele's "Hometown Glory" and Boobie's prelude dialogue are examples of Big K.R.I.T.'s ability to rework compositions and his "invocation of another's voice to help you say what you want to say."[88] Big K.R.I.T.'s revised authorship and originality produces a new, alternative text and context for seeing Boobie and—in this medium specifically—hearing the cinematic Boobie. As Rose reveals, the relationship between Black oral traditions and sampling technologies produces communal narratives, making sampling "a process of cultural literacy and intertextual reference."[89] Released as a mixtape, "Hometown Hero" boastfully eschews *Friday Night Lights'* industrial machine of secured rights and licensing. The Boobie sample underscores not only how "[reusing] portions of copyrighted material without permission undermines legal and capital market authority" but also un-sutures the character from its fixed visuality into a new sonic playing field.[90] Boobie is framed as a venerated Black football folk hero, the everyday stuff made of street legend in rural and urban inner cities.

Dissimilar to Berg's film's coding of Boobie's defeat as the reason the Panthers can "win for losing," Big K.R.I.T. adopts Boobie in quotation as an extracted persona and performance of "virtuosity that is born in the face of failure."[91] Virtuosity, conceptualized via Black vernacular culture, provides a frame in which to think through how Big K.R.I.T. untethers Boobie's bravado from a cinematic text that always moves his body forward to its undoing, playing out the tape of his embodied defeat over the course of the film's run time. Cut and remixed as the opening sonic force in "Hometown Hero," the intertextual Boobie refuses to be anything but "distinguished now." The temporality of Boobie's narrative of being shifts to Big K.R.I.T.'s moment of becoming through the reiterative power of performativity. Boobie is a body that matters *again* through his hip hop hailing in the rapper's flow. Through this revision, a re-signification, Big

K.R.I.T. introduces both his rap persona and the cinematic figure to a Black familiar world as hometown heroes that people of color identify with and celebrate.

"Hometown Hero" is not the last time nor the most well-known occasion Big K.R.I.T. uses Boobie Miles as a pop and sports culture reference. In 2012, the hip hop artist released the song titled "Boobie Miles" from his mixtape *4 Eva N a Day*. "Boobie Miles" samples "Morning Tears'" by MFSB, and this composition draws more abstractly on the cinematic football player. The song's title functions as a signifier, a code about the cultural politics of sporting success and failure. When asked why he continues to be inspired by *Friday Night Lights*, Big K.R.I.T. explains:

> That movie was extremely impactful for me. Being from a small town, being the kind of person where I really thought sports was going to be it for me, and then not being able to do that all my life. What would you [sic] considering falling down and having to pick yourself back up? Or knowing something was 100%, and then not being 100%, and you have to start all over again. That's the story of a lot of people's lives. It was like, this is something I want to stick to, as far as the aspect of getting up, getting out, and doing something with yourself. It's so many people that either can't, or tried, and weren't necessarily succeeding but still struggled and made it happen. The story of Boobie Miles is crazy. *Friday Night Lights* is crazy to me. I was so inspired by that movie. The actual title track, to do the song, I was like, it's gotta be inspirational. If you get your opportunity, your 15 minutes to say something important, you better really take advantage of it.[92]

The track's lyrics and music video mainstream Boobie's narrative into a generalized inspirational tale in keeping with the film's telos and themes. This version of Boobie's narrative is set in a hyper-stylized video with Big K.R.I.T.—signaled by the moniker on his shirt—as the "champion" (figure 14). While the lyrics and music video do not quote the film as explicitly as "Hometown Hero" does, the name-dropping title, athletic metaphors, and sporting imagery directly and indirectly connect the anthem to Berg's film. The line—"ACL torn, and you're a couple yards short from a Super Bowl championship and it was down 4"—most explicitly references a football player, but the title alone means the song is about the cultural and sporting politics surrounding Boobie. If "Hometown Hero" produced an alternative world in which failure does not define him, the eponymously titled "Boobie Miles" provides a counter-logic on his sporting failure, a somewhat commonplace idea that if at first you fail you should try again. In the black-and-white video montage of male athletes missing shots in their respective goals, Big K.R.I.T. raps:

FIGURE 14. Big K. R. I .T. becomes the champion in the music video for "Boobie Miles."

Get money, don't be no lame
Bench warmers never ride foreign, so play the game
Never drop the ball, never accept a loss, get back up if you fall
And when your numbers called, you better give your all
I hope you give your all
You gotta play until the end
The only difference between a winner and a loser is a winner plays
    until he wins

Unlike the novice confidence and reflective lyrics in "Hometown Hero," "Boobie Miles" references the cinematic football player through the discourses of success and failure, replicating the dialogic in *Friday Night Lights'* film and television adaptation. The song's motivational anthem makes it a catchy workout tune but not necessarily a counter-hegemonic discourse on losing even if it does have a cultural critique within its narrative.

However, like "Hometown Hero," Big K. R. I. T.'s "Boobie Miles" narrativizes Boobie's discourse through collaged intertextual resonant metaphors that show how rap music bridges identification as a kind of sonic critical muscle memory of shared experiences. Sampling here both pays homage and, for Bissinger, who encourages Boobie to "sue the motherfucker" for using his name without asking, constitutes identity theft.[93] Thus, alongside the commercial aesthetics and capitalist impulses articulated within the lyrics, the song simultaneously conforms to and challenges the tendency toward avarice in hip hop and athletics. Big K.R.I.T.'s "Boobie Miles" sonically stakes out a potentially progressive stance on losing as a critique of those racialized financial structures that require young Black people to use their bodies to economically advance. And yet, there is some resistance to this reductive narrative as well when one considers the logics of the lyric "only difference between a winner and a loser is a winner plays until he wins" in relationship to the film. As iconic iterations of the Black familiar, the song "Boobie Miles" and by extension the other transmedia versions of Boobie "makes us want to *do* something," to play until we win—defined against cultural institutions and productions that punish losers.[94] "Boobie Miles" engages and rebuffs the fixed scripts of sports, race, and masculinity that circulate in *Friday Night Lights*. Big K.R.I.T. refuses to lose on the film's terms. Instead, he will play until he wins, a rewinding of the start until the outcome proves favorable.

For Big K.R.I.T., Boobie's virtuosity and his own are doubly defined through rap music as a sonic cultural expression that imagines and reimagines. It calls upon, calls out to, and calls back Black people pushed to the margins. It is cinematic Boobie's "distinguished" self, his diegetic rhetoric and sporting stylistics, that sets the tone for Big K.R.I.T.'s own rhetorical and performative agency. On both songs, alternative logics on failure are expressed. To different ends and with different aims, "Hometown Hero" and "Boobie Miles" offer a radical refusal for Boobie's beautiful, Black, and strong body to be defeated. In the reclaiming of the former, now fallen, racial icon, Boobie has become a Black football folk hero: real, fictional, and mythological. Flowing to the beat of Big K.R.I.T. and circulating in Black forms of cultural expression, Boobie is transformed from Bissinger's book and Berg's adaptation to an imprinted character in Black popular culture and consciousness.

Finally, with all of Boobie's transmedia re-significations at play, it comes as no surprise that artists such as Big K.R.I.T. and countless other everyday people invoke and affirm Boobie's athletic and cinematic history, purchasing and dressing in his unofficial jersey and quoting lines from Big K.R.I.T.'s songs and the film to reference his iconic memory in their daily lives. On social media, fans of Boobie proudly recite the lines: "Let Boobie shine Coach!" and "Y'all wanna win? Put Boobie in!"[95] Embracing the character's swagger, the cinematic Boobie, previously iconized, later pathologized and in need of televisual redemption, is reclaimed within the Black familiar as a football folk hero whose (de)feats on the field have become remembered and celebrated in Black popular culture.

This chapter's attention to Boobie's intertextuality and intratextuality forms a critical transmedia meta-representation of sporting blackness and muscle memory as literary, cinematic, televisual, and sonic projection: failure as moral fate, social abjection, moral deficiency, and something otherwise. In his last mediated form in Big K. R. I. T.'s songs, Boobie's sonic textuality provides expressive space for the subversive arts of reclamation, not predicated on Boobie's redemption or white recuperation of his failures, as seen in film and on television, respectively. Instead, Black creative consumption, spectatorship, identification, and reworking represent an oppositional theorizing that makes Boobie, as he once boasted in *Friday Night Lights*, "distinguished" in the then, now, and future.[96]

3. Black Female Incommensurability and Athletic Genders

Imagine *A League of Their Own* sequel that starts with the scene of the black woman throwing the ball back from the stands and you stay with her and it becomes a biopic on the 3 black women that played in the Negro Leagues (Toni Stone, Mami 'Peanut' Johnson & Connie Morgan).

—MATTHEW A. CHERRY

To consider the paucity of Black women's representation in sports films, I want to draw attention to a brief but profound scene in Penny Marshall's *A League of Their Own* (1992), one that illustrates the incommensurability of Black female sporting blackness in the genre. Critically acclaimed and the highest grossing baseball movie to date, *A League of Their Own* fictionalizes the history of the All-American Girls Baseball League (AAGBL), a woman's professional baseball organization initially created as the All-American Girls Softball League by chewing gum mogul Philip. K. Wrigley.[1] The league existed from 1943 to 1954, beginning in four midwestern cities and, at its peak, included teams in ten cities with a legion of fans. Wrigley founded the AAGBL during World War II as a "wartime surrogate" for men's professional baseball, as he was concerned that men's absence from the major leagues would have irreversible damage on national interest in the sport.[2] A comedic melodrama set during the War, *A League of their Own* tells the fictional tale of two sisters, Dottie (Geena Davis), a homemaker and stand-out catcher, and Kit (Lori Petty), a fiery yet immature pitcher, as they try out and play for the Rockford Peaches, coached by women sports–hating and disgraced Chicago Cubs player Jimmy Duggan (Tom Hanks).

While celebrating the groundbreaking history of women's professional sports, the film attempts to capture the fraught gender dynamics of the AAGBL, especially "the cultural dissonance between 'masculine' athleticism and 'feminine' womanhood" that the league's regulations contributed to maintaining.[3] *A League of Their Own* is attendant to the AAGBL's strict rules of conduct, which included, among others: always appearing in feminine attire when not playing, no "boyish bobs," no smoking or drinking in public, and all social outings to be approved by chaperones.[4] These codes of gender and social propriety, geared toward promoting and maintaining "women's baseball as a spectacle of feminine 'nice girls' who could 'play like a man,'" engender moments of dramatic tension and comedic relief in the film as the women come into conflict with these "femininity principles."[5] While the film memorializes AABGL history, including the gender expression that came from blending "mannish" qualities off and on the field with traditional white femininity, *A League of Their Own* also captures the prohibition of Black women from the league. In doing so, Marshall's film confronts the double exclusion of Black women because of their race and gender in sports history, subtly and powerfully critiquing the gender equity narrative the film celebrates.

Black women appear in only one brief scene in *A League of Their Own*, specifically during a montage that illustrates the AAGBL's rise in popularity. In this scene, there is a cut to the edge of a baseball field where a solitary Black woman dressed in a printed frock and white hat stands in the outfield near the fenced-in foul line. On the other side of the fence stand four Black men and two Black women adjacent to a set of battered green bleachers. The entire group of Black spectators is far from the arena's covered stadium seating that houses the scores of white fans waiting for the game to begin, emphasizing the Jim Crow policies that segregated public spaces, including sports arenas, during this time. Opposite the other Black spectators, the lone Black woman stands out on the field of play. The action begins as she kneels to pick up a baseball that has accidentally rolled into the outfield. The camera reverses to reveal Dottie and her teammates with the white populated stadium behind them. Dottie lifts her glove, gesturing and then calling out for the Black woman to throw the ball a modest distance back to her. The camera reverses to capture the Black woman as she plants her foot and hurls the baseball (figure 15). Bypassing Dottie, the ball goes over her head, with great accuracy, directly into the mitt of teammate Ellen Sue (Freddie Simpson), who is standing a substantial distance away from both Dottie and the Black woman. Catching the ball, Ellen yelps, removing her hand from her glove and shaking it out to infer the power of the Black woman's throw. Dottie, taken aback by the woman's athletic ability and precision, looks back at the Black woman with surprise. The camera reverses back to a medium close-up of the Black woman; her pursed lips appear to be in between the gestures of a smile and a smirk as she looks off into the distance at Dottie. Nodding, knowingly, she turns around to walk away.[6] The scene ends as quickly as it began, cutting to footage of the Peaches' second baseman Marla Hooch's (Megan Cavanaugh) wedding recessional.

FIGURE 15. Sidelined Black female athletic prowess in *A League of Their Own* (Penny Marshall, 1992).

This brief scene of sidelined Black female athletic prowess is a mere thirteen seconds long in a film that runs 128 minutes. While minimal in time, the scope of this moment is significant to understanding Black women's incommensurability within sports films. Like the ball flung by the Black woman, this scene could have easily been tossed out of the film by Marshall, having no narrative function necessary for telling this feminist tale of women's neglected sports history, the upending of traditional gender roles, and America's national pastime. Its deliberate inclusion, then, is telling and far-reaching in its impact, despite its brevity, in part because of how it scripts the Black female sporting body into the mise-en-scène of white women's athletic empowerment as a diegetic critique of the league's racial apartheid. At the margins of the baseball field, the Black woman, who goes both unnamed and uncredited in the film, surfaces within and outside the bounds of dominant sports history, and her presence and athleticism paradoxically address the absence of her body and subjectivity within AAGBL history and the sports film genre more broadly.

The unnamed Black woman stands out within the all-white narrative, which is predicated on an unequal gender divide and the spectacle of gender contrast. Analogous to her lack of a place in the league, she also has no point of comparison on screen, as other Black female sporting bodies are nonexistent in the film. However, she represents a history of discrimination by the AAGBL against Black female athletes. Her visual placement at the margins and deft sporting performance implicitly critiques the explicit racism and segregation in women's professional baseball. As sports historian Susan K. Cahn explains: "The AAGBL also had an unwritten policy against hiring women of color, though it did employ several light-skinned Cuban players. Not until 1951, five years after the integration of professional men's baseball, did the league openly discuss hiring black women. Torn between the need for skilled players and a desire to promote a particular image of femininity, officials decided against recruiting African Americans 'unless they would show promise of exceptional ability.' This decision, and the fact that no black players were ever recruited, reflects the pervasive racism in American society during the 1940s and 1950s."[7] Despite the fact that Jackie Robinson and Larry Doby integrated men's professional baseball's International League and American League in 1947, the AAGBL refused Black women entry into women's professional baseball, maintaining "an image rooted in white middle-class beliefs about beauty and respectability" that "[excluded] and [deprecated] black women, making black athletes almost by definition less likely to meet league standards."[8] *A League of Their Own*'s narrative economy is true to this history but also aware and critical of its racist protocols. The film accounts for Black women's absence within the league and its storyline through a Black women's transgressive athletic performance. She not only flexes her abilities in a "man's sport" but also foregrounds her displacement within a white woman's sporting world.

In describing Black women's incommensurability, Michele Wallace employs the celestial metaphor of the black hole, extending Houston Baker's thoughts on Richard Wright's books *Native Son* and *Black Boy* and his short stories as "a black w/hole, satisfying and complete."[9] Attending to the physics of black holes as not empty but dense, accumulative spaces, Wallace builds on Baker's trope for her own counter-hegemonic understanding of Black women's invisibility and, yet, ubiquity in the creative arts, explaining that black holes "may give access to other dimensions."[10] A black hole, then, becomes understood "as a process, as a progression that appears differently, or not at all, from various perspectives."[11] The metaphor is not only, as Wallace proffers, illustrative of the incommensurability of Black feminist creativity, where all people see is the void and not the mass(ive) inventory of content/creators, but also applicable to our understanding of Marshall's rendering of Black female athletes' critical muscle memory.

The Black woman's presence in the film surfaces a "black w/hole," an absent-present history of Black female athletic practices, leagues, and teams, including the places and communities where her abilities were taught, learned, and honed. Her sporting blackness points out and uncovers the virtual non/existence of itself in recorded (sporting and cinematic) histories "in the way that black holes were nonexistent until they were discovered by science."[12] If black holes have the possibility of providing access to other dimensions, as Wallace's embrace of the cosmic metaphor proposes, the unnamed Black woman's athletic body projects this possibility, critically staging sporting blackness as an aperture to known and unknown Black women's sporting history. In fact, the Black woman's sporting performance, alongside the two other Black women standing near the sidelines, reifies Black female athletes' positioning at the periphery but also yields versions of the historical bodies of Black women baseball players Toni Stone, Connie Morgan, and Mamie "Peanut" Johnson.

Stone, Morgan, and Johnson were "African American women who, after being turned away from the AAGBL, played baseball for the Negro Leagues. The women played for three seasons (1953–55) and added a measure of much-needed publicity to a black baseball league slowly in decline."[13] In *A League of Their Own*, the short scene of the Black woman in action standing adjacent to her fellow Black female spectators advances a shared sporting experience, a critical muscle memory of these women's sporting history of exclusion from the AAGBL and inclusion in the Negro Leagues. In her analysis of this opening scene, sports historian Amira Rose Davis suggests that the unnamed Black woman's "nod and sardonic smile as if to say 'I can play too'" alludes to "the image that has developed of these women's [Stone, Morgan, and Johnson] lives: silent, nodding, and half-smiling—saying everything and nothing at all."[14] The unnamed character, then, not only silently gestures at her knowingness but also gives purview to Black women's physical and symbolic labor as present but unaccounted for in American sports and society.[15] With a minuscule number of fictional films about Black women athletes, a thirteen-second scene in *A League of Their Own* becomes foundational to our understanding of Black female incommensurability in sports films in terms of their in/visibility. The lack of Black sportswomen is a common convention of the genre. In this mode of non-representation, their invisibility describes not only a physical "absence" in sports films but also the structural impact that the denial of Black women's "presence" in sporting history has on the genre's content and form.[16]

THE GENDERED MODES OF SPORTING BLACKNESS

Gender is consequential to our understanding of sporting blackness. In chapter 2, I framed Boobie's transmedia sporting blackness, particularly his athleticism and bodily integrity, within his racial iconicity, detailing how the Black *male* physique is emblematic in sports popular culture. To this point, Kobena Mercer describes how "the black man as sports hero" is defined in tropified terms as "mythologically endowed with a 'naturally' muscular physique and an essential capacity for strength, grace and machinelike perfection: well hard."[17] This mythologization hinges on the "sexual and racial fantasy which aestheticizes the stereotype" of the Black male athlete, and his body is objectified, reified, and commodified in the realm of sports.[18] Sports films traffic in these sexual and racial tropes, displaying, idealizing, and fetishizing images of Black men's muscularity: flexed arms, toned back, hard chest, sculpted legs, and chiseled abdominals. "The fact that it is the black male and not black female body that has become iconic," Ben Carrington speculates, "demonstrates the contradictory ways in which black masculinity can be afforded a 'privileged' status further illustrating how regimes of representation can simultaneously marginalise black femininity whilst valorising black masculinity."[19] As the films about Black male athletes decidedly outnumber films about Black women athletes, analyses of sporting blackness in film and visual culture disproportionately favor thinking through the matrices of gender in terms of Black masculinity.

Nicole Fleetwood's examination of the precarious racial iconicity of the Black athlete provides a requisite template to address the representational imbalance and consider Black women and racialized femininities in sports. Fleetwood centers the Black female body in the discussion of iconicity through an analysis of Serena Williams's athletic prowess, musculature, fashion choices, and defiance of tennis's gendered and racialized notions of propriety. Through attention to Williams's physicality and style, Fleetwood advances the gendered stakes of racial iconicity, concentrating on the performative aspects of women's sporting blackness in the public imagination that challenges, unsettles, and broadens the scope of gender, racial, and sporting norms. She explores these aspects through the lens of intersectionality, or the overlapping social categories and interlocking systems of power that specifically affect Black women.[20] In doing so, Fleetwood insists that Williams's sporting blackness "highlights how sports, race, and convention work together to buttress ideals of gendered physicality, racialized femininity, and performative aesthetics."[21] I want to extend her consideration of these ideals to my study here on the gendered modes of sporting blackness in order to address the (de)construction of Black female subjectivity, embodied performance, and critical muscle memory in sports films.

Representations of Black female athletes in sports films are scant, a consequence of women's contested place in sports history and our sporting imaginary. Instead of being foregrounded as athletes in sports narratives, they are, in a manner similar to the Black woman in *A League of Their*

Own, sidelined. Black women in sports films exist mostly as minor characters such as wives, mothers, and cheerleaders, if they are not absent all together. Their peripheral treatment is "not fortuitously occurring at the margins," as Stuart Hall notes of marginalized Black experiences, "but placed, positioned at the margins, as the consequence of a set of specific political and cultural practices."[22] In this chapter, I first address Black women's position on the sidelines of sports films, examining the gendered and racialized representational politics and practices that circumscribe Black women's roles and sporting bodies in the genre.[23] This exclusionary pattern in sports films, I argue, functions formally and ideologically as "variations on negation," or what Michele Wallace theorizes as the ways in which Black women have been rendered and effaced in various cultural arenas. The delimited representational space for Black women athletes as characters and subjects in sports films underscores the importance of feminist and intersectional approaches to sporting blackness in narratives about Black women in sports. These approaches, which theorize the doing and undoing of racialized gender norms, speak to performativity within "a scene of constraint."[24] In this case, scenes of constraint include not only sports film conventions, or the ways that gender difference is addressed in the genre, but also the limited number of sports films—as of this writing, a little over a dozen—about Black women athletes.[25] Because of the small concentration of films, brief but potent moments such as the one in *A League of Their Own* become of central importance to the w/hole of Black women's incommensurability and, thus, (in)visibility in the sports film genre. But what can sports films about Black women athletes who challenge social conventions and athletic traditions reveal about the gendered modes of sporting blackness? In this chapter, I turn from a broad consideration of Black women athletes' lack of representation on screen and its impact on the genre to focus closely on two related and yet very different feature films about Black women's sporting bodies, examples that push against and reify the normative genre conventions and discourses of gender in sports films: Gina Prince-Bythewood's *Love and Basketball* (2000) and Jesse Vaughan's *Juwanna Mann* (2002).

VARIATIONS ON NEGATION

The relative void of films about Black sportswomen has created a deliberate if not defining absence within sports cinema. Despite the dominance and celebrity of Black female athletes from Althea Gibson to Florence Griffith Joyner to Serena and Venus Williams, Black women are almost never the subject of biopics, the most common sports film subgenre, which generally privilege stories of heroic white male athletes with a subset of stories about legendary Black male athletes. Black women's vacant place on screen characterizes their paradigmatic "invisibility blues" within a vast representational void that Ed Guerrero once described of Black men in contemporary film as an "empty space in representation."[26] This exclusionary pattern of the cinematic Black female athlete has produced "variations on negation" that structure the denial, rendering, and effacement of Black women athletes on screen.

Michele Wallace describes variations on negation as the contradictory ways Black women have been made invisible in critical theory and the public imagination despite their ubiquity in various arenas.[27] In her treatise, Wallace attends to the denial of Black women's artistry and intellectual discourse within dominant traditions and the difficulties of presenting a Black female perspective in cultural criticism, a consideration I apply to sports cinema's racialized and gendered regimes of representation that characterize the incommensurability of the Black female sporting body, who is made to be "other" to the already "othered" white women athletes and Black male athletes in the genre. In sports films, Black women's variations on negation occur in the ways in which their bodies—sporting and otherwise—are paradoxically made invisible and visible in the genre. If, as Wallace attests, "variations on negation confront the 'impossible,' the radical being and not being of women of color," then tracing the historical and generic patterns of this denial, rendering, and effacement that contributes to Black women athlete's marginal positioning on screen can challenge while centering the mattering—both in terms of materiality and significance—of the Black female sporting body on screen.[28] As well, confronting these moments of impossibility, what Wallace calls the incommensurable, such as I did in my analysis of the brief scene of Black women's sporting prowess in *A League of Their Own*, provides the opportunity to later consider the gendered modalities of sporting blackness and critical muscle memory in films such as *Love and Basketball* and *Juwanna Mann*.

The lack of sports films about Black women reflects the broader marginalization of all women athletes in the genre. Women (mainly white women) are situated in sports narratives relative to the male athlete-hero as mother, wife, daughter, sister, or groupie: supportive, unsupportive, constructive, or destructive forces for, usually, (white) male self-definition. Women's positioning at the margins of sports film narratives, however, is a consequence of the idea of sports as a masculinist site of competition, one that has shaped women's historical struggles to participate as subjects and agents within this arena. For centuries, sports have been thought to be the domain of men, where mastery, dominance, aggression, control, pleasure, and power are expressions and affirmations of masculinity. "Sport and masculinity," Dayna B. Daniels acutely explains, "have become entwined to the point that the normative characteristics of a masculine male and the normative characteristics of an athlete are nearly identical."[29] To be an athlete is to be a man.

Historically, women were actively discouraged from athletic involvement. It was thought that "women could succeed only by sacrificing what was seen as their natural femininity for masculine qualities of body and mind."[30] For example, in the nineteenth- and early twentieth-century, "health cautions around physical activity of white, middle- and upper-class, heterosexual women" limited female participation in sports to informal recreational leagues or non-strenuous activities for fear that vigorous exercise and athletic activity "exposed the female body to public view and damaged a woman's reproductive organs, possibly ruining her chances for future motherhood."[31] Concerns ranged from panic over bodily injury and sexual impropriety to fear and anxiety that women's perceived masculine sporting behaviors undermined their heterosexuality. The stereotype of the mannish lesbian athlete was used to discredit and discourage women athletes. These apprehensions over women's bodies, particularly their reproductive capabilities and sexuality, were not applicable to all women's bodies; instead they were wielded "to protect the alleged superiority and desirability of white people as central to the leadership and development of American society."[32] Black women's sporting bodies, as Cahn argues, were viewed through racist frames: "African American women's achievements in a 'mannish' sport also reinforced disparaging stereotypes of black women as less womanly or feminine than white women."[33] Nonwhite, indigenous, and immigrants' physical labor, sporting or otherwise, were ignored, misshaping historical records and collective memories about women of color athletes during this time. This gendering and racializing of sports, Daniels attests, has engendered "incorrect beliefs about the histories of games and sports, and the invisibility of girls and women as participants, [that] have created a foundation of myths upon which the contemporary culture of sports and the construction of masculinity have been built."[34]

Sports cinema and its gendered and racialized regimes of representation have imported, crystallized, and projected these myths, justifying the cinematic exclusion of Black women athletes on the basis of historical realism. In other words, Black women athletes cannot appear in films about sports history they were not a part of because that would sacrifice the film's claim to veracity. Unlike *A League of their Own*, most sports films do not embed the histories of racial segregation into their narratives unless the films themselves are about integrationist topics. Sports films, however, take much license with sports history, changing events, games, participants, and facts (even when they are biopics) to serve narrative and emotional beats, often seeming unconcerned with historical accuracy in favor of cultural and affective resonance. Despite the hypervisibility and achievement of a few Black women athletes in sports visual culture, sports films rarely recognize these exceptional female athletes in sports history at all. Black hypervisibility produces a kind of overrepresentation and visual currency that "simultaneously announces the continual invisibility of blacks as ethical and enfleshed subjects in various realms of polity, economies, and discourse, so that blackness remains aligned with negation and decay."[35] Thus, the hypervisibility of Black sporting women in popular culture eclipses scores of Black women athletes, paradoxically leaving them hidden from history and cinematic view as another Black w/hole. There can be, in other words, no criticality or memory where no history or visuality takes place or is recorded/projected, only invisibility and negative space in the genre. Therefore, Black sportswomen—despite their game-changing records in a panoply of athletic activities—are a structuring absence of the sports film genre.

In sports cinema more generally, stories of (white) female athletes make up only a small segment of the sports film genre.[36] Within this gender economy, Black women's bodies exist but are hardly sporting. They principally are present in fictional stories about Black male athletes: cast as dutiful or negligent mothers in films such as *The Jackie Robinson Story* (Alfred Green, 1950) and *The Blind Side* (John Lee Hancock, 2009), respectively; baby mamas in conservative tales like *Coach Carter* (Thomas Carter, 2005); love interests in male-centered biopics such as *Glory Road* (James Gartner, 2006); or doting and steadfast wives as seen in *Remember the Titans* (Boaz Yankin, 2002) and *42* (Brian Helgeland, 2013). When Black female athletes' stories are given cinematic treatments, these films still adhere to sports film and television's generic conventions of sublimating larger structural/gender/racial issues into narratives that champion individual success for wide audience appeal, especially since they are principally made-for-television biopics such as *Wilma* (Bud Greenspan, 1977), *Run for the Dream: The Gail Devers Story* (Neema Barnette, 1996), *The Loretta Claiborne Story* (Lee Grant, 2000), *The Gabby Douglas Story* (Gregg Champion, 2014), and *The Simone Biles Story: Courage to Soar* (Vanessa Parise, 2018).[37]

While not outside of the racialized gender processes that code the sports film genre and Black women's (dis)placement therein, *Love and Basketball* and *Juwanna Mann* explicitly engage, challenge, deflect, and ultimately capitulate to the categorical range of Black women's representation in sports films. The characters in *Love and Basketball* and *Juwanna Mann* function antagonistically within a genre that more often than not positions Black sporting women as nonexistent (or off the court as wives or girlfriends) or masculinized athletes. In the first case, Black women are invisible/sidelined, and in the second, Black women are coded in ways that underscore how they have been historically considered not "real" women at all in sports or society.[38] Both protagonists, Monica and Juwanna, exist within and outside of this "accusatory space," a positioning diagnosed by Jacquie Jones to describe the narrow two categories Black women are allowed to cinematically occupy in 1990s cinema.[39] In sports films' corollary realm, *Love and Basketball's* and *Juwanna Mann's* main characters' sporting bodies and performances represent, transgress, exaggerate, and reaffirm these gender lines, constraints, and spaces on and off the basketball court.

ATHLETIC GENDERS

Because of the incommensurability of the cinematic Black female sporting body, the analogous sporting narratives of *Love and Basketball* and *Juwanna Mann* make these two films, despite their glaring differences, apposite examples of sporting blackness, especially when juxtaposed. Both films are about basketball, heterosexual romance, redemption, and the gendered dynamics of sports. *Love and Basketball* is a romantic sports melodrama about a tough-nosed Black female baller who attempts to navigate her love of basketball and her desire for the basketball-loving boy next door. *Juwanna Mann* is a sports comedy about how a male professional basketball player, whose unsportsmanlike conduct gets him kicked out of the men's league, pretends to be a woman in order to play in the women's professional basketball league. In both films, I examine how a Black woman's and a Black man in drag's body on the court, respectively, challenge cultural norms about the athletic performance of gender, calling into crisis our understandings of gendered sporting and nonsporting ideals. I argue that in *Love and Basketball* these crises are resolved by making the Black woman properly feminine and thus desirable via discourses of Black on Black heterosexual love and feminist gender equity. In *Juwanna Mann*, they are heightened and lampooned for comedic effect, resulting in portraits of Black femininity as garish, laughable, and easily discarded.

However, both films do encourage more capacious and consequential readings of sporting blackness at the intersections of race and gender, acts and aesthetics. If sporting blackness allows for a mutable self and fluid subjectivity, then reading the Black female sporting body, not in terms of biology, which attempts to naturalize difference, but, instead, in terms of performativity or constitutive acts advances a larger critical project about the apposition of gender in/and sporting blackness as constructed identities and corporeal actions that constitute athletic activity. As Judith Butler explains, "Gender is in no way a stable identity or locus of agency from which various acts proceed; rather, it is an identity tenuously constituted in time—an identity instituted through the stylization of the body, and hence, must be understood as the mundane ways in which bodily gestures, movements, and enactments of various kinds constitute the illusion of an abiding gendered self."[40] Gender, a socially and historically transitive construct, manifests as a set of imperatives and strategies to read sporting blackness not only as a state of being but also as an action, mode and modality, or occurrence of bodily expression that is constantly being repeated, reinforced, risked, and revised within the constraints of the sports film genre's staging of gender ideals. Critical muscle memory, then, manifests in athleticism as performativity, or in Butler's terms as "athletic genders," sedimented cognitive and embodied repetitive sporting acts of social fiction about bodily comportment and ideals that are always in flux.[41] In other words, muscle memory is the illusion and allusion of the gendered self. It manifests in physical movement and is always being contested in fields of play. As sporting acts/action, critical muscle memory reveals, consolidates, dissimulates, enables, disables, mimes, reworks, eroticizes, and re-signifies conventions of racialized femininities and masculinities. When intertwined with Black femininity in *Love and Basketball*, muscle memory becomes acritical in order to comply with the gendered expectations of the straight Black romance film; whereas in *Juwanna Mann* muscle memory casts Black femininity as a joke, a hoax and enforced amnesia of ethical Black athleticism.

To analyze the Black female sporting body in *Love and Basketball* and *Juwanna Mann*, I attend to the stylization of the body through gesture, movements, and enactments to see how the athletic body contours meaning, exercises imaginative possibilities, and exhaustively embodies ideas about racialized and gendered sporting identities on and off the court. Attendance to athletic genders signals the ways in which "gender is a field in which a variety of standards, expectations, relations, and ideals compete with one another."[42] In *Love and Basketball*, Monica, played by Sanaa Lathan, is the film's protagonist. Her assigned sex is female and her gender project is firmly situated within the traditions and strictures of Black middle-class life and mores. Whereas *Juwanna Mann*'s lead character, Jamal, played by

Miguel A. Núñez Jr., is a Black man in drag posing as a woman, as a deceptive means to a competitive end, not as a mode of gender identification. While the latter film pushes the boundaries of what constitutes a traditional woman's sports film as well as the idea of a Black female protagonist in ways that expose how tenuous and contested gender is in sport, society, and on screen, both examples invite us to reject claims of facticity and consider how "gender identity is a performative accomplishment compelled by social sanction and taboo."[43] *Love and Basketball* and *Juwanna Mann* center on their respective characters' athletic genders, illustrating how sporting blackness functions to embody and play out constructs, limits, and possibilities of racialized femininity, masculinity, and binary and nonbinary embodied epistemes.

Both films require engagement with "nonce taxonomies" that "challenge hegemonic models of gender conformity" and classifications of physicality, desire, and subjectivity, specifically female masculinity and drag femininity for, respectively, "playing like a man" and "suiting up" on the court.[44] In this register, sporting blackness can be analyzed in terms of athletic genders, a motor for bodily comportment and athletic style of play that can unsettle gendered expectations in and through sports. This motor, however, stalls out a shared critical muscle memory of gender performance in *Love & Basketball* in order to suture the narrative to the heterosexual contract between Black men and women, while in *Juwanna Mann* it motors a clown car with a cargo of gendered clichés and ridiculous jokes. In the end, the drama and comedy in *Love & Basketball* and *Juwanna Mann*, respectively, are narrativized and embodied in the characters' affront to and anxiety about normative gender expression within the marked spaces of athletic competition and straight relationships.

"PLAYING LIKE A MAN" IN *LOVE AND BASKETBALL*

Gina Prince-Bythewood's *Love and Basketball* is a rare sports film about a Black female baller that tackles the ways in which women athletes have come to realize themselves as subjects and agents in the male-dominated world of sports. Imagined by Prince-Bythewood as a "Black" *When Harry Met Sally* (Rob Reiner 1989), the film is a romantic sports melodrama.[45] That is, it intertwines elements of Black love stories and "women's films" into a women's sports film. Describing a range of contemporary women's sports films that emphasize emotional and sporting intensities to promote audience identification with female athletes, Jean O'Reilly explains that women's sports films, including *Love and Basketball*, have particular tropes that align them with classical melodrama's gendered modes and plot structures—particularly sexual transgression, the redeeming power of love, and sacrifice and tears evidenced in earlier films such as *Stella Dallas* (King Vidor, 1937) and *All That Heaven Allows* (Douglas Sirk, 1955).[46] "In the woman's sports film," O'Reilly details, "gender conflict is the biggest issue, and female protagonists must often struggle to simply defend their desire to play sports, to be 'mannish,' in the dominant male society. The very fact of playing sports thus provides the main social and sexual transgression in the melodramatic plot structure that many of these films adopt."[47]

Love and Basketball incorporates these melodramatic plot structures, invoking and resolving anxieties around expressions of racialized femininity and masculinity on the court through the female protagonist "playing like a man" and then, later, failing to do so as a means to affirm sporting and gender hierarchies and claims of naturalness via Black heterosexual coupling. At the same time, the film's interest in women's sports expands on our understanding of the capacity of women's sports to unsettle cultural norms and productively call into crisis stable gender ideals. This is because "women's sports," as Butler insists, "offer a site in which this transformation of our ordinary sense of what constitutes a gendered body is itself dramatically contested and transformed."[48] An analysis of athletic genders in Prince-Bythewood's film registers the transitivity of gender as the projection of possibilities and prohibitions of a Black girl who can ball. Playing basketball in the film, then, becomes a site and citation for these moments of social, cultural, and gender transgression and regression.

Broken up into "four quarters" in keeping with the game's structure, *Love and Basketball*'s narrative spans fifteen years of the protagonists' lives, following the growing relationship between two neighborhood basketball players, Monica Wright (Sanaa Lathan) and Quincy "Q" McCall (Omar Epps). The "first quarter" begins in 1981 when Monica, eleven, moves next door to Quincy into the wealthiest Black neighborhood in the United States, the exclusive View Park area of Baldwin Hills in Los Angeles. Following a tense pickup game between the two, Monica and Quincy go from rivals to friends to boyfriend/girlfriend to enemies before the film shifts to the "second quarter" set in 1988. At that time, Monica and Quincy are seniors in high school. Both are on varsity basketball teams for Crenshaw High School in Los Angeles. Playing point guard, Monica hopes that her basketball skills land her an athletic scholarship. She has yet to be recruited, possibly because her aggressive play and surly temper sometimes gets the best of her on the court. In contrast, Quincy, who is both popular on and off the court, is a rising star at Crenshaw, following in the footsteps of his father, Zeke (Dennis Haysbert), a current Los Angeles Clippers player in his final years of professional play. Unlike Monica, Quincy is being heavily recruited by top basketball programs as well as Ivy League schools, though he favors the former over the latter in the hopes of competing for a collegiate national championship. Against the backdrop of their diverging basketball careers, Monica and Quincy's relationship takes a romantic turn by the end of the quarter, when she finds out she is being recruited by the University of Southern California (USC) where Quincy plans to attend as well.

The "third quarter," 1988–89, chronicles Monica and Quincy's freshman year together at USC and the tenderness and turmoil of their new relationship. Monica struggles as the backup point guard for the Lady Trojans, while Quincy shines as a starting freshman for the men's program. However, the basketball balance shifts for the two of them as the year progresses. Monica's high school antics, particularly showboating after scoring, are not tolerated by her college coach. Improving her skills through a reinvigorated work ethic, Monica catches a break when the Lady Trojan's starting point guard is injured during a game and she gets a chance to play. Monica later wins the starting spot on the team. In contrast, Quincy's college career is cut short, choosing to prematurely enter the NBA draft after finding out about his father's philandering ways. The quarter ends with the breakup of Monica and Quincy's relationship, largely because he claims that Monica puts basketball before him.

The final and "fourth quarter" begins in 1993 with Monica, unable to play professionally in the United States, taking her skills abroad to Barcelona, Spain, where she becomes a celebrity. Monica's love of basketball wanes, however, despite winning several championships. Homesick, she returns to Los Angeles and gets a job working at her father's bank, turning in her Nikes for heels she can barely walk in, as it seems her basketball playing days are over. Quincy, who entered the draft and bounced around from several teams, is rarely playing for the Lakers, mostly from the bench, until he tears his ACL, seemingly ending his basketball career. Monica visits Quincy in the hospital, where she finds out he is engaged to another woman. Devastated because she is still in love with him, a week before his wedding, Monica challenges Quincy to a high-stakes one-on-one game: playing for Quincy's heart and the dissolution of his engagement. The two play a first-to-five match. Although Monica loses, they romantically reunite. The film ends with a cut to the Lakers' stadium, half-filled with fans—among them—NBA legend Earvin "Magic" Johnson, as the Women's National Basketball Association's (WNBA) Los Angeles Sparks take the court, including former Sparks' player Lisa Leslie in a cameo role. Wearing her sports hero Magic's number 32, Monica, whose last name now reads Wright-McCall, plays professional basketball for the Sparks as her husband, Quincy, and their baby girl sit courtside to watch her play.

Love and Basketball's romantic melodrama depicts Black women as agents of their own destiny while still circumscribed within the limitations of gendered expression and sporting opportunities. Monica's tense and supportive relationships with other women, particularly her mother and sister, as well as her friendships/rivalries with her female teammates, situate this film as a charged Black feminist woman's sports film in keeping with late twentieth-century Black independent film projects and Prince-Bythewood's oeuvre. However, the heterosexual A-plot of romance, marriage, and reproduction delivers a fairly standard urban contemporary love story in the manner of *Brown Sugar* (Rick Famuyiwa, 2002) and *Love Jones* (Theodore Witcher, 1997), for example.

In *Love and Basketball*, Monica's sporting performances on the court illuminate the tensions around discourses of masculinity and femininity in sports. Despite how others gender her sports performance, Monica pugnaciously identifies herself as just a "ball player." It seems Monica must disavow her femininity altogether in order to retain her athleticism and muscularity. However, her claims to a neutral sporting identity—one easily inhabited by men and therefore considered a masculine ideal—is an attempt to denaturalize gender and gender-segregated sports. Monica's surly insurgence nonetheless leads to difficulties for her in both love and career. When Quincy tells her that her bad attitude (read aggressive and masculine behavior) on the court is why she's not being recruited, Monica retorts: "You jump in some guys face, talk smack, and you get a pat on your ass. But because I'm female I get told to calm down and act like a lady." Monica is aware of and disgusted by the gendered politics that code her sporting performance as well as the Black middle-class respectability of ladylike behavior and heterosexual female comportment. Her reply to being told to tone it down on the court signals how women in sports are physically hemmed in by these gender expectations regarding style of play. Monica's indignation at such a request qualitatively contests gendered fields of play, asking, as Jennifer Doyle does, "What is it we are looking for in a women's game? Surely not a confirmation of the 'femininity' of the people on the pitch [or court]. It must be something else—like how the women's game allows us to escape narrow ideas about who and what women are."[49] In the end, Monica's insistence on being considered a ball player and nothing more is an attempt to script herself and her comportment as polygendered. In this sporting context, polygenderism enacts "a new lens through which the pictures of femininity and masculinity blur, fade, and metamorphose into a new way of accepting ourselves" outside of a gender sporting binary.[50]

On the basketball court, Monica's polygender play embraces the modality and subject position of female masculinity, whereby hegemonic models of gender conformity are challenged through the logics of embodiment.[51] Her corporeal actions, embodied gestures, movements, and enactments challenge dimorphic gender constructions that craft the athletic and non-athletic female body. Monica's sporting body creates a fluid subjectivity where being and becoming are put into motion on the court and, in turn, so are our expectations of acceptable gender performances. Her muscle memory is present tense and signals the possibility of Black women's cinematic futurity and athletic multiplicity. In *Love and Basketball*, there are four scenes of Monica on the court in particular that dramatically stage and register the ways in which athletic genders are exercised through bodily comportment and style of play.

First, in the quarter when Monica and Quincy initially meet, her body on the basketball court is read as male because of the baggy shirt and jeans she wears and the cap covering her long hair. This initial act of misrecognition transforms into shock for the boys she competes against because of her "surprising" ability to play basketball. On the court, it is obvious that she is the best player, even better than Quincy. Her defiant sporting performance, in this case "playing like a boy" instead of derogatorily "playing like a girl," makes Quincy step his game up as they play two-on-two basketball. Monica and Quincy verbally spar throughout the game about gender expectations. Quincy chastises Monica, calling her names and telling her that girls can't play ball. Telling him that she can ball better than him, she allows her skilled play to "do the talking." The heated game continues mostly between the two, but Monica outperforms Quincy, who grows frustrated with Monica's athletic ability and starts to miss several shots. With Monica taking the ball out on game point, Quincy switches with his teammate to guard her. Dribbling the ball with Quincy defending her, Monica tells Quincy that she's going to be the first girl in the NBA. Quincy lashes back that he will be the one in the NBA and she will be his cheerleader, reinforcing the structural marginalization of women on the sidelines of the basketball court. With a quick give-and-go with her teammate, Monica gets around Quincy and takes the ball to the basket. But before she can get the shot off to sink the game winner, she is fouled by Quincy, who pushes her to the ground. Monica is bloodied with a cut on her face, and the game and scene ends abruptly.

This sequence structures the film's discourses around embodiment, gender performance, and the basketball court as a privileged space for expressions of masculinity. As a tomboy, Monica represents "an extended childhood of female masculinity."[52] Monica's athleticism and dominant performance challenge the ways in which sports are considered an arena for boys and men. Her insistence that she is going to be in the NBA (at the time there was no WNBA) simultaneously illustrates women's limited access to professional sport opportunities and asserts her own imagined gender transitivity outside the bounds and binaries of courted norms. As long as she can ball better than the boys, she can stylize herself as the first woman in the men's league, paradoxically making visible the segregation of the sport and the incommensurability of her "difference" through her comparable and compatible sporting performance. In the end, the fact that she is thwarted by Quincy's deliberate foul reveals not only the tension around her female masculinity and athletic prowess but also his fear of the success of such a performance. The muscle memory developed in this standoff and shut down are resolved by the later abnegation of Monica's female masculinity and her later compliance with the strictures of proper Black femininity and maternity as the new route toward successful Black women's sportsmanship.

Two more scenes of Monica's sporting performance on the court evince the complex ways in which female masculinity manifest the broader scope of athletic genders in the film. These two scenes occur during the "second quarter" when Monica is on her high school women's varsity basketball team (figure 16). Both scenes depict the tensions between femininity and masculinity as an embodied sporting performance. The "second quarter" begins with a black screen as MC Lyte's song "Lyte as a Rock" fills the soundscape. The nondiegetic music ushers in the image of Monica on the court as MC Lyte questions:

Do you understand the metaphoric phrase "Lyte as a Rock?"
It's explainin' how heavy the young lady is

The camera cuts to a blurry image of the teenaged Monica playing for Crenshaw High School. Before the image can come into focus, the shot changes to a close-up of her Nike Air basketball shoes with Magic Johnson's number "32" handwritten on the side. A brief montage intercuts close-up shots of various parts of Monica's body with her actions on the court, illustrating how her stylized play is a literal and figurative sum of her parts. The cinematography vacillates between a music video aesthetic and the home-video of her family's recording of the game. As MC Lyte's song continues, it becomes apparent that Monica is the obvious leader and star on her team. Her sporting performance marks her as an exemplary athlete. As the other team is on offense, Monica works hard to defend the opposing point guard. Despite losing her man when the other team puts up a screen, Monica spins off the screen and runs to cover her player. In a decisive move as the opposing player goes up for a shot, Monica forcefully blocks the basketball. After the play, Monica stares down the girl, walking up and brushing past her in an intimidating manner. The referee instantly gives Monica a technical foul for taunting and unsportsmanlike conduct, and she is benched for the rest of the game.

The second scene example occurs during Crenshaw's championship game. With the camera angled from her vantage point, Monica's perspective on the game is privileged. After the tip-off, the scene cuts to the final minutes of play. The Lady Cougars are down, and Monica sinks a basket to cut the opposing team's lead to one-point. Throughout the scene we can hear Monica's thoughts as she goes through each play, sizing up her opponents and telling herself what to do next. After stealing the ball and sinking another shot, she puts her team up by one-point. Playing strong man-to-man defense, Monica is charged with a foul for reaching in, sending the player to the free throw line to shoot one-and-one. The opposing player sinks both shots and now the Lady Cougars are down by one. With ten seconds left in the game, Monica feels the pressure all on her, telling herself: "It's on you Mon. Come on. Get there. You just need to get there." She pulls up and throws up a shot that hits the rim, missing the basket. She is forced to foul the opposing player to stop the clock and preserve any chance that her team could stage a successful comeback. With five fouls, Monica fouls out of the game, and the team loses.

The gender tensions around Monica's sporting performance in both high school basketball games are evident in her athletic prowess on the court. In the first example, Monica's athleticism, aggression, and dominant play are what makes her a gifted basketball player, evidenced in the block she makes. However, she is given a technical foul for her lack of sportswoman-like behavior, conduct that is much more prevalent and tolerated in men's basketball. Here, her "playing like a man" signals not only the limits of women's athletic gender expression and the conditioned experiences of femininity and masculinity but also the ways her play is read as excessive "for a girl." Despite walking in shoes marked in reverence for her basketball "Showtime" hero, Magic Johnson, Monica is too much drama and her experiences are judged differently, causing problems on and off the court. In the game, Monica is punished for her unsportswoman-like conduct in a

FIGURE 16. Monica "playing like a man" on the court in *Love and Basketball* (Gina Prince-Bythewood, 2001).

sport that distinguishes men's and women's teams through the use of "lady" before the team mascot name (she plays for the Lady Cougars). Off the court, her excessively masculine-coded play causes panic over her sexuality. In the scene following the first game described, Monica is at home with her family, and her mother, Camille (Alfre Woodard), a housewife, admonishes Monica for her behavior on the court. Camille explains that she wishes Monica would grow out of her tomboy phase, to which Monica replies: "I won't. I'm a lesbian!" Her statement causes a moment of shock for Camille, until Monica adds: "That's what you think isn't it? 'Cause I'd rather wear a jersey than an apron." While Monica goads her mother by calling out the two options that exist for a woman athlete such as herself, this moment relates back to her performance on the court, one that is deemed too "mannish" and deviant and implies a heterosexual failure. As a combative body on the court and in her childhood home, Monica's sporting performance challenges fixed styles of play predicated on gender comportment that punish her for articulating an alternative to the gendered scripts in sports as well as society.

In both games, Monica's sporting female masculinity signifies how women's visibility on the court "brings wreck" to the idea of who gets to embody being an athlete. Gwendolyn D. Pough describes the hip hop modality and rhetorical practices of "bringing wreck" as "moments when Black women's discourse disrupt dominant masculine discourses, break into the public sphere, and in some way impact or influence the United States imaginary."[53] In the first game scene, the juxtaposition of the court's mise-en-scène and MC Lyte's "Lyte as a Rock" visually and aurally disrupt dominant masculine sporting discourses and the framing of sports as a male domain. Sporting blackness in this scene becomes visually and sonically defiant, female, and aggressive. Monica's muscle memory here is critical and disruptive. As Monica's sporting body and skilled play are profiled, Lyte raps:

> Must I say it again, I said it before
> Move out the way when I'm comin' through the door
> Me, heavy? As Lyte as a rock
> Guys watch, even some of girls clock
> Step back, it ain't that type of party
> No reply if you ain't somebody
> Get out of my face, don't wanna hear no more
> If you hate rejection, don't try to score

The verse "Lyte as a rock" gets at the dialectical frisson of Monica's bodily comportment. She embodies contradictions with a willed insurgency: "I am a lesbian" even as Monica, like Lyte, disavows that claim: "it ain't that type of party." A ball player above all else, Monica's stylized body and sporting performance "brings wreck" to the masculine gender codes that structure the court as male by drawing attention (through the block) to her deft skills and right to be in the public and game sphere.[54] Just as the presence of female MC's in hip hop culture "[opened] the door for a wealth of possibilities in terms of the validation of the Black female voice and Black women's agency," so does Monica's sporting performance on the court expand the imagined field of athletic genders.[55] Monica's critical muscle memory stands in for, invokes, and makes visible a genealogy of Black women athletes on the court, in sports media, and in sporting and popular culture at large. For example, Monica's sporting prowess rearticulates the history of basketball phenom Cheryl Miller, who played at USC from 1978 to 1982. Miller was drafted into the United States Basketball League (USBL), a men's league that operated from 1985 to 2007, where many future NBA players got their professional start. While Miller never got to play in the WNBA, she did coach the Phoenix Mercury, a WNBA team.

Moreover, in her championship game performance, Monica's point-of-view is often privileged to demonstrate her sporting agency. In the final moments of the game, Monica is in her "flow" and light as a rock. Sports studies scholar Susan A. Jackson and psychologist Mihaly Csikszentmihalyi describe the concept of "flow" as "a state of consciousness where one becomes totally absorbed in what one is doing, to the exclusion of all other thoughts and emotions. So flow is about focus. More than just focus, however, flow is a harmonious experience where mind and body are working together effortlessly."[56] Monica's fully engaged performance, or flow, (with and without M.C. Lyte's track) is depicted when she steps on the court. Shutting out the noise of the arena, she is fully concentrated on the moment. Time both slows down and lapses as the final minutes of the game are shown. With her internal monologue filling the soundscape, the film depicts how her mind tells her body what to do as she faces her opponents. The camera privileges her point-of-view as she dribbles the ball. As we see the court from her perspective, she tells herself: "Don't get tight. . . . She's laying off . . . pull up." Monica sinks the shot over her opponent and the camera switches to show her triumphant reaction. While the game does not end in her team's favor, Monica's virtuoso sporting performance in the film is one of mastery over body and mind, where her internal narration details and designs her stratagem. This dramatic focus on interiority reimagines the contours of Monica's embodied agency. It is not merely an imposed exterior but a self-stylization from the inside out that instructs, improvises, and enacts new moves and ways of being for her on the court.

Monica's female masculinity challenges sports as solely defined for masculine achievement, pleasure, and enjoyment. However, the film's ending is a capitulation, underscoring the classical melodramatic plot that structures the film's depiction of sexual/gender/sporting transgression and the containment thereof. In the end, Monica claims to have stopped playing basketball because she is no longer in a relationship with Quincy, and thus the game is no longer fun. In the final scene of her on a court, Monica challenges Quincy to a game of one-on-one, ostensibly, for him to call off his planned wedding and be with her instead. While at first Quincy refuses to play her, Monica apologizes for their breakup in college, explaining that she did not know how to be in relationship and still be dedicated to basketball. With Quincy still hesitant, Monica reminds him that he once told her that the only reason she beat him when they were children was because he wanted her to win. Therefore, if she wins the one-on-one match, it would be because deep down Quincy knows he is about to make a huge mistake and wants her to stop him (figure 17). They suit up and play best to five, with Monica taking an early 3–0 lead before Quincy stages a dominant comeback and takes the lead 4–3. Stealing the ball and scoring to tie the game once more, Monica has the opportunity to win but misses the layup, and Quincy dunks the ball on his next turn, an aggressive move that codifies his sporting performance as stereotypically dominant and reestablishes

FIGURE 17. Monica plays Quincy one-on-one for his heart in *Love and Basketball* (Gina Prince-Bythewood, 2001).

him as the one in control. Stunned, Monica begins to walk away before Quincy calls to her and says: "double or nothing," remaking the terms of their relationship at his request and not hers.

This sporting scene is meant to be romantic (if not sexually charged), but it also undoes a lot of the narrative about Monica's sporting prowess and agency. She reframes her childhood win as a willful loss by Quincy. Playing against him as an adult, Monica no longer wants to dominate him—like her eleven-year-old self—but be dominated, allowed to win the game by his technicalities and his heart by benevolent gesture. This affirms the idea that while girls can play with/beat boys, women cannot compete at the same level as men. Monica chooses to stop playing like a man and to start playing like a girl who is about to lose her man, letting him set the terms of their reconciliation. While her ability on the court affords her the opportunity to play professional women's basketball abroad and later in the United States with the WNBA, the film reasserts her traditional femininity through the erasure of her female masculinity by losing to Quincy and then winning via maternity and the nuclear family depicted in the film's final moments. While it is Quincy on the sidelines holding their daughter at the end as Monica plays pro ball, *Love and Basketball*'s double-dribble—its challenge to and capitulation to sporting/gender norms—runs afoul to Monica's insistence of being a ball player (period) as the film celebrates the more capacious post-feminist idea/ideal that she can "have it all"—love, basketball, and motherhood.

"SUITING UP" IN *JUWANNA MANN*

Jesse Vaughn's *Juwanna Mann* is a sports comedy that pushes the boundaries of what constitutes a traditional woman's sport film, largely because the film is about a Black male professional basketball player pretending to be a Black female professional basketball player. Taking on Black women athletes as its subject and comedic object, *Juwanna Mann* depicts the world of women's professional basketball using a female ensemble of actors and women's professional basketball players in the cast, making the film analogous to (even as an anomaly of) the woman's sports film. In fact, the film explicitly depicts athletic genders in such a way as to push—even as it pokes fun at—the categories of masculinity and femininity as limits to be embodied and surpassed on and off the court.[57]

Counterposed to *Love and Basketball, Juwanna Mann* is not an acclaimed sports film by any stretch of the imagination and was a critical and commercial failure upon its release. The film was panned by critics, who described Vaughan's first feature as "formulaic" and "predictable."[58] One critic went so far as to call the film "sloppily edited, the gags limply staged, the dialogue and jokes stiff and stale. Even the action on the basketball court is unimaginative and boring."[59] *Time Out* characterized the comedy's narrative as "an unpersuasive moral journey, with a smattering of laughs, that fails to justify the insulting premise that only a man can help the ladies win at both basketball and love."[60] *Entertainment Weekly* punned that Vaughan's film is "a Tootsie-role sports farce that's a drag in every which way," claiming that "as anyone who has peered in on the actual WNBA for five minutes knows, professional women basketball players are as tough as men. That the film treats this as a joke isn't funny—it's the height of lame condescension."[61] As these scathing reviews indicate, *Juwanna Man*—in similar fashion with other gimmicky basketball films such as *Like Mike* (John Shultz, 2002) and *Uncle Drew* (Charles Stone III, 2008)—has, understandably though unwisely, been discarded from popular and academic discussion, relegated to what media scholar Racquel Gates calls the "metaphorical gutter" of respectable Black media representations not worthy of attention in either sports film studies or Black film criticism.[62] Unlike *Love and Basketball*, a film that has been taken up in both fields as a privileged object of study, *Juwanna Mann* has almost no body of scholarship and only a smattering of caustic reviews.[63]

My attention to *Juwanna Mann* is meant not only to demonstrate how this film offers an acute study of athletic genders but also to offer a recuperative gesture to center a sports film pushed to the margins because of its "negative" representations. As an example of a disreputable media text, *Juwanna Mann's* crude narrative, simple characters, and plot holes should not foreclose analysis but, instead, be an invitation for critical inquiry into the pragmatic and problematic ways in which gender is constructed in sports films. This is not about salvaging the merit of negative texts. As Gates explains, "[negative texts] may not necessarily offer much in the way of aesthetic or political contributions, but they are still 'great artifacts,' to quote Jeffrey Sconce, because of the ways they crystalize particular debates around black representation at a given moment."[64] Gates vitally encourages us to apply negativity as a theoretical frame for the study of Black images in popular culture, utilizing it as "a mode of analysis for *seeing* the work that these texts are doing in the first place. For, rather than cut off the analysis at the first sign of a stereotype or politically regressive construct, negativity seeks to move the discussion past this first level of scrutiny and on to the question of what meanings these texts hold relative to the culture that produces both them and their positive complements."[65] Negative images, as Gates argues, are not necessarily subversive or challenging, and *Juwanna Mann*, to a large degree, reinforces normative and phobic understandings of race, gender, and sexuality. But, as she suggests, we do not have to "read against the grain" to understand how negative representations have moments that challenge normative subjectivities on the surface even if they lack depth.[66] The broad jokes and bad drag of *Juwanna Mann* expose not only the stereotypes that litter its narrative but also the failings inherent in the dominant and dimorphic structuring of Black gender comportment and its compulsory enforcement by leagues, institutions, corporations, and communities. The fact that the film failed as a site of pleasure or entertainment for critics parallels the society's wide failing of Black sporting bodies, on and off the court, in and out of drag.

   Juwanna Mann is a fictional sports film about professional basketball player, Jamal Jeffries (Miguel A. Nuñez Jr.), whose egomaniacal, recalcitrant, and arrogant behaviors get him kicked out of the men's professional basketball league. In the film's opening, it is obvious that fame has gone to Jamal's head. He lives a lavish and indulgent lifestyle, arriving to a home game in an ostentatious stretch hummer that bears a photo of him on the front bumper. When a young boy asks Jamal for an autograph, he acquiesces with a stamp of his name, cementing Jamal as a flashy and spoiled athlete of little substance. Coming off a six-day suspension, Jamal's job with the United Basketball Association (UBA) is put into jeopardy during the game. After receiving a foul for grabbing an opposing player (former NBA star Tyrone "Muggsy" Bogues in a cameo role), he is benched by his coach. Acting out and declaring himself the leader of the team, he curses out the coach, stating that any team in the league would like to have him as a player. Yanking off his jersey and throwing it at his coach, Jamal stalks away as the arena of fans turn on him, booing as he jumps onto the scoreboard table. Yelling at the fans, Jamal removes his shorts to "give them something to boo about," as he stands proudly in his jockstrap before throwing the shorts into a white woman's face in the stands. He proceeds to do a series of pelvic thrusts while yelling "boo you" to the crowd. Upping the ante of this unsportsmanlike striptease, Jamal removes his last stitch of clothing, baring himself completely, to the shock of his teammates and the game's sportscasters and to the delight of at least one female fan shot in a close-up. As with his shorts, Jamal flings his jockstrap into the crowd, landing—not without irony—on a patron's hot dog. While he proudly displays himself, Jamal is forcibly dragged from the court by security.

Jamal's naked antics are significant, not solely because his public exhibitionism results in his being barred from playing men's professional basketball. By "showing his ass" through his outrageous behavior and exposing his "manhood" in every sense, Jamal performs the deviant, naturalized, and sexually menacing comportment negatively associated with Black men in professional basketball. His unruly actions, ego problem, and bad boy behavior reify "the rhetoric of poor sportsmanship, that shapes the media discourse of the NBA."[67] While Black men's bodies are sites of desire and fetishization in sports, Jamal's full-frontal act is an overdetermined and aberrant transgression. His naked male aggression conjures up cultural stereotypes. Exposed and hung, Jamal embodies too much blackness and maleness for the masculinist team sport. The fact that he later resurrects himself as a player in feminine form is telling of the film's body panic narrative. Suiting up as a woman, his fractious behavior is domesticated on the court in ways that trouble the precarious gender politics that shape both men's and women's sport.

Suspended indefinitely, Jamal's contract is null and void because he violated its "morals clause." Jamal, however, takes no responsibility for his behavior. His white agent, Lorne Daniels (Kevin Pollak), who has failed to exert control over him, quits, opting not to represent him now that Jamal is basically unemployable. Losing money, friends, his house, his model girlfriend Tina (Lil' Kim), and having most of his belongings repossessed by the bank, Jamal is forced to move back in with his aunt, Ruby (Jenifer Lewis). On a trip to the grocery store, Jamal stumbles upon young kids playing a pickup game of basketball. Their ball ends up rolling down the driveway toward him. Led by the only girl playing, the group admonishes Jamal for his selfishness on the court. The kids go back to playing and Jamal, admiring their play, stares at them. While at first it appears that he is simply appreciating the pure love of the game that their play signifies, Jamal is actually enamored by the skills of the young girl dominating the boys on the court. In that moment, Jamal hatches his plan to make his way back into professional basketball.

The idea of athletic genders is literally represented in the mise-en-scène of the Black girl among the boys. Jamal does not respond to the young girl's ethical critique of him and his behavior on and off the court, but instead it his interest in the girl's play that engenders his devious devising and pursuant strategic drag. The young's girl's sporting body is viewed as vessel and vehicle for Jamal's self-advancement, a new, femininized ideal of athletic morphogenesis. Calling up his ex-agent Lorne, Jamal explains that he has found a phenomenal basketball player he wants him to meet and, shockingly, that player is a woman.

The film presents Jamal's cross-dressing transformation into Juwanna Mann through a comical treatment scored to Diana Ross's "I'm Coming Out." The scene's use of Ross's iconic gay anthem scores Jamal's transformation within a sonic appropriation of queer identity and sexual pride. At the same time, however, it underscores the performativity of athletic genders as a transgressive sonic interpolation that is formative and performative, where normative behaviors are cast out in favor of being and becoming something new.[68] The song's self-expressive pageantry inaugurates and frames the cross-dressing comedic farce as a power play, an offensive tactic and spectacle of gender bending that rescripts the "closet" narrative as he pulls wardrobe items out and on in a dramatic fashion. Wearing a stuffed brassiere and holding a dress, Jamal dances around his aunt Ruby's bedroom, thrusting his pelvis and saying he is going to get paid. In this sartorial reveal, his power thrusts reassert the charade of dominant masculinity into his process of femininization. Interrupted by Ruby, Jamal convinces her to help him transform into a woman for the sake of his basketball career and not an expression of queer identification. In this scene, "drag as high het[erosexual] entertainment" provides "a ritualistic release for a heterosexual economy that must constantly police its own boundaries against the invasion of queerness, and that this displaced production and resolution of homosexual panic actually fortifies the heterosexual regime in its self-perpetuating task."[69] And, at the same time, his drag imagines a female ideal that is transformative in the sense of his own sporting identity.

"Coming out" and up with his alter ego, Jamal, now as Juwanna Mann, tries out for the Women's United Basketball Association's (WUBA) team the Charlotte Banshees (a mascot based on the mythology of a shrieking

FIGURE 18. Jamal Jeffries suits up in drag as Juwanna Mann in *Juwanna Mann* (Jesse Vaughn, 2000).

woman), blackmailing (or as he puts it, Black-female-ing) his former agent, Lorne (figure 18). Juwanna makes the team, even though she displays the same showboating and selfish play Jamal did in the men's league, which, as we recall, make Monica a liability in *Love and Basketball*. His spectacular sporting abilities are not seen as too much or too masculine for the sport, even if they are shocking. Instead they constitute new standards of play. However, Jamal's behavior is seen as unacceptable in much the same way that the actual women's professional basketball league, the WNBA, is cast as morally superior to the NBA.[70] Befriending the Banshee's team captain, Michelle (Vivica A. Fox), Juwanna learns how to be a team player. While Michelle has a philandering boyfriend named Romeo (Ginuwine), Juwanna's interest in Michelle is more than platonic, and the film contains several scenes with Juwanna implicitly/explicitly expressing sexual interest in Michelle. However, Juwanna is also being pursued, much to her annoyance, by a brazen, gold grill–wearing lothario named Puff Smokey Smoke (Tommy Davidson). From *Some Like it Hot* (Billy Wilder, 1959) through *Tootsie* (Sydney Pollack, 1992), this weathered comedic trope of a man hiding in drag plays up a formulaic homophobia and homosexual panic that a conventionally straight man would have amorous intentions toward a "woman" barely hiding her masculinity while, simultaneously, the cross-dressed character becomes enamored of a female ingénue whom he befriends through supposed shared circumstance and sisterhood.

Juwanna becomes a fan favorite in the women's league because of her dominant and, sometimes, scene-stealing style of play. In one game sequence, Stevie Wonder's "Isn't She Lovely" rings out to confirm Juwanna's impressive individual and team play. With a kinder demeanor and as a more ethical and equitable team player than Jamal, Juwanna becomes a liked and likable public figure, and her fame and marketability grow. This causes a problem when Jamal is given a hearing with the UBA to overturn his expulsion from the men's league that is on the same date as the first playoff game for the Banshees. Choosing the Banshees over himself and thus demonstrating the kind of self-sacrifice associated with femininity, Jamal goes to the women's playoff game and disregards his future prospects in the men's league. His final play of the game helps carry the Banshees over their opponents but also reveals his "true" identity. Instead of doing a layup, Juwanna dunks the ball, breaking the backboard and shattering glass all over the court. Undoing the implicit gender rules of basketball (the idea that girls don't dunk) to the praise of her teammates, when Juwanna breaks the glass backboard, she symbolically breaks the glass ceiling of women's "below the rim" sporting performances. In this sense, Juwanna's sporting performance defamiliarizes gendered expectations (the dunk over the layup) and yet, as the next beat reveals, reestablishes the traditional binaries and gendered associations attached to women and men's basketball styles of play. As the team cheers her winning dunk, the joy is short-lived when her teammates notice that her wig, as described in Black and drag vernacular and queer parlance, has been "snatched." With the coif off her head, the truth is revealed that she is not what she appears but what she allegedly plays like: a man (figure 19). The team, fans, and sports commentators gasp aloud because they finally notice that Juwanna Mann is actually Jamal Jeffries, and he is promptly kicked off the team.

At first abandoned by the Banshees once his identity is revealed, Jamal eventually makes amends with them prior to their next playoff game, giving them a pep-talk explaining that they could win without him. He tells them: "You never needed me to win this and you don't need me now. I needed you." Inspired by his apology, the Banshees win not only that game but also the championship. Later, Jamal has a hearing with the UBA basketball board to discuss his actions. During this hearing, Jamal's agent touts him as a true basketball star and future role model who should be allowed to rejoin the men's league because he is a changed man, a metamorphosis engendered by his cross-dressing experience. The commissioner of the board accuses Jamal of having disgraced both the men's and women's professional leagues, touting essentialist claims to stable gender referents in

FIGURE 19. Juwanna's wig has been snatched and the truth is revealed in *Juwanna Mann* (Jesse Vaughn, 2000).

segregated sports. However, at that moment, the Banshees, led by Michelle, enter the room and dispute the commissioner's claim. Michelle explains that the team forgives Jamal and that board should too. Michelle gives Jamal his own WUBA championship ring, recognizing his contribution to their successful season. Confirming her support, Michelle kisses Jamal, who is allowed to return to playing in the UBA. The final scene shows Jamal on the basketball court. As the crowd cheers him on, the announcer declares that Jamal is the only man who's played for the men's and women's professional leagues. Returning for his second year in the UBA, the film ends with a triumphant looking Jamal ready to run on the court as fireworks and screaming fans welcome him back to the world of men's professional sports.

The film's negotiations of athletic genders in Juwanna's sporting performances are often rendered for comedic effect. Allegedly there is nothing funnier than a man having to learn to play like a girl, especially when he is dressed like one. Through Juwanna's sporting excellence, the film reifies misogynistic sports culture ideals about gender normativity, specifically the notion that men are better than women at sports. As the film's tagline explains: "The only way he can stay pro is to play (like) a girl." Jamal having to both play a girl and play *like* one is negotiated in his and others attempts to get him to stop "playing like a man" in both men's and women's professional sports. Yet these tropes reveal the ways in which idealized athletic gender norms depend on imagined embodied practices to be repeated, recognizable, and intelligible because they are fundamentally unstable, in flux, revisable, and surpassable by and through sporting performances.

Juwanna Mann's drag is not an example, however, of gender subversion but of appropriation that "calls into question whether parodying the dominant norms is enough to displace them; indeed whether the denaturalization of gender cannot be the very vehicle for a reconsideration of hegemonic norms."[71] Taking the film at face value, Juwanna's (dis)embodied performance of Black sporting femininity does not completely challenge male hegemony but hyperbolically affirms gender hierarchies, naturalized gendered difference, and heterosexual norms. Like many films in the American cinema canon that use cross-dressing as a mode of deception and cover for fallen men, humor is produced by relying on fixed and intransient notions of sex and gender, femininity and masculinity. This is redoubled within the lineage of Black male comics and actors—from Flip Wilson to Redd Foxx to Richard Pryor to Eddie Murphy to Martin Lawrence to Tyler Perry—who have "suited up" as Black women characters, mostly to poke misogynistic fun at Black women as they rely on the most tired conventions of classed Black womanhood: loudness, sexual aggression, and inability to comport as proper ladies. Similar to the subset of films starring Black men in female fat-suits, *Juwanna Mann* "functions as cinematic palimpsest upon which layers of cultural history and meaning are scripted."[72] What remains under the drag pageantry is the histories about and meanings attached to Black women's athletic bodies, ones that were predicated on biological fallacies based on racial difference. Juwanna's obvious masculine appearance embodies the stereotypes of Black womanhood and athletic females as mannish, unattractive, sexually unappealing, and animalistic.[73]

For comedic effect, several of Juwanna's sports performances play up the past and present histories of successful Black women athletes being unjustly attacked as "*not* biologically [female]s," an idea that "rested on the deep conviction that superior athleticism signified masculine capacities that inhered in the male body."[74] For example, in her initial tryout with the Banshees, Juwanna arrives late, dressed in a full face of makeup and a track suit, giving off the perception of femininity through her manufactured image. When she hits the court, she dominates with Jamal's typical show-boating and selfish playing style, making her look appear "off" of gendered expectations. Going head-to-head with the butch lesbian Latisha Jansen (Kim Wayans), whose sexuality is viewed as predatory, Juwanna is sexualized on the court as a means to highlight both players perceived deviance. Latisha tells Juwanna that she hopes her game is as tight as her ass and that she can make the ball bounce like her breasts. Juwanna's sporting performance is one that simultaneously has her being read as female, thus as an erotic object to be sexualized by men and women, and as male/masculine through her exceptional athleticism. Moreover, though she is playing with other gifted female athletes, Juwanna literally and figuratively stands out in the game's implicit battle of the sexes. Her game is beyond everyone else's on the court, substantiating the idea that the women's league is a substandard one to the men's professional game.

The film attempts to balance these moments of sexual tension and gender sporting hierarchy with Juwanna's "comedic" drag semi-embodiment. During the practice, her fake boobs flop all over the place, suggesting both the need for an adequate sports bra but also reminding us that she is poorly costumed. As well, she is forced to rearrange her "package" on the court. The film constantly broadcasts Juwanna's true identity as Jamal for comic effect, and the fractured dissimulation is always meant to remind us that Black women's sporting bodies, not Jamal's, are the joke. Juwanna's muscle memory is always already figured as belonging to Jamal, foreclosing the possibility of Black women's athleticism and achievement in a film ostensibly centered in such a world. Her athletic prowess is unparalleled to her soon-to-be teammates and she is positioned as an outsider on the team. Juwanna, in effect, cannot help but to "play like a man." For this reason, Lorne makes Jamal promise to not have Juwanna dunk because women do not dunk in the league due to either implicit prohibition or inability.[75] Juwanna's contained play (no dunks) thus represents an attempt at gender stability and conformity. Her embrace of the "inhibited intentionality" that circumscribes women's sporting comportment and bodily existence signals the ways in which women's muscle memory is a kind of physical, phenomenological, and social constraint.[76]

The gender humor in the film operates on multiple levels because humor "unlike humorlessness, can admit how exceptional bodies, in their incongruity, hold potential insights into the non-congruence of all bodies into any purported norm."[77] Put differently, Juwanna's athletic genders on the court comically manifest and violate a set of norms that hem all Black athletes' bodies into acts of compulsory comportment. For example, throughout the film, Juwanna's selfish and hyperstylized play (she does 360-degree lay-ups) draws criticism from her teammates, who, while aggressive and hardworking, play a "purer" form of the game: team-based basketball associated with women's sports. When she is "playing like a man," Juwanna draws the unwanted attention of the minstrel character Puff Smokey Smoke, who says he "likes a girl with ball control." However, when Juwanna accidently passes the ball to a teammate and is rewarded with a pat on the butt, she finally becomes a team player, largely so she can grab women's behinds. This moment of camaraderie, while ridiculous and played for laughs, illustrates how Juwanna's sporting performance goes from "playing like a man" to "playing like a girl." As she passes the ball and lets others score, Juwanna finally is able to be visible and render Jamal invisible through her style of play. Juwanna here negates Jamal and becomes one of the girls, albeit through a queer reworking of heterosexual desire and object choice. The consequence of this sublimation of Jamal is the ways in which gender becomes recognizable and legitimized through athletic performance in ways that can affirm, alter, and even exceed what we expect from women's and men's sports. However, as mentioned, Juwanna's dunk is the aspect of her sporting play that is policed for fear it will be clocked for gender "realness," "a standard that is used to judge any given performance within the established categories."[78] Juwanna's shocked teammates accept the aberrant dunk as a newly established feat of Black women's athleticism, but the move breaches the court's social contract of female comportment. The dunk, as a presumed legible male sporting performance, engenders his exposure, evidenced by the wig falling off after doing the play. In this sense, Juwanna's decision to decidedly "play like a man" and dunk reestablishes gender norms and hierarchies even as it challenges them. The act makes Jamal's body visible while Juwanna's body is turned into a fraudulent body, diminishing what it means to play as/like a woman in sports.

In the end, *Juwanna Mann* is a problematic if not predictable film. Jamal's drag produces laughs and comedic anxiety around gender identity, reducing drag, Black femininity, Black women's sportsmanship, and gender masquerade to jokes that are invariably tinged with homophobia and misogyny and wholly ignorant of transgender embodiment and materiality. The film's use of women and women's sport for the self-definition of men reifies the limits of its gender discourses and hierarchizes men's athleticism as better than women's athleticism. Notwithstanding these points, the film's ending with Jamal back in the men's league, in some ways, pushes back against its own constriction and, thus, the ideology of essentialist gender construction as comportment and style of play. In marking his re-debut, the announcer proclaims that Jamal is the only man who has played in both men's and women's professional leagues. The announcer's statement and Jamal's look of pride does not suggest the notion of a battle of the sexes that ends solely in male conquest but an intergender and intragender theater that exposes the biological as well as morphological ideals of advantage/disadvantage that standardize, regulate, and segregate women and men's sporting performances. His embodied farce, however ridiculous and downright offensive, has changed him and his muscle memory, producing a style of play that has set a new standard for his game on the court. His duplicitous and, later, institutionally sanctioned access to both "playing like a man" and "playing like a girl" in both men's and women's sporting arenas simultaneously reveals how gender performance is imitative, contingent, fluid, and transformative and how athletic genders outside of constrictive binaries that structure leagues and life have the possibility of appropriating and subverting cultural stereotypes and sporting norms.

THE INTRAMURAL SOCIALITY OF SPORTING BLACKNESS

While *Love and Basketball* and *Juwanna Mann* both conclude in ways that reinforce heterosexual gendered norms, both films articulate athletic genders as a mode of sporting blackness, where critical muscle memory is the tense, constricted, contested, and flexed performances of racialized femininities and masculinities. Their affirmations of and challenge to specifically normative feminine conventions expose how race and gender, along with other axes of identity such as sexuality, become distilled through discourses and performances on and off the court. And while Black women–centered sports films such as *Love and Basketball* and *Juwanna Mann* are formal challenges to a genre invested in the invisibility of Black female athletes, both films still conform to the categorical gender norms of the genre and society via narratives of gender panic on the court.

Despite both films' conclusions, *Love and Basketball* and *Juwanna Mann* provide an opportunity to conceptualize the gendered modes of sporting blackness as embodied acts and stylized aesthetics on screen. Monica's female masculinity and Juwanna's drag embodiment cast the Black female sporting body as virtuosic, malleable, and contingent, unsettling gender and sex expectations "in ways that are not reducible to chromosomes or chemistry" but are rendered, disciplined, suspended, and surpassed by and through the body's athletic performances.[79] As Tavia Nyong'o explains, "whether devious, or simply deviant, the freakishly virtuosic [gender-bending] body is a spectacle and a threat."[80] The fact that both films contain the spectacle and threat of gender instability attest to the epistemic crisis that these competing, culturally elaborated ideals produce even as their overriding heterosexual romance plots (a kind of gender-disciplinary machination of the genre) are meant to affirm sporting and gender hierarchies.

In the end, an analysis of sporting blackness, Black female athlete's representations, and athletic genders confront the gendered and racialized dynamics of the sports film. This mode of inquiry is what Hortense Spillers calls the "*intramural* aspect of culture analyses [which] is both necessary *and* evaded, for it would force us to confront what is suppressed in the public discourse of the analysis, indeed, what the politics of 'race' customarily require to be censored here: the *strong* line of gender, as 'race' 'within' runs a broken line from one actant to another, a positioning in discourse overlaps a strategic class formation."[81] While Spillers is describing academic tensions around gender as a kind of "intramural sport," her description is no less apt for understanding the discourses and scholarship about race in sports films that suppress "the *strong* line" of gender and its critical capacities to think through the enactments and entanglements of blackness.

My attention to racial and gender performativity propels this chapter's analysis of sporting blackness and critical muscle memory as athletic genders, reifying "the symbolic significance of the body as a metaphor of social relationships," not to suggest that gender identity is fixed but that an analysis of embodied movement and mobility, scripted as comportment and style of play, can lay bare the constructions and contestations of gendered Black being, becoming, and belonging.[82] Finally, the gendered mode of sporting blackness also evinces conditions of possibility, a critical mode of athleticism where "blackness is transected by embodied procedures that fall under the sign of gender."[83] These procedures are both courtside and interior, iterations of the changing same in gendered Black life and sports. Sporting blackness, in this capacity, is embodied in variant possibilities of motion and contestation, like gendered norms themselves. Black masculinities and femininities constitute a more capacious lived and imagined and, in Spillers terms, gendered and ungendered sporting blackness rooted in and outside of the bounds of cultural norms and generic constraints.[84] As metaphors for intraracial sociality, both *Love and Basketball* and *Juwanna Mann* conceptually evince critical muscle memory as commensurable understandings of what it means to be Black, competitive, in love, and play ball. In the specific instances of Black women's athletic gendered expression from Monica to Juwanna to the uncredited woman in *A League of Their Own*, these embodied experiences are both mandated and insurgent, a kind of shared, unequal, and (in)visible placement in sports and Black society.

4. The Revolt of the Cinematic Black Athlete

What has happened is that the black athlete has left the façade of locker room equality and justice to take his long vacant place as a primary participant in the black revolution.

—HARRY EDWARDS, *The Revolt of the Black Athlete*

This final chapter is an experimentalist interrogation of sports films' raced tropes and representational codes of cinematic sporting blackness. These conventions, even when deconstructed or disavowed in the other works discussed throughout this book, still prevail in the aforementioned films through the structural discipline, psychic shortcomings, gendered tropes, and/or moral failings of the cinematic Black athlete. I begin the chapter by invoking a mediatic moment of world-historical import, a scene that serves as an epistemic break in Black sporting iconicity. It is the Summer Olympics. It is Mexico City. It is 1968. And there are two Black men, Olympic champions who have raised their gloved hands during the playing of "The Star-Spangled Banner" in what would come to be known as the Black Power fist and salute. Prior to that moment, Harry Edwards had proposed a boycott of the 1968 Olympics to highlight the gross racial and economic inequities in the United States. While some Black athletes did stay home in protest, sprinters Tommie Smith and John Carlos devised the layered symbolic stance and gestural act, changing for all time the easy containment of rebellion in Black athletes. This dramatic scene and televised spectacle contour the imagery and discourse of revolt in this chapter's analysis of Haile Gerima's 1971 avant-garde sports film *Hour Glass*.

THE REVOLT OF THE BLACK ATHLETE

To understand the revolt of the cinematic Black athlete in *Hour Glass*, it is critical to set the scene for and unpack the staging of one of the most popular and pivotal visual spectacles of Black resistance in sports history. In 1968, sociologist and activist Harry Edwards called for a revolt of the Black athlete.[1] Edwards, a former standout athlete and honor student at San Jose State University, organized to fight the abusive and dehumanizing actions he and other Black athletes experienced from white coaches, teammates, spectators, and sporting institutions. He characterized "both collegiate and professional sports in the 1960s as 'slave systems' of control and exploitation of Black athlete talent."[2] In such a system, utility and machine-like physical excellence defines Black athletic opportunity. This means that many Black athletes, Edwards argued, know "that once their athletic abilities are impaired by age or injury, only the ghetto beckons and they are doomed once again to that faceless, hopeless, ignominious existence they had supposedly forever left behind."[3] He denounced the structural inequalities—housing, employment, policing, and discrimination—facing Black athletes, inequities that mirrored the broader domestic realities for Black people in the United States.

Edwards's outspoken indictment of Black athletes' maltreatment underscores the interface of sports, race, and social issues. At this nexus, he linked Black athletic struggles to both a history of civil rights campaigns and the Black Power movement in the 1960s.[4] Instigated by civil unrest and situated within a lineage of Black freedom movements, Edwards positions the revolt of the Black athlete teleologically within a history of Black liberationist efforts, a nationalist struggle predicated, for him and others, on the gendered politic of "reclaiming manhood."[5] Joining the likes of Martin Luther King Jr., Malcolm X (El-Hajj Malik El-Shabazz), Stokely Carmichael (Kwame Toure), Huey P. Newton, and H. Rap Brown (Jamil Abdullah Al-Amin) as activists, organizers, and revolutionaries, Black male athletes, guided by Edwards, were to lead this phase and faction of Black revolution, staging resistance in a way that reinforced the already present connections between sports and the politics of race on a national and global scale.

For Edwards, the 1968 Summer Olympic Games in Mexico City was to be a critical opportunity for Black resistance. Campaigning against Black athletes' participation, Edwards attempted to use America's dependence on Black athletic talent to assert dominance in sports and project the illusion of racial equality against itself. He organized the Olympic Project for Human Rights (OPHR) to counsel and mobilize Black athletes to boycott the Olympic Games.[6] Edwards and OPHR's primary spokespeople, sprinters Tommie Smith and Lee Evans, wrote in the organization's founding statement:

> We must no longer allow this country to use a few so-called Negroes to point out to the world how much progress [America] has made in solving her racial problems when the oppression of Afro-Americans is greater than it ever was. We must no longer allow the sports world to pat itself on the back as a citadel of racial justice when the racial injustices of the sports world are infamously legendary. . . . Any black

person who allows himself to be used in the above matter is a traitor because he allows racist whites the luxury of resting assured that those black people in the ghettoes are there because that is where they want to be. So we ask why should we run in Mexico only to crawl home?[7]

With this rejoinder, Smith and Evans highlighted the paradox of Black athletes competing on behalf of a nation that promulgated segregation, discrimination, and unequal opportunity. As an act of patriotism, an attempt to hold America to her own constitutionally pledged standards, OPHR strategized to challenge racial injustice in one of its most popular cultural realms, the sports arena, which had been considered by many to be an already integrated domain of fair play and equality. The boycott was to be a mass media spectacle whose "visual power," Martin Luther King Jr. remarked to athlete John Carlos, "was in the void it would create: an Olympics without black athletes."[8] Challenging America's national subjectivity and claims to democracy, the OPHR "fashioned embryonic political actions with older, incomplete civil rights struggles, synthesizing antediluvian tactics, such as the boycott, with the newfound dominance of Black Power popularized both by SNCC and the Black Panthers, as well as by the litter of identity movements that followed."[9]

A list of sporting and policy demands accompanied OPHR's threat to boycott the Olympics.[10] However, the demands were not met, and the threatened boycott did not occur for many reasons, though notable athletes including UCLA basketball star Kareem Abdul-Jabbar (Lew Alcindor) did refuse to participate in the international sporting competition. Instead, during the Games many Black Olympians demonstrated their solidarity with OPHR's concerns through various gestures (wearing Black berets, OPHR pins, etc.), and, conversely, some athletes like George Foreman and Jesse Owens countered these political acts with their own beleaguered patriotic ones. The most iconic mix of political activity and athletic achievement was evidenced by the Black Power protest of Olympic sprinters Tommie Smith and John Carlos. Their historic and defiant stance in Mexico City "dislocated the normative staging of the nation, as well as the sprinters' own place as national subjects, and had heavy consequences for all it chose to represent."[11]

The reception of Smith and Carlos's rebellious actions must be framed, first, within the broader geopolitical moment and social movements for which they are historically situated. The late 1960s was a time of international antiwar, anti-imperialist, anti-racist, anti-capitalist, and anti-sexist mobilizations. Student, worker, new left, feminist, and Third World advocates organized and struggled globally for liberation and equality. The sociopolitical tenor worldwide was turbulent and decidedly against US imperialism, underscored by America's calamitous intervention in Vietnam. These US and global political antagonisms were exacerbated by a range of events from the Tet Offensive in Vietnam and the Prague Spring to the assassinations of Martin Luther King Jr. and Robert F. Kennedy. New left political action shaped the global atmosphere, directly affecting Mexico City where the Olympic Games were to be held. On October 2, 1968, about ten days before the Olympics, hundreds of Mexican students and leftist protesters—fighting against repression and violence by the government— were fired upon and killed by police and troops in the Tlatelolco massacre, while athletes from around the globe awaited the start of the Games at the Olympic Village. Therefore, Smith and Carlos's defiant actions were enmeshed in a heightened and consequential moment and site of national and international political struggle and resistance.

When the Games commenced, Edwards's call for a revolt of the Black athlete was amplified by Smith and Carlos, OPHR members, and US track and field sprinters. On October 16, 1968, Smith and Carlos competed in the 200-meter Olympic final. During that race, Smith shattered the world record, finishing the 200-meter sprint in 19.83 seconds, winning the gold medal for team USA. Clocking in a final time of 20.06 seconds, Carlos took the bronze medal, coming in third place after Australian sprinter Peter Norman, whose last kick in the final moments of the race propelled him to second. Following their spectacular feats, Smith and Carlos made their way to the podium for the awards ceremony. Taking the stand, the American flag was raised and "The Star-Spangled Banner" played in recognition and reverence of the first-place victor's achievement and citizenship. As the anthem rang out, Smith and Carlos bowed their heads and each raised one arm in the air with their fists clenched in the Black Power salute (figure 20). Their uplifted hands, clad in Black gloves, politicized the moment even further than the already politically and nationalist-tinged rituals on display.[12] As historian Amy Bass explains, the stadium of onlookers and millions of viewers worldwide watching on television "listened to the national anthem while watching two American athletes powerfully display both their connection to and their criticism of the United States."[13] Their Black Power salute was met with jeers from the packed stadium crowd, booing their militant image. Their gesture on the stand, however, would go down in history as a potent and symbolic act of Black opposition to racist national and imperial scripts that attempt to project Black athletes as metonyms for the mediation of US racial harmony.

The posture of revolt from Smith and Carlos was not only evidenced in the corporeal spectacle of their raised fits but also in the insurgency of their

FIGURE 20. As the US national anthem plays following the 200-meter track and field finals, gold medalist Tommie Smith (center) and bronze medalist John Carlos (right) raise their gloved fists in the Black Power salute on the podium at the 1968 Olympic Games in Mexico City. Australian sprinter and silver medalist Peter Norman (left) wears an Olympic Project for Human Rights (OPHR) pin in solidarity. Photo by NCAA Photos/Getty Images.

self-fashioning. Holding their shoes, the two medalists wore long black stockings to signify Black poverty. According to Carlos, he and Smith "wanted the world to know that in Mississippi, Alabama, South Central Los Angeles, [and] Chicago that people were still walking back and forth in poverty without even the necessary clothes to live in."[14] Smith wore a black glove on his right hand and Carlos wore the matching black glove on his left hand. "My raised right hand," Smith attests, "stood for the power in Black America. Carlos' raised hand stood for the unity of black America. Together they formed an arch of unity and power."[15] Smith fastened a black scarf around his collar while Carlos wore a strand of beads around his neck. For Smith, the scarf signified blackness and for Carlos, the beads represented "those individuals that were lynched, or killed, that no one said a prayer for, that were hung [and] tarred. It was for those thrown off the side of boats in the Middle Passage."[16] Carlos, the son of a migrant worker, also unzipped his jacket to show solidarity with working-class people. He explained: "I was representing shift workers, blue-collar people, the underdogs. [. . .] Those are the people whose contributions to society are so important but don't get recognized."[17] Smith's slightly bowed head, he later confided to Harry Edwards, "was in remembrance of the fallen warriors in the black liberation struggle in America—Malcolm X, Martin Luther King, Jr., and others."[18] "The totality of our effort," as Smith notes in an interview with Howard Cosell following the protest, "was the regaining of black dignity."[19] To revise the popular idiom, if the *dignity* is in the details, the minutiae of their accoutrement and comportment—the carried shoes, long black socks, unzipped jacket, black gloves, scarf, beaded necklace, clenched fists, raised arms, and bowed heads—embroidered the political stakes and cultural struggles already present into the existing fabric and design of the Olympic Games.

Smith and Carlos's actions evince a complex dissonant visual strategy, one that proved, as Bass's invocation of Toni Morrison suggests, that "spectacle is the best means by which an official story is formed and is a superior mechanism for guaranteeing its longevity."[20] Smith and Carlos's raised fists and fashioned metaphors projected a complex symbolism, a radical iconography of dissent in the most popular international sporting arena. They replaced individual victory and national glory with the "silent gestures" of collective resistance against what Stuart Hall calls "societies structured in dominance."[21] They transformed the victory dais into a protest platform, one that used "the dominant ritual, acknowledged its accompanying symbols, and then proceeded to revolutionize it, subverting the normative presentation of the nation-state with its own tools."[22] The tableaux of

Smith and Carlos, as well as Norman, who wore an OPHR badge on his jacket in solidarity with the cause, turned all three of their bodies into an interracial and international beacon of discontent.[23] This staged and, even more imperatively, televised spectacle produced an "imagined community," addressing the plight of Black Americans to a national audience within a global arena, inviting solidarity from other athletes and the world's citizens. Because the Olympics are a major television broadcast event, one that required Mexico City to expand its global television connections, Smith and Carlos's actions were viewed by a television audience of nearly four hundred million people worldwide on ABC. As Bass explains:

> Their action took place in an international, televised realm, forcing a crucial role upon the media in amplifying the tension of their act of insubordination by bringing it directly to the living rooms of America and, on the next morning's sports page, to breakfast tables where it was digested alongside coffee and eggs. It was a moment of central significance to both sport and politics, forever frozen in full-color during the unprecedented Olympic coverage by ABC, with strains of the national anthem providing the audio backdrop. The protest created what became the defining image of Mexico City, an image that has had residual effects on the sports world as well as a more generalized historical and cultural resonance that fuses the racialized anger of 1968 with the broader imagery of black masculinity in American society.[24]

Their mediated and photogenic bodies became canvases of representation able to signify and supersede the iconography of Black Olympians as symbols of US democracy.

The visual and aural spectacle of the alterity of Black people in America underscores questions of marginality addressed by W. E. B. Du Bois's notion of double consciousness and what Trinh T. Minh-ha refers to as the challenges of "hyphenated identities" and "hyphenated realities," or the in-between realm of "us" (Black people) and "them" (the nation) that shapes the challenges of *becoming* Black-American.[25] Repudiated for their actions by US Olympic officials, Smith and Carlos were punished for their protest. They were stripped of their medals (though the nation still counted their accomplishments), suspended from the US Olympic track and field team, and expelled from the Olympic Village. When they returned home, the two were met with some praise but mostly criticism and ostracism, and they struggled for years to find decent employment and opportunities after the Games, a situation that reproduced what their protest was about in the first place.[26] The social and sporting opprobrium extended to Norman as well, who was reprimanded by Australian Olympic officials and later denied a spot on the Australian national track team despite qualifying for the 1972 Olympic Games.[27] Even with the vicissitudes of triumph and tribulation they faced, the legacy of Smith and Carlos's sporting defiance reverberates in the halls of Black history and indelibly shapes the images and imaginings of what it means for Black athletes to revolt.

The above account of Edwards, the OPHR, and Smith and Carlos's Olympic protest provides a historical grounding and the originating "muscle memory" critical to this final chapter's analysis of sporting blackness in terms of the revolt of the cinematic Black athlete. The spectacle of Smith and Carlos's Black Power salute, which reflected Edwards and OPHR's recognition of television's burden of simulcasted liveness, produced a corporeal subjectivity of resistance for mass media audiences. Smith and Carlos's embodied protest demonstrates how to read the Black sporting body's performative gestures on screen as defiant, linking the body's actions to the making and remaking of racial meaning through the mediating power of visual sports culture. Sporting blackness, in this real-life "postgame" context, constitutes a kind of somatic and televisual visibility and intelligibility.[28] In other words, Smith and Carlos's sporting blackness on screen marks the visual and discursive ways the turbulent tenor of 1968 shaped Black sporting bodies and, concomitantly, the way Black sporting bodies shape visual discourses of being and becoming politicized figures. It is Smith and Carlos's rebellious sporting blackness—a rage against sporting and social comportment—that structures this chapter's analysis of *Hour Glass* and the cinematic Black athlete in revolt.

HOUR GLASS'S BOLD OMISSIONS
AND MINUTE DEPICTIONS

In what follows, I analyze how Haile Gerima's 1971 experimental film *Hour Glass* pictorializes a revolt of the Black athlete, where sporting blackness is constructed in the nexus between athleticism and consciousness. In a manner simultaneously didactic and opaque, the fourteen-minute short film cinematically responds to Edwards's call in 1968 for Black athletes to lead the newest phase of Black Power in American society. Gerima describes *Hour Glass* as a "paradigm on sponsored guidance about a young guy who's raised in a foster home, in an Anglo-Saxon culture, and how much he is alienated from his own cultural essence. As a result, he ends up playing basketball at a university, but he's not a normal participant of the sport and soon realizes that he's the new modern gladiator."[29] In doing so, he becomes a different kind of contestant. Gerima describes this is as the arrival point:

"He finally leaves this densely white school as a gladiator and goes into the community, where he needs to go for his own peace and security."[30] The protagonist goes from being a lone athlete to becoming part of the Black populace, converting athletic motion and sporting contest into physical movement and everyday political contestation.

As the chapter's opening description suggests, the image of Smith and Carlos at the 1968 Olympics is a popular and potent visual symbol that circulates in the cultural imaginary, particularly when one considers a representation of a defiant Black athlete. *Hour Glass* culls this history of Smith and Carlos's protest, relocating the revolutionary imagery and sounds of 1968 into *Hour Glass*. The film's documentary impulse, or its gestures to the racialized sporting events of 1968, is oblique yet glaringly apparent in its narrative of the quotidian experiences of alienation and abnegation of Black athletes in all-white university settings, a central critique also made by OPHR, Edwards, Smith, and Carlos. Gerima's fidelity to the historic moment manifests in an unconventional way. The historicity of Gerima's *Hour Glass* operates within a dialectic of what Trinh T. Minh-ha describes as "bold omissions and minute depictions," telling popular memory through aural illusions and sonorous representations.[31] The film lacks an explicit representation of the 1968 Games or Smith and Carlos. Instead, its historic and popular televisual memory resonates in the film's experimental, dense, and highly symbolic visual and sonic representation of a Black athlete in revolt. *Hour Glass*'s visual and lyrical metaphors construct its cinematic language in terms of small fixations that are apertures to broader narratives about race and diasporic (be)longing. The film's asynchronous sound and image function in narrative tension with each other, disrupting the audiovisual cohesion in the diegesis and driving the perceptual and ideological imaginings of the protagonist's critical awakening. *Hour Glass*'s bold omissions and minute depictions structure the film's critical muscle memory. A close reading of the film requires attention to symptomatic and intertextual cues, the critical muscle memory of 1968, that also inscript the interrelated histories of UCLA, Black college athletes/university athletics, and other attached sporting and non-sporting narratives to the profilmic space.[32]

Made as a student first-film assignment at UCLA, *Hour Glass* can be situated within the production practices of the L.A. Rebellion to address the film's formal methodology. A basketball film more aligned to Third Cinema aesthetics than classical Hollywood styles of continuity and narrative closure, *Hour Glass* is a significant example of how experimental sports media operate as an antidote and challenge to the generic codes and conventions presented in mainstream sports films.[33] As such a case, I consider the film's formal practices and representational politics in relationship to the sporting imaginaries it engages, refuses, and finally subverts toward its own communitarian and scopic aims. The revolt of the cinematic Black athlete in *Hour Glass* becomes both the protagonist's refusal to play the game of basketball and the narrative's refusal to be a sports film. Drawing on George Lipsitz's work on how race disrupts generic categories and erupts racial discourses on screen, I use the film's doubly defiant strategies to think through its undoing of genre conventions associated with traditional sports films.[34]

L. A. REBELLING AGAINST CINEMATIC CONSTRAINTS

Seldom discussed in L.A. Rebellion scholarship, *Hour Glass* is considered an incubator of narrative and formal ideas about transformative self-realization that Haile Gerima would learn from and later refine in his more recognized short and feature-length works such as *Child of Resistance* (1972), *Bush Mama* (1975), *Ashes and Embers* (1982), *Sankofa* (1993), and *Teza* (2008).[35] Born in Gondar, Ethiopia, Gerima came to the United States in 1967 to attend the Goodman School of Drama in Chicago. After meeting UCLA professor Teshome Gabriel in Maine, he enrolled in UCLA's Theater Department before transferring to the Film Department. "Although the context from which he began to write, produce, and direct his films arose from the political and economic terrain specific to blacks in the United States," Mike Murashige explains, "Gerima has remained grounded in the traditions of Ethiopian culture and artistic practices of his childhood."[36] At UCLA, Gerima set out to create work that was about collective experiences and the advancement of consciousness, particularly for Third World people. In doing so, Gerima's *Hour Glass* is a provocative representation of defiant sporting blackness, one that reflects and rebels against the production culture at UCLA, where it was created, and evinces the complex representational strategies indicative of Gerima's body of work.

Gerima made *Hour Glass* during a milestone in Black American independent cinema. He is part of a groundbreaking cohort of UCLA-trained filmmakers, including Charles Burnett, Julie Dash, Billy Woodberry, Larry Clark, Jamaa Fanaka, Barbara McCollough, Bernard Nichols, Ben Caldwell, and Alile Sharon Larkin, among others, who were committed to rethinking Black content and film form in both cinematic theory and practice. These filmmakers, retrospectively grouped and named as the L.A. Rebellion by Clyde Taylor, ushered in a new moment in American cinema, one that led him to declare: "By the turn of the next century, film historians will recognize that a decisive turning point in the development of Black cinema took place at UCLA in the early 1970s. By then, persuasive definitions of Black cinema will revolve around images encoded not by Hollywood, but within the self-understanding of the African American population."[37] In both a serendipitous and hard-fought moment where social and institutional forces aligned to open up admission opportunities at state universities such as UCLA, these artists forged a collaborative and heterogeneous cinema practice in productive tension with the machinations of the university setting and Hollywood's film industry.[38] They were neither a uniform film movement nor a cohesive, group-identified collective of film and video artists; however, they embraced a shared range of aesthetics and politics to create a diverse filmography that reimagined Black lives on screen in new modes and liberating paradigms, often connecting diasporic Black domestic culture and politics to anti-colonial struggles and Pan-African traditions. In sometimes very experimental work or through avant-garde, documentary, or neorealist techniques, many L.A. Rebellion filmmakers depicted working-class and quotidian urban Black subjects and communities to contest systemic social, economic, and political inequities. These filmmakers were influenced and challenged by a range of cinematic models that drew on global film movements; Black film, art, literature, and oral traditions; and were engaged with theories of Black cultural nationalism and internationalism, Third World Marxism, and Pan-Africanism.[39] Despite their differing articulations and syncretism of these modes and concepts, L.A. Rebellion filmmakers collectively aimed to imagine, reflect, interpret, and represent Black life and their experiences outside of classical Hollywood cinema practices and models while attending to national cultures and politics, regional specificities, and global class, race, and gender struggles.

Gerima wrote, directed, and edited *Hour Glass* as his "Project One," a required first assignment for all UCLA MFA graduate film and undergraduate Ethno-Communication students. Project One assignment guidelines included specific technical parameters: shooting in 8 mm with nonsynchronous sound and an optional 16 mm magnetic soundtrack to be mixed in postproduction. This means that sound is indirectly wedded to the image, revealing rather than concealing the sonic work of the apparatus in ways that are projective, hyperbolic, and imagined. Within these analog technological constraints, Project Ones allowed student filmmakers to explore subject matter of their own choosing and experiment with the medium's formal and sonic elements as sensory materials. *Hour Glass*'s asynchronous polyphonic soundtrack functions to produce, like Gerima's later work, a "symbolic reality" that "disrupts realist illusions of narrative transparency and closure by calling attention to the labor necessary in the construction of a narrative."[40]

Allyson Nadia Field's comprehensive study of L.A. Rebellion Project Ones explains that these student films, while uneven and difficult to categorize, "reflect the cultural environment in which they were made and its affiliated political movements, social concerns, and problematic gender expectations."[41] The formal constraints of Project Ones meant that L.A. Rebellion filmmakers were not subject to classical narrative structures and were able to experiment with combinations of sound and image. Dialogue, usually privileged in sound cinema, is subordinated, and sound effects are used to spatialize, localize, and give depth to characters and activity on screen.[42] As a first assignment, these artistic works functioned as an initiation into film production, one where students learned cinematic processes (writing, directing, shooting, and editing) and experimented with the medium to find their individual voice and unique directorial vision. The final films, which were meant to be approximately three minutes long—though L.A. Rebellion films like *Hour Glass* at almost fourteen minutes often exceeded that length—were screened and critiqued by faculty and fellow students. L.A. Rebellion Project Ones (and their later films) reflect the group's diverse politics, varying backgrounds, and differing aesthetic and representational choices. There is no unifying style, but they all attempt to render Black visual and expressive culture anew by teaching themselves to rework a medium that historically framed blackness in abject, perfunctory, and racist ways.

Field argues that Project Ones like Gerima's *Hour Glass* necessitated that L.A. Rebellion filmmakers radically "*un*learn" classical cinema codes and conventions that reinforce racial, social, and gender hierarchies:

> As much as the process of studying film in a university consisted of learning the necessary skills, techniques, and history of filmmaking, working with a medium that had historically been mobilized in the persistent marginalizing and dehumanizing of people of color necessitated approaching film with circumspection. In these students' work, as [Clyde] Taylor observed, "Every code of classical cinema was rudely smashed—conventions of editing, framing, storytelling, time, and space." They were likewise committed to questioning cultural assumptions about representation, as well as challenging institutional practices and many aspects of the film school curriculum.[43]

Gerima confirms this notion of radical unlearning while also schooling oneself in the filmmaking process. "Western teachers were teaching me,"

Gerima recalls, "not the technique of filmmaking, in terms of the technology, but molding and shaping me to make me a story teller in their cultural context, and thereby neutralizing me as another American filmmaker with no 'accent.' This happens not only to Third World filmmakers, but also to whites when they study filmmaking."[44] Gerima's self-reflexive filmic temperament here reflects "the accented cinema" of postcolonial, diasporic, exiled, and Third World filmmakers living in the West.[45] As a self-identified Third World filmmaker, Gerima cultivated a practice beginning with *Hour Glass* that emphasized counterhegemonic, international strategies of cinematic resistance.

Filmed under these conditions, Gerima's *Hour Glass* exhibits radical formal choices. Its dynamic and disruptive use of sound and image evinces the ambitions of L.A. Rebellion filmmakers, as James Snead notes, "to rewrite the standard cinematic language of cuts, fades, frame composition, and camera movement in order to represent their own 'non-standard' vision of black people and culture."[46] Directly inspired by African filmmakers like Ousmane Sembene and progressive works in Cuban cinema, *Hour Glass* insists on a film language of liberation, what Teshome Gabriel's theorizing of Third Cinema emphasizes as an aesthetic form articulated through the politicizing of cinema.[47] Using the familiar cultural arena of sports as his subject matter, Gerima inculcates an aesthetic of liberation in *Hour Glass* via his fusion of avant-garde tropes (asynchronous sound, rapid editing, nonlinear narratives) born from Project One's parameters but in the service of his own cinematic style and political outlook. Thus, US film school training and European cinematic experimentation meet and are shaped and reworked by Gerima's adherence to Third Cinema principles of radical consciousness and conscious engagement with anti-imperialist struggles. Fusing political and ideological content and aesthetics, *Hour Glass* inaugurates his cinema of resistance through sonic dissonance that figures and morphs the Black sporting body into a different kind of contestant on screen.

THE SONIC DISSONANCE OF THE BLACK SPORTING BODY

Hour Glass obliquely depicts the psychological experiences of a Black male college basketball player's journey toward racial and political consciousness. His *prise de conscience* is achieved symbologically and materially, as we follow him from a racially isolating white campus into the Black community of South Central Los Angeles. An unnamed character, the basketball player (played by Mel Rosier) is akin to the protagonist in Ralph Ellison's novel *Invisible Man,* who has no name because "none seemed to fit, and yet it was though I was somehow a part of all of them, had become submerged within them and lost."[48] Like all the representations of Black sporting bodies examined in this book, Gerima's athlete functions as an individuated multiplicity, the one and the many and the one of many. Sonically, the dialogue-less *Hour Glass* begins with The Last Poets' spoken word track "Niggers Are Scared of Revolution" and ends with Elaine Brown's Black Panther Party anthem "Seize the Time." The film's acoustic interjections and visual projections propel the protagonist's processes of critical awakening and leave-taking. A polyphonic soundscape of poetry, speeches, songs, and effects blends black-and-white and color sequences within the narrative diegesis into a fantasmic audiovisual space.

This "sonic visuality" coupled with recurring, atemporal dreamscapes—as diegetic breaks—creates a dense and symbolic montage, expanding the narrative into surrealist and Third Cinema–inspired allegory.[49] Without the hierarchy of the visible over the audible, *Hour Glass* stresses what Bhaskar Sarkar's reading of Richard Dyer argues are the nonrepresentational aspects of representation that impinge on the protagonist's and the viewer's senses. Affect and meaning are orchestrated non-representationally "at the auditory level—tonal progression, rhythm, dynamics, pitch, fading in and out, echo and reverberation effects—and the visual—colour, texture, camera movement, angle and framing."[50] The film's deployment of radical politics mobilizes Third Cinema modalities, particularly the insistence on political and ideological content, critique, and critical analysis. In *Hour Glass,* these tactics position the lead character's sporting blackness as destructive, constructive, and productive of Black quotidian futurities.

Hour Glass opens with a blank screen and the sound of a ticking clock. The pulsating frequency of the sonic hourglass instigates the film's visual and aural montage sequences. Framed in a black-and-white medium shot at an extremely low-angle, the film's unnamed protagonist is a Black man who towers above the camera. He is dressed in a trench coat with a hangman's noose around his neck. The protagonist slightly tilts his head down, looking directly into the camera before walking out of the frame with the rope dragging behind him. The film cuts to a basketball court and the sonic ticking ceases as a new aural and spatial framework structures the film. This inaugural image positions and dramatizes the Black body as "conditioned and circumscribed by historical convention."[51] A representation of critical muscle memory as shared Black experiences, Gerima's protagonist stages Black history in sporting and horrific terms of "hang time," invoking the tales of countless Black bodies that were the victims of the spectacular racialized violence and public ritual of lynching in American society, while also connecting these histories to the modern sports arena.[52]

Mounted on the backboard, the camera, now perched above the rim at the court's baseline, frames the athletic setting and its resonance. The acoustics of the court—dribbling, shooting, shuffling, players talking—and the basketball activity in progress are aligned though not perfectly sutured. On the court, a player pulls up at the free throw line and shoots a jump shot, sinking the ball. The camera angle, now positioned high in the stadium stands, shifts to an establishing shot that reveals the full length of the court as two teams compete against one another.

The camera's static position is fleeting. Now unfixed, its jerky motions capture the frenzied movements and phonics of the basketball game being played before finding its locus, framing one player specifically. Shot from an extremely low angle thereby echoing the film's opening visuals, the on-screen basketball player is revealed as the same Black man from the film's beginning. As the stadium lights beam down and the sounds of a roaring crowd amplify, the player momentarily takes center stage before losing the ball. The camera shifts visual planes and aural dimensions, focusing on the legs and rapid, squeaky footwork of the cohort of players on the court. As the editing dynamically cuts to the full-bodied play and players, the sound editing layers the noises of dribbling, stadium roars, and activity into a sporting sensorium.

The scene's sonic sporting effects, however, are disrupted. The sounds of the court are faded out as the soundtrack segues to The Last Poets' spoken-word recording "Niggers Are Scared of Revolution" performed by Omar Ben Hassen. An assemblage of musicians, poets, and activists based out of New York, The Last Poets were influential in the Black Arts Movement and recorded albums of politically and socially conscious poetry accompanied by instrumentation in the 1960s. The use of the Last Poets provides structuration to orchestrate meaning and affect in the film, connecting the sporting activities to Black cultural nationalist movements that are later shifted toward a revolutionary Black internationalism. The track also tethers the connection between basketball and various idioms of Black music. The soundscape links basketball's styles of play with improvisational or free jazz and proto-hip hop. The virtuosity in both basketball and vernacular Black music foreground their mutual use of ensemble, structure, improvisation, and showmanship. Significantly, The Last Poets' track operates as a sonic and radical intervention in the complex disciplining strategies represented by and through sports mechanisms and the cinematic apparatus. "Niggers Are Scared of Revolution" challenges not only how we are to understand the basketball game being witnessed but also the cinematic vocabulary of complementary sounds and images used in mainstream sports depictions.

The asynchronicity between The Last Poets and the basketball play not only underscores Project One films' curricular constraints but also breaches the sporting imaginary on screen. Carter Mathes's extension of Fred Moten's theorizing on Black radical aesthetic intervention clarifies the fusion of the sporting activity with The Last Poets' spoken word as an "embrace of the sonic 'asynchronicity' of black radical consciousness, framing the political and critical capacity of sound as an evasion of sedimented or regulated reading."[53] The Last Poets' radical Black subjectivity shapes our understanding of the cultural struggles explored in *Hour Glass*. As the basketball play continues, Hassen's recitation of "Niggers Are Scared of Revolution" provides a sonic conceptual field of meaning, amplifying the lower frequencies of Black radicalism within the sporting mise-en-scène. The film plays only a small excerpt of the song's political critique:

> Niggers are scared of revolution
> Niggers are players, niggers are players, are players
> Niggers play football, baseball and basketball
> While the white man is cuttin' off their balls
> And when the nigger's play ain't tight enough
> To play with some Black thighs

With the percussive accompaniment of Nilaja's African drumming, the exhortation of "Niggers Are Scared of Revolution" is directed at the Black community and the players on the court. As a music sample, the lyrics castigate Black athletes who allow themselves to be exploited as players in sports and society. Similar to Harry Edwards's accusation of hubris about apathetic Black athletes who ignored the sporting, social, and economic realities they and/or others faced, The Last Poets' spoken-word poetry suggests that the advancement of individual athletes through sports is not enough for the revolutionary needs of the larger Black community.

The play of basketball in *Hour Glass* is complexly rendered within The Last Poets' soundscape. The film's aural textures and mise-en-scène reverberate a dissonance and counternarrative on the Black sporting body. The basketball player in the film is sonically scripted as the "nigger" in American society, a signification and subjectivity that will change as he becomes more aware of his rarefaction and dehumanization. As the basketball play on the court suggests, he is an active participant, even if unwittingly so, in his own exploitation and subjection for material success and assimilation. Rejecting the Cartesian dualism that splits the mind and body, the juxtaposition of visual and aural imagery link the two for the protagonist. The basketball player must learn to think on and, as the film progresses, off his feet. Gerima uses the interplay of the athletic activity and the music to transform the body's individuated action on the court through The Last Poets' demand for action into social commentary, a process that begins to show the critical capacity of Black thought to resist subjection and shape a Black radical consciousness. In this regard, the track's polemical critique recodes the film's visible components. The spectacle of the basketball game's contest becomes newly confrontational. The frequencies of Black radical sounds raise the volume of political urgency and construct its resonance for both the protagonist and the audience. The caustic lyrics engage the spectator to "[resist] the primacy of the ocular in favor of embracing the complexities of visual and aural exchange within black cultural production."[54]

As the excerpt of "Niggers Are Scared of Revolution" trails off, the soundtrack transitions to The Last Poets' "Run, Nigger" performed by Abiodun Oyewole. The speed of the basketball game maintains its even flow as the song's kinetic energy via the ticking clock sonically pushes the kinesthetic charge to "run, nigger." Recruiting the protagonist to move with haste, the entire track of "Run, Nigger" plays, and the lyrical figuring of the basketball players is framed within the poetry's fugacious temporality:

I understand that time is running out
Running out as hastily as niggers run from the Man
Time is running out, on our natural habits
Time is running out, on lifeless serpents reigning over a living
   kingdom
Time is running out of talks, marches, tunes, chants, and all kinds
   of prayers
Time is running out of time

The song also employs the repeated phrase and beat of "tick tock." This syncopated temporal machination aligns the depicted athletic activity with both the construction of sports time and the need for, in Amiri Baraka's words, "nation time."[55] Sports time is structured by the authority of the clock, "the actual time of the game, a configuration of temporality that literally measures every tick of the clock precisely and absolutely, a temporality that conducts itself as not only independent of but also as operating distinct from 'real time.'"[56] Gerima disallows this exceptional space of sports time by situating the body within and of historical time where, as The Last Poets declare, things are changing rapidly. As the tempo increases, the song charges

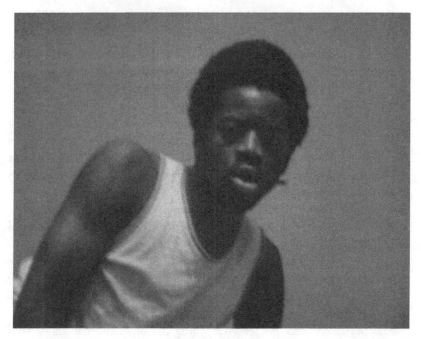

FIGURE 21.   The Black athlete falls on the basketball court as The Last Poets exclaim that "time's done run out" in *Hour Glass* (Haile Gerima, 1971).

the listener to act: "run, nigger!" The mix of the athlete's body in action and the track's warning that "time is running out" equates Black percussive movement as a catalyst for temporal instability, an anarchic and multisynchronic muscle for counter-memory and Black insurgency.

When Oyewole expresses that "time's done run out" and the protagonist falls to the floor on the court, his body is halted amid sports' incessant demand for perpetual motion and contest, evidenced by the play continuing around him (figure 21). The music disorients the athlete's flow of movement and reorients his body outside of the disciplinary logic of sports time into historical time(s), a simultaneity distinguished by what M. Jacqui Alexander calls the construction of post-, neo-, and colonial time which interrelate in palimpsestic ways.[57] This moment of disorder and stasis in the film provides an occasion to imagine and project the psychic state of the Black athlete as an "event," an unexpected instance and disruption of routine into an historical occurrence with multiple resonances.

Drawing on the work of Alain Badiou and Jacques Derrida, Grant Farred argues that the stilled Black sporting body (in his case that of Ron Artest during the "Palace Brawl") provokes a temporal dilemma and has the ability to reframe sports time and white public space—such as the basketball arena—by allowing for it to "arrest time" and "step out" of its disciplinary logic.[58] Farred's theorization on the temporal paradigms and embodied histories of inert Black sporting bodies can be grafted onto *Hour Glass*. When "time runs out" for the Black basketball player, he falls to the ground and is stilled momentarily. The soundtrack cuts back to the cacophony of stadium noise. The flow of sports play in *Hour Glass* ends in its entirety, which occurs in just under three minutes of the film's duration. The fall functions as a disruption to sports time and cinematic logic, generating a supplemental irreality in the visual projections that follow. *Hour Glass* demonstrates this through a break in the diegesis that engenders a process whereby the student athlete "steps out" of sports time's interplay of control and regulation and "steps into" a new domain of critical awareness born out of his newfound perspective on his sporting performance.

As the sound of a roaring crowd grows, this critical awakening is depicted literally as the protagonist gazes into the stands and stares directly into the camera. From the athlete's point of view, the camera reveals a crowd of white patrons in the stands, with particular focus on a white couple in the final row of the arena. The film cuts back and forth between black-and-white and color film stock as patriotic music fills the soundscape. The couple in the arena is flanked by two American flag decals. The white man wears an ivy wreath around his head, the woman a crown (figure 22). He gives her a torch and she hands him a scepter with an eagle head. This image renders the couple as king and queen alongside emblems and echoes of Americana, iconography that should be read in tension with The Last Poets' earlier sonic social indictments. As presiding rulers in this hegemonic fantasy, the white man and woman function as agents of the racial nation-state; they are the proverbial "white man" cutting off balls (or basketball play) that the protagonist should run from. The camera zooms in on the couple as they both slowly lift their arms up to give a "thumbs down" gesture with their hands toward the fallen Black player. The scene ends with the camera cutting back to him still sitting down on the court, rubbing his head in frustration.

While it is presumed that contact with another player caused the athlete to fall to the ground, Gerima depicts this moment as one that involves not only physical injury but also psychological trauma for the protagonist, who is sonically defined by The Last Poets' lyric and visually delimited by the white couple's voyeuristic denouncement in the stands. In doing so, Gerima constructs the sporting body outside the confines of its own embodied and temporal finitude. A canvas of representation with critical muscle memory,

FIGURE 22.   In *Hour Glass* (Haile Gerima, 1971), university athletics are pictured as gladiatorial contests where white patrons look down on the Black athlete before condemning him with a thumbs-down gesture.

the protagonist's play and pause works out and through a broader history of Black bodies performing for the entertainment and consumption of white fans and on behalf of nationalist bourgeois values.

In the scene, Gerima shows how the racially bifurcated basketball world is divided "between 'the black court' and the 'white arena.'"[59] In this domain, the athlete, as Field describes the scene, "imagines the white spectators as modern-day Roman emperors, deriving sadistic pleasure from the physical battles of combatting slaves."[60] The protagonist's vision casts university basketball programs as gladiatorial institutions where many Black bodies participate in sports for the scopic, financial, and visceral delight of white audiences. Refusing to register as a player that white spectators champion on the court and root against in real life, the athlete figuratively steps out of the temporal and disciplinary logic of sports time to see the people behind the machinations of such control and power. The Last Poets provide an acoustics of awakening, a tonal strategy that is embodied and intersubjective and that produces social consciousness.[61] *Hour Glass* shows how non-diegetic sonic propulsion can provide a radical diegetic intervention for its protagonist, one that produces unexpected new actions and activities—a newfound muscularity producing counter-memory that marks critical muscle memory as lyrical and communally driven actions to be taken.

As an entire sequence, *Hour Glass*'s basketball opening signals the "double movement of containment and resistance" that shapes the protagonist as a composed yet contested figure.[62] Gerima later frames his body as defiant and unruly in a way that does not reinscribe onto the cinematic Black body racist tropes—such as a subhuman gladiator—but recodes his disruptive body within new temporal and diegetic paradigms. Significantly, his moment of embodied rest engenders a profound moment of ideological unrest within him, and it is in that instant that the protagonist's diegetic performance of revolt begins.

MINUTE DEPICTIONS OF REVOLT

The performance of revolt in *Hour Glass* is the minute refusal to play the game of basketball, and Gerima depicts this performance as an erudite, meditative, and introspective process of being and becoming a politicized subject. No longer a body to be watched and consumed on the court but alienated in the classroom and society, the protagonist, a *student*-athlete, returns to his dorm room resolved to learn about US, African, and Caribbean colonial histories, politics, and collectivities. Grabbing a book from his shelf and taking a seat at his desk, he studiously begins to read J.C. Furnas's *Goodbye to Uncle Tom*, which combines sociology with literary criticism to dismantle Harriet Beecher Stowe's mythification of slave life by delving into the material history of Black enslavement.[63] As the first book to counter the protagonist's miseducation on and off the court, Furnas's text helps the student-athlete understand his role on the basketball court as connected to systems of slavery, both of which extract Black muscle as raw material for the labor and capital interest of white-ruled economies and institutions.

While the opening basketball sequence experimented with asynchronous sound and image, the more subdued timbre—a rhythmic drum beat—in the dorm room scenes slows the film's auditory pace down to mirror the contemplative acts of the protagonist. This reflection becomes formalized with the camera zooming into a close-up of his face. With a quick cut, the diegesis breaks down into dream logic as the protagonist imagines a horrific scene where a young, naked Black boy is imprisoned in a stark white room filled with liquor bottles, a small cot, and a toilet. Lying in a fetal position, the small boy cringes as an elderly white woman rips a sheet displaying the

FIGURE 23.   The student-athlete's revolutionary literacy includes Black nationalist, Marxist, anti-colonial, and Black internationalist texts in *Hour Glass* (Haile Gerima, 1971).

face of Malcolm X off his unclothed body. Throughout this ordeal, Malcolm X's speech "Message to the Grassroots" plays on the soundtrack. As the old woman goes to hang the sheet portrait of the devout Muslim and leader of the Organization of Afro-American Unity, Malcolm X's disembodied voice is drowned out with screams and gunfire before the scene shifts back to the diegetic present. The camera zooms out from Furnas's *Goodbye to Uncle Tom*, connecting the imagined dreamscape to the protagonist's consideration of the book's revolutionary content.

As the film continues, an assemblage of books piled on the protagonist's bed fill the camera's frame (figure 23). While some titles are obscured, others are clearly in view, including W. E. B. Du Bois's *The Souls of Black Folk* (1903); Eldridge Cleaver's *Soul on Ice* (1968); Frantz Fanon's *Black Skin, White Masks* (1952), *Wretched of the Earth* (1961), and *Toward the African Revolution* (1964); and Immanuel Wallerstein's *Africa: The Politics of Independence* (1961).[64] Alongside Furnas's book, these imaged texts provide a meta-textual rescripting of the film's narrative of revolt, one that catalyzes the protagonist's decision to escape from the court and later depart from the university to the Black community. Black critical thought and practice become the forces of physical and narrative momentum in the film.

Even a cursory examination of this cohort of scholarship reveals the protagonist's process of erudition as well as gives insight into the film's narrative construction and ideological themes. Du Bois' *The Souls of Black Folk*, an intertextual and polyphonic amalgam of literary modes and genres, provides a complementary structure to *Hour Glass'* like-minded narrative about double consciousness. The protagonist comes to critical awareness in a manner akin to Cleaver, who writes about his incarceration in *Soul on Ice*; their activation to activism is accomplished through reading.[65] In doing so, the basketball player perceives, as Fanon suggests in *Black Skin, White Masks'* psychoanalytic reading of the Black psyche formed and disfigured by colonialism and racism, that "there is one expression that has become singularly eroticized: the black athlete."[66] Reeling from this recognition, the protagonist suffers the effects of mental instability—an aspect of colonialism explored in *The Wretched of the Earth*—during the diegetic breaks as he attempts to liberate himself through his newfound and acute revolutionary literacy. The film's sonic atmosphere inhabits and repudiates a colonial state, and the protagonist, employing the kind of "combat breathing" described in *Toward the African Revolution*, suffers under his conditions of exploitation.[67] In the protagonist's fall on the court and later in his tossing and turning in bed, *Hour Glass* shows how colonialism attacks all aspects of the bodily schema from the inside out and the outside in. The basketball player must free himself by considering what it means to think about US Black experiences in an internationalized context of liberation and decolonization signaled by Wallerstein's *Africa*.[68] With all the imaged books, Gerima represents the protagonist's individuated performance of revolt as connected to global Black freedom struggles, framing him as both an individual Black body and a part of an expansive, diasporic Black-African body politic.

Following the camera's shot of this cohort of books, the protagonist finds himself on his bed, holding his head in confusion and contemplation, as if he is grappling with the synergies and contradictions within and among these Black nationalist, Marxist, anti-colonial, and Black internationalist texts in the context of a North American education and dorm room. As the camera zooms in again, as if to convey his internal subjectivity, the film intercuts images of him on the basketball court and in his dorm room. On the court, two players wrestle a ball from each other. There are jump cuts to the white couple in the stands. These scenes shift from black-and-white to color, moving from shots of the protagonist to shots of the books to the surreal dreamscape inhabited by the little Black boy and elderly white woman. With these juxtapositions, the film conveys the idea that the protagonist is internally wrestling with his two-ness, that of being a Black athlete whose individual exceptionalism is exploited on the court and that of becoming a politicized individual attuned to the global struggles of Black freedom.

The diegetic break into dream logic returns as the protagonist's psychological turmoil continues. This time, the sheet portrait snatched from the little boy—who sits up slightly as if to confront the woman as she grabs it—is of Martin Luther King Jr., whose "I Have a Dream" speech plays on the soundtrack. As the white woman takes the sheet to nail to the wall behind a wooden X, in a manner similar to the Malcolm X portrait, King's voice is cut down amid gunfire and screams. In the final nightmare, the voice of Angela Davis is heard speaking about the events surrounding Jonathan Jackson's armed and fatal attempt to free the Soledad Brothers in a hostage situation at the Marin County Courthouse in 1970. This time, when the elderly white woman tries to take the sheet with Davis's portrait off the young boy, he jumps up and wrestles it away from her. The agency of the young boy mirrors the awakened political consciousness of the protagonist within the film's "real-life" diegesis, illustrated through the cut to the student-athlete standing between the camera and a poster-image of Davis as a "natural woman" on his wall. The character's direct, suspect look into the camera underscores what Field describes as the film's masculinist "fantasy of protecting Angela Davis."[69]

This dorm room sequence illustrates not only the double consciousness of the protagonist but also the double movement of containment and resistance in society that the athlete struggles to overcome. In the racially hostile basketball court and university setting, the film's protagonist is constricted. Through political consciousness and social awareness, he becomes mobilized to resist his literal and figurative confinement. Thus, Gerima depicts the performance of revolt in *Hour Glass* as not only a refusal to play the game of basketball but also a refusal to play the game of racial injustice and inequality. The student-athlete's body is transformed into a different kind of contestant within the film. No longer solely playing in futile sporting competitions for the pleasure of white audiences, the Black student-athlete's body is reconfigured as a questing body in Fanonian terms: "O my body, make me always a man who questions!"[70]

As *Hour Glass* continues toward its end, the student-athlete-turned-wayfarer packs his books and clothes in a suitcase and leaves his dorm in search of Black community. Breaking out of the constrictive white university setting and surrounding community, his once literal investment in athletic motion and contest is transformed into an active consideration of Black social movements and political contestation. Off campus, his sojourn is depicted in a chromatic centrifuge, spinning him in circles as he moves along a platform. Red and white vertical stripes bordered in blue trap him as he walks by photos of assassinated figures like King, Malcolm X, Abraham Lincoln, and John F. Kennedy and FBI-wanted Black leaders, including Huey P. Newton, a scholar, author, activist, and cofounder and leader of the Black Panther Party (BPP). Wearing a noose around his neck again, the protagonist is aligned with what Newton describes in *Revolutionary Suicide* as the actions needed to challenge the system, ones that could result in death but would be for the greater movement of social change.[71]

In addition to this imagery, the sound of the ticking clock returns to exaggerate the importance of the film's temporal logics. As the film's title suggests, an hourglass structures and measures time but is not time in and of itself. As a container, it—like the swirling Americana mise-en-scène around the protagonist—is panoptic and part of the Western telos and Enlightenment ideals that the depicted Black nationalist and Pan-Africanist books reject in order to construct anti-colonial arguments and temporalities. Moving off the court with its precisely timed quarters and free throws and departing the university campus, the antihero of Gerima's film shatters the ideological hourglass, refusing to labor in white time as he chooses to be enveloped in the Black quotidian: traveling without a seeming destination other than Black communal life and liveness.

As he gets on a bus and travels outside of the alienating, affluent neighborhoods of Brentwood and Beverly Hills, Elaine Brown's "Seize the Time" plays on the soundtrack. Brown was the first and only woman to serve as chair of the BPP. Here again, Gerima uses underground music frequencies to politicize the protagonist's actions. If The Last Poets operated to arrest time and resist the playful images on screen, then "Seize the Time" functions similarly as a call-and-response musical strategy within the diegesis. Brown's song calls out to the protagonist, "the time is now," to which he must respond and seize the moment in order for him and, in turn, the audience, to construct themselves within a new cinematic subjectivity. He is no longer exhausting himself for "the man"/the team/the machine. He switches from a bus carrying only a few white people to one filled with Black travelers, fixating on the non-goal-oriented flight of boys on their bikes as he stares out the window. The protagonist makes his way into and through the Black community of South Central Los Angeles. The film ends with him

FIGURE 24.   Enveloped in the Black community of South Central Los Angeles, the student-athlete walks into an unknown future in *Hour Glass* (Haile Gerima, 1971).

walking down the street before turning into an alley where he stops at an unmarked door. Opening it, he looks into the darkened space (figure 24). His entrance through the door is a literal and symbolic move to show that he is ready to face the unknown head-on. Closing the door behind him, the darkness envelops the frame and the film abruptly cuts out. *Hour Glass*'s elliptical ending and the protagonist's sporting blackness is the journey of being and becoming connected to and a socius of the Black community.

BOLD OMISSIONS AND HISTORICAL INSCRIPTIONS

Hour Glass's experimental form blurs the cinematic and social world to interrogate sporting blackness in terms of Black cultural nationalism and Pan-African anti-colonial struggles. The minute depictions of Black resistance illuminate the film's bold omissions in terms of the "text's historical referentiality, representationality, and meaning."[72] And yet, how does *Hour Glass*, in Leerom Medovoi's terms, "assume the presence of textual depth, a register of meaning that remains unspoken, unwritten, or unrepresented, yet structures by its very absence all that *has* been spoken, written, or represented"?[73] While the structuring absent historical referent, I argue, is the revolt of Black athletes in 1968 and the actions of sprinters Tommie Smith and John Carlos, *Hour Glass*'s critical muscle memory, or shared Black sporting and non-sporting experiences, extends to the historicity of represented, tangential, and repressed narratives. In the film's diegesis, Gerima's minute visual and sonic depictions connect the protagonist's sporting blackness in motion and stasis with Black social histories of lynching, athletics, intellectual communities, and revolutionary figures. These critical muscle memories are rendered through avant-garde techniques and as explicit diegetic content. We can also, however, read *Hour Glass*'s story of revolt as symptomatic, in that it refers to and registers other contiguous and latent cultural histories that it does not narratively depict. In addition to the history of 1968, there are overlapping, invisible histories and omitted plots that frame and signify in the film: Gerima's and others' experiences at UCLA, stories of Black collegiate athletes, and the spatiotemporal politics of the late 1960s and 1970s.[74] These histories and events are *Hour Glass*'s critical muscle memories, inscripted—even while unscripted—in the film's narrative about a Black athlete in revolt.

Gerima was inspired to make *Hour Glass* after witnessing the ways in which many Black athletes at UCLA were apathetic toward their own education and the social issues facing Black people on campus and in broader society.[75] He was also influenced by his own racial alienation at the university, which occurred simultaneously with the celebration of athletics at UCLA, particularly its men's basketball program made famous under NCAA championship-winning coach, John Wooden. As the Bruins created a basketball dynasty, students of color protested for the implementation of ethnic studies and affirmative action programs to assist in enrolling students of color at the starkly white university. The film, while not biographical, references many of Gerima's own struggles at UCLA, feeling like an outsider and being in confrontations with UCLA's Film Department. "At UCLA," Gerima explains, "I had to defend myself from teachers who didn't like my story. I'd read it to other 'tribes' to see if a teacher was looking at *my* work in context of *his* culture, rather than pointing out legitimate technical difficulties."[76] Like the film's protagonist, Gerima took the bus to campus, each trip back home was, like the student-athletes', a return to the Black community that can be linked to his sustained interest in doing work directly related to and for Black and Third World people.

Additionally, the film's representation of the protagonist's coming of consciousness through reading anti-colonial theory and Black liberation literature mirrors the dynamic intellectual environment Gerima and other L.A. Rebellion filmmakers were engaged with at the time. "Heavily indebted to the ideas of Malcolm X and the Black Panther Party," Cynthia Young explains, "the African Americans in the group tended to be cultural nationalists who believed that the source of culture derived from African diasporic experience. By contrast, [Ntongela] Masilela, [Haile] Gerima, and [Teshome] Gabriel tended toward Marxist revolutionary internationalism, insisting on the interrelation of race and class domination."[77] While depicted as an individual intellectual experience in Gerima's film, L.A. Rebellion filmmakers valued "robust ideological debate" about many Black theoretical texts, especially Fanon's *The Wretched of the Earth* (pictured in *Hour Glass*), which, as Ntongela Masilela explains, "was a central text, for it clarified the historical moment in which these filmmakers found themselves."[78]

Hour Glass fictionalizes the social and political atmosphere on campus at the time for Black students, one that was a period of unrest following many racially charged incidents on campus, including the firing of Angela Davis (pictured and heard in the film). Davis, who was an assistant professor in the philosophy department at UCLA, was fired by the Board of Regents of the University of California in 1969 for her membership in and allegiance to the Communist Party USA. She was later rehired, and then fired again in 1970 for what they called her use of "inflammatory language" during her lectures and speeches. *Hour Glass*'s diegetic visual and sonic reference to Davis underscores Gerima's interest in her as a radical figure, a characterization he takes up again in his following film *Child of Resistance*, inspired by a dream he had after seeing Davis on television in handcuffs. Additionally, the images of BPP members, principally Huey P. Newton, highlight not only their struggles for social justice but also the growing factions of the organization on UCLA's campus, especially because of the on-campus murder of two student BPP members. Black students protested on campus following the murders of two Panthers, Alprentice "Bunchy" Carter and John Huggins, in Campbell Hall in 1969 by members of the Black nationalist group, the United Slaves (US) Organization. The campus was a place for unequal race relations on a Black-white binary, but it also was a contested site for Black-on-Black politics. *Hour Glass*'s narrative of a Black student-athlete's resistance and defiance reflects and rearticulates the institutional history of social, political, and inter- and intracultural unrest at UCLA during this time. A post-1965 Watts rebellion film, *Hour Glass* conceptually renders the communal and political discontent and conditions, both social and interior, that were the roots of revolt for many Black athletes and people in South Central Los Angeles.[79]

Beyond the narrative's resonance with the recognizable sporting and social reality at UCLA, *Hour Glass*'s critical muscle memory of revolt aligns the film's protagonist with fellow basketball player Lew Alcindor, known today as Kareem Abdul-Jabbar. Abdul-Jabbar led the Bruins to three consecutive basketball NCAA national championships during the late 1960s. He experienced success on the court and discrimination on campus and in society, leaving him feeling isolated and alienated like *Hour Glass*'s student-athlete. Resisting his rarefaction, Abdul-Jabbar, alongside Edwards, Smith, and Carlos, stated at the founding conference for OPHR:

> I'm the big basketball star, the weekend hero, everybody's All-American. Well, last summer I was almost killed by a racist cop shooting at a black cat in Harlem. He was shooting on the street—where masses of people were standing around or just taking a walk. But he didn't care. After all we were just niggers. I found out last summer that we don't catch hell because we aren't basketball stars or because we don't have money. We catch hell because we are black. Somewhere each of us have got to make a stand against this kind of thing. This is how I take my stand—using what I have. And I take my stand here.[80]

While still playing for UCLA, Abdul-Jabbar decided to boycott the 1968 Olympics, refusing to play for the US Men's Olympic Basketball team as a protest against racial inequality in all sectors of society, stating in *Sports Illustrated*:

> I got more and more lonely and more and more hurt by all the prejudice and finally I made a decision. . . . I pushed to the back of my mind all the normalcies of college life and dug down deep into my black studies and religious studies. I withdrew to find myself. I made no attempt to integrate. I was consumed and obsessed by my interest in the black man, in Black Power, black pride, black courage. That, for me, would suffice. I was full of serious ideas. I could see the whole transition of the black man and his history. And I developed my first interest in Islam.[81]

This statement mirrors the actions of the student-athlete in *Hour Glass* who rejects the normal college life and setting in pursuit of his own Black identity and cultural awareness. The film's protagonist, like Abdul-Jabbar, reads his way out of distress into consciousness.

As well, connections can be made to basketball players beyond UCLA. For example, the two-ness experience and leave-taking of *Hour Glass*'s protagonist aligns with the experience of former NBA star Chet Walker, who played basketball at Bradley University in the 1960s. In his memoir *Long Time Coming: A Black Athlete's Coming of Age*, Walker describes his desperation to leave his college campus: "Bradley had me as its employee; they had me as a commodity for as long as I was of use. If I publicly expressed my anger or desire to leave, they would destroy me.... One minute I was an All-American basketball player as full of myself as a powerful young man could be. But the next minute, I was reduced to the nigger in the doorway. No amount of sports heroism in America could change that. Early on I understood this doubleness and that it would never truly change for me."[82] Gerima depicts this doubled experience for *Hour Glass*'s protagonist in the montage of him playing and the couple in the stands, the court functioning as a space where he is both celebrated and condemned. Coming to critical consciousness, the student-athlete in the film is empowered to leave his racially divided college campus and reconnect to the Black community. Gerima's film also reimagines the atmosphere of protesting Black university athletes in the wake of the events of 1968, including the "Black 14." Recently chronicled in Darius Clark Monroe's short documentary *Black 14* (2018), the "Black 14" are Black student-athletes who were kicked off the University of Wyoming's football team in 1969 for wanting to wear black arm bands during their upcoming game against Brigham Young University as a protest against the racist policies of the Church of Jesus Christ of Latter-day Saints.[83] In the end, *Hour Glass* registers these popular and obscured memories of Black athletic consciousness and protest. These athletes' and others' cultural histories highlight the broader tropes that code most sports films about Black athletes, ones that Gerima's film upends in order to tell a different kind of story.

THE REVOLT OF THE CINEMATIC BLACK ATHLETE

Hour Glass is an anomalous sports film. The film clearly has an allegorical structure that rejects the typical allegorical structure of most sports films. With a soundtrack that interrogates and shapes the protagonist's psyche and actions, the film explores not only the dynamics of kinesthetic movement but also the potential and kinetic energy—reflective repose and movement into Black communal space—of coming to radical Black consciousness. *Hour Glass*' aberrant sports narrative is one that privileges a performance of revolt, a refusal to participate in and be an object of exploitive pleasure, sporting entertainment, and racial subjection. It is a refusal to discipline the body to sports time in order to "seize the time," a transgressive temporal articulation of Black consciousness within and as social movement. The film's Black sporting body is a rebellious one, a sports antihero that resists control and regulation in his anti-sporting performance.

If *Hour Glass*, in terms of its content and production, required a radical *un*learning of classical codes and modes of representation, I want to consider how Gerima's *un*conventional sports film affords the chance to address the negating capacities presented in the film's performativity— "what it *means* in the sense of what it *does*."[84] In this line of thinking, I extend Field's emphasis of the "un" in Project One's *un*learning as a mode of undoing. My emphasis on the "un" in *un*convention signals this formal countermanding process in racialized terms. *Hour Glass*'s representation of sporting blackness and critical muscle memory activates what Michael Gillespie theorizes as the consequential ways blackness can operate as an animating force within a genre.[85] With its minute depictions and bold omissions, *Hour Glass* demands that we work through the discursivity of race in sports cinema, how sporting blackness shapes and can possibly break—to the point of undoing—the codes and conventions of sports films. This focus on patterns and systems of representation is intended to put pressure on the deliberate construction and deconstruction of cinematic and racial codes, tropes, and iconography used in the sports genre more broadly. *Hour Glass* critically illustrates how radical *un*conventions can engender liberatory possibilities of sporting blackness on screen.

George Lipsitz makes the case that race plays a crucial formative role in generic representations.[86] Popular American genres such as sports films rely on racial imagery to structure the narrative and its ideologies in terms of racial hierarchies while reiterating stereotypes and affirming colorblind racist logic. Lipsitz argues that race can subversively be used to disrupt and restructure static genre conventions such as these through a formal engagement with the racial concerns and histories that shape the vicissitudes of social life. He suggests that uncommon racial elements in conventional genre films can disrupt the normative ways genres and generic codes are understood, familiarized, and found pleasurable. Lipsitz calls this eruptive force "genre anxiety," a symptom or spasm induced by social crises or tremors that become dynamically and unexpectedly registered in American cinema, particularly in the 1970s.[87] In its representation of a Black athlete in revolt and associated critical muscle memory, *Hour Glass*'s generic spasms reflect Gerima's deliberate engagement with Black realities and conditions in sports and society. His experimental sports film vivifies, in Lipsitz's terms, how "the task confronting oppositional filmmakers from aggrieved racial communities comes into sharp relief when we study the images and genre conventions they have to displace in order to tell their stories their way."[88] *Hour Glass*'s avant-garde form and anti-sporting sports story evinces the complex disruption, deconstruction, and displacement of conservative sporting conventions, cresting in its rejection of its sports narrative altogether. The film's polyphonic and imagistic rendering of sporting blackness unsettles cinematic and sporting illusions with its protagonist abandoning its sporting world in favor of a meditation on critical self-awareness and communal envelopment.

As an *un*conventional sports film, *Hour Glass* demonstrates the critical negating capacities of sporting blackness to destabilize and disregard generic representations. This is the ability to undo sports film conventions that encode conservative ideologies and racial and gender hierarchies into idealized stories of sporting success. The diegetic deviances are intensified by a refusal of sporting conventions and cinematic telos. The revolts in *Hour Glass* are many—from asynchronous sound and image to the protagonist leaving the court indefinitely to Gerima dismissing the film's sporting narrative in favor of exploring blackness as critical thought that moves forward without a cinematic end and toward an elliptical new beginning. As such, *Hour Glass* operates as a critique of the traditional ways in which we envision certain texts, codes, and conventions about race and sports cinema.

The film rejects common sports tropes about Black male athletes specifically. Gerima dismisses these tropes, repudiating the genre's melodramatic emphasis on utopic tales of heroic male achievement. *Hour Glass* is about a refusal to "play the game." Playing the game, here, means taking part in sports' formal structures of regulation and competition, where fixed rule exists for those participating in systems that tout notions of individualism, meritocracy, and fair play in sports and society. Playing the game also means adhering to sports cinema's formal codes, conventions, and cultural assumptions. Upending the mythos and conventions that characterize "playing the game" in most popular sports films, Gerima reconstructs the sporting world on screen from a Black point of view to challenge both cinema, sports, and society's racializing projections.

Hour Glass, however, is not an *un*conventional sports film solely because of its experimental aesthetics and the sports codes it incorporates and then rejects. It also is *un*conventional because it *is* and then purposely *is not* a sports film. In its cinematic subterfuge, the revolt of the cinematic Black athlete in *Hour Glass* is a revolt against sporting blackness on sports films' terms, an alignment with and then rejection of the genre's visual economy of expression. Here, sporting, is not just athletic and embodied performance but is also "the enunciative function of blackness," a kinesthetic embrace of kinship and critical being.[89] It is the questing for communion and fellowship and a questioning of all cultural arenas where competition creates hierarchies. The film calls for a consideration of how the Black sporting body can supersede its own athletic iconography to mean and then mean something else entirely; and, thus, sporting blackness may require an athlete *not* to play if the games, like the generic codes and conventions, are already fixed.

RESISTING A FINISH LINE

Hour Glass is the shortest and, perhaps, least-known case study in this book. The film was once considered "bonus material," a special feature included on the DVD of Gerima's feature-length film *Bush Mama*, released by Mypheduh Films in the early 2000s.[90] UCLA's Film & Television Archive played a critical role in expanding audience access to *Hour Glass* and other L.A. Rebellion Project One films as a part of its preservation efforts.[91] *Hour Glass* has since been digitized in standard and high definition, available not only in the Film & Television Archive's reserves but also on its website or on YouTube. These streaming platforms alongside its availability as a DVD special feature have brought new and contemporary audiences to Gerima's film, helping it to resonate with and in relationship to analogous representations of Black athletes in revolt in the modern sports age. *Hour Glass*, as Clyde Taylor instructs about the preservation of L.A. Rebellion films, is not a cinematic time capsule; rather, to revise Taylor's words, the film is still radioactive in the present sporting landscape.[92] Newly digitized, *Hour Glass* re-signifies in this current moment of sporting protest and alongside contemporary sports popular culture about past and present defiant Black athletes.

In recent sports media, there has been a lot of attention to genealogies of socially, politically, and culturally conscious Black athletes, evidenced in films such as Clark Monroe's aforementioned 2018 short documentary *Black 14* and Showtime's three-part docuseries *Shut Up and Dribble* (Gotham Chopra, 2018), which examines the relationship between the NBA and civil rights issues and highlights the stories of athlete-activists and game-changers including, among others, Bill Russell, Kareem Abdul-Jabbar, Craig Hodges, Mahmoud Abdul-Rauf, and LeBron James.[93] Additionally, there have been a number of recently produced hagiographic fiction and nonfiction films about the political pugilist Muhammad Ali, specifically detailing his refusal to be inducted into the US military during the Vietnam War on April 28, 1967.[94]

The renewed media interest in stories about resistant Black athletes is, in part, because of the spectacle and controversy over Colin Kaepernick repeatedly taking a knee during the national anthem to protest racism, social injustice, and police brutality in a manner reminiscent of Smith and Carlos's singular action at the 1968 Olympic Games.[95] As I've explained elsewhere, the former NFL San Francisco 49ers quarterback's act "became a subject of conversation, celebration, consternation, and condemnation" and "Kaepernick's resistant posture is a counter-signal, an embodied sign that refuses to emit as it was trained to and for which it was (once) handsomely paid. In repose, a gesture both meditative and provocative, Kaepernick's (and later others') pregame protests have become the bigger contest than the game itself."[96] This sentiment is echoed in the 2018 "Dream Crazy" commercial advertisement for Nike, where Kaepernick, as narrator, delivers an inspiring narrative about tenacious athletes who have dared to dream beyond sporting expectations.[97] The athletes depicted in the commercial all have faced adversity in and outside of their respective sports. Dressed not in a sports uniform but in a beige trench coat with his prominent afro filling the frame, Kaepernick stands on a street facing a projected image of the American flag. He turns and stands silently as his voiceover proclaims: "Believe in something, even if it means sacrificing everything."[98] Having been blackballed from playing in the NFL, Kaepernick is a modern figure and symbol of sporting blackness as a refusal to "play the game" dictated on racist terms, teams, and turfs.

With its digital resurgence, *Hour Glass* circulates and re-signifies in this new era of protest and alongside these and other media representations of defiant Black athletes: from Michael Bennet and Eric Reid to players in the WNBA to Serena Williams to the University of Missouri and Northwestern University's football teams to countless amateur players. Black athletes are continuing to revolt against inequality, police brutality, exploitation, and dehumanization, demonstrating time and time again their exigent humanity and how sports function as an "allegorical terrain for other kinds of contestation."[99] Sitting down, taking a knee, calling out injustice, and refusing to play, these contemporary Black athletes have, like past sportsmen and women, challenged, disrupted, and boycotted sports in the tradition of Black civil rights and freedom struggles. In its past and present tenses, *Hour Glass*'s critical muscle memory of revolt is connective tissue that binds these contemporary actions to a real and imagined insurgent cinematic history of rebellious acts of sporting blackness.

Conclusion

The Fitness of Sporting Blackness

With *Sporting Blackness*, I offer a hermeneutic to analyze race and embodiment in sports films to read beyond the surface of race and racial stereotyping. This pivot from "skin in the game" to "skin in the genre" allows for an accounting of the formal and political consequences of the sports film and its rendering of the Black athletic body. Within these critical entanglements, the Black sporting body's historical braiding becomes a *counter*narrative plaiting that productively goes against the straight visual, sporting, and cinematic stories, tropes, and telos presented on screen. Sporting blackness and critical muscle memory have been my modes and motor of representational and formal analyses to take on the popular fare associated with Hollywood sports films and mainstream media (the *Friday Night Lights* media franchise, *A League of Their Own, Love and Basketball,* and *Juwanna Mann*); avant-garde and experimental work (*Overtime* and *Hour Glass*); and nonfiction modes of production (*On the Shoulders of Giants; This Is a Game, Ladies; Hoop Dreams;* and *Hoop Reality*). In both close and contextual readings of these media texts, I have worked to inflect how and where and to what degree history, sports, blackness, and cinematic-athletic stylistics disrupt static notions of race and when they buttress such dominant ideology.

Revealed in these examinations are the more transgressive devices and representational strategies that conventional and alternative sports films and media have employed to render blackness on screen in formally distinct and disruptive ways. These devices and strategies register the repertoire of diasporic traditions that emerge from Black popular culture, ones that Stuart Hall reminds us can shift the kinds of Black cultural criticism presented by scholars studying commodified and stereotypical representations of blackness in popular culture. As Hall suggests:

> However deformed, incorporated, and inauthentic are the forms in which black people and black communities and traditions appear and are represented in popular culture, we continue to see, in the figures and the repertoires on which popular culture draws, the experiences that stand behind them. In its expressivity, its musicality, its orality, in its rich, deep, and varied attention to speech, in its inflections toward the vernacular and the local, in its rich production of counternarratives, and above all, in its metaphorical use of the musical vocabulary, black popular culture has enabled the surfacing, inside the mixed and contradictory modes even of some mainstream popular culture, of elements of a discourse that is different—other forms of life, other traditions of representation.[1]

The films discussed in this book surface the contradictions and pervasive influence of recurring representations of the athletic Black body, but also, through sporting blackness and critical muscle memory, the potential for countering, contesting, and revising those portrayals. Black sports documentaries, as I have argued, use historical and social contexts, embodied authorship, and first-person narration to contest historical representations and sedimented readings of Black athletes. Arthur Agee's appearance and voice-over in *Hoop Reality*, for example, turns the former *Hoop Dreams* star into an iconoclastic historical contestant. Additionally, many of the nonfiction and fiction sports films and related media I discuss foreground Black vernacular culture where music, specifically, is used to formally rework texts in ways that unsettle racist cinematic and sporting logics. For instance, Haile Gerima deploys the subversive sounds of The Last Poets and Elaine Brown to aurally animate a counternarrative strategy in *Hour Glass*. In Big K.R.I.T.'s "Hometown Hero," Black cultural geography inflects the local and frames the milieu as both lived and sonic space. We can also make note of the ways in which Black presences on screen can reveal Black absences and traditions of representation within the genre itself. The underrepresentation of Black women in sports films, specifically, makes a brief scene in *A League of Their Own* a critical "Black w/hole" in the genre's depiction of Black female athletes. Moreover, formal innovation gives way to contextual history and radical unconventions. Aesthetic experimentation in *Overtime*'s avant-garde Black basketball hauntings vivifies sports and social history; while the experimentalist undoing of generic codes in *Hour Glass* rejects sports films "rules of the game," showing how radical aesthetics can be connected to the radical politics of Black athletes. As this cursory catalog of formal devices and representational strategies suggests, sports cinema and media's stereotypic regimes of framing Black athletes are regularly disavowed, critiqued, revised, and refused by progressive media makers and scholars attuned to the repertories of Black popular culture.

Many of these elements are rendered to powerful effect in Steven Soderbergh's basketball drama *High Flying Bird* (2019). With a narrative reminiscent of *Hour Glass*, *High Flying Bird* likewise responds to Harry Edwards's call for a revolt of the Black athlete; however, the film situates its narrative of resistance not within the world of amateur collegiate sports but squarely within the current power struggles Black athletes face in the NBA. Less interested in the typical sports film elements and tropes that make up the genre, *High Flying Bird* takes on the "game above the game," or the capitalist-driven and white-controlled business of basketball's professional league that commodifies Black male bodies for play and profit. With a screenplay by Oscar-winning screenwriter and playwright Tarell Alvin McCraney, *High Flying Bird* explores the political economy of the NBA, finding its main protagonist not in a Black athlete but in Ray (André Holland), a Black sports agent trying to help his clients weather a professional basketball lockout between the players association and the league's owners. The lockout, which privileges the obscenely wealthy white owners as they attempt to broker a television deal, has gone on for over six months and left the league's players in financial binds. This is especially so for newly drafted rookies, who have yet to be able to cash in on their athletic careers. Ray's urgency for the lockout to end is not only because his livelihood is on the line but also because his rookie client, the number one draft pick, Erick Scott (Melvin Gregg), is in dire financial straits and out of cash. At the film's outset, Ray admonishes Erick for taking a high-interest loan from a stranger he met a party who is now hounding him for repayment. While Erick hopes to receive some money to hold him over until the lockout is resolved, Ray, instead, provides him with a sealed package that he calls a "bible" and tells Erick that he should open it at the right time.

With so much on the line for himself and his clients, Ray engineers a way to end the lockout by showing that the players, specifically the Black players that make up the majority of league, could become autonomous agents and reap financial rewards by taking the game into their own hands. To successfully move players, owners, and associates as pawns in an ingenious scheme to end the stalled negotiations, Ray stages an "accidental" one-on-one game between Erick and fellow rookie teammate Jamero Umber (Justin Hurtt-Dunkley), with whom Erick has clashed on social media over who is the better player. We only catch a few seconds of their game, as the film is more interested in the higher stakes at play. This absence of game footage aligns the film's politics, where, as one critic explains, on the "basketball court, 'give me the rock' mean 'pass the ball'" but in *Highly Flying Bird* it connotes "something akin to 'the workers should seize control of the means of production.'"[2] The video of the one-on-one goes viral, and the owners are forced to reckon with the idea that they are losing control of the players and the game itself. In a press conference following the unsanctioned one-on-one game, Ray explains to the reporters in attendance and the players and owners watching: "What you all saw on your smartphones and tablets was raw. It was palpable and it was real. It was the beginning of change. Change of this game that's been played behind the game. What you saw yesterday was just a glimmer, a lightening flash of what could be the beginning of a whole new industry."

According to Ray, this player-run industry could end the "game they made over the game," where the absence of owners, player's associations, and even agents exploiting players in their prime earning years makes way for a player-controlled economy of the sport. While he tries to make Erick see his vision, Ray realizes that the future of player autonomy in the league is not currently feasible, as it would require all players to buy into the sporting socialism and sell-out the capitalist machine of the NBA. His recognition becomes most pronounced in a meeting between him and his mentor, local basketball coach, Spence (Bill Duke). In the scene, Ray stands in an empty court. There is a sign on a wall behind him of a silhouetted jumpman with the text "Rise up" plastered alongside the basketball image. The insurgent politics of the sporting and social dictum are not lost on Ray as he talks to Spence about the sustainability of all-Black basketball leagues before the integration of white professional leagues. They discuss what it meant and what it would mean to put Black people (back) in control of the game:

SPENCE: The whole game grew based on our hunger, our hunger for it.
RAY: Whoa. But you couldn't pay for it?
SPENCE: Not enough.
RAY: Man. For a second, man, I could see a whole infrastructure that put the control back in the hands of those behind the ball instead of those up in the sky box.
SPENCE: Nah. It can't sustain, man.
RAY: It never had to.
SPENCE: Don't hit me with that Ivy League talk.
RAY: Spence, man, Rutgers ain't no Ivy League.
SPENCE: Black Ivy, man. Why set it up if it's not gonna last forever?
RAY: Why make a man if only to watch him die?
SPENCE: Playin' God now?

RAY: Nah, man. I just wanted to snatch the game out they hands for a minute. I don't need it. I just wanted to hold it, for just a second. So they know . . . like I know.

For Ray, his knowing is significant and symbolic of the change he desires even if he cannot fully hold on to "the game" at the moment, especially since he is aware that many players, including Erick, are "no revolutionaries" but players who need the league and its structures even if it does not fully benefit them.

The film concludes with Ray, over the course of seventy-two hours, orchestrating the end of the lockout. A different kind of "local boy makes good" sports ending, the film's deal-making climax is presented in flashbacks that take place off the court: in offices, a sauna, and a church. The film's end, however, plays like the beginning of a new film. After explaining his actions to his soon-to-be ex-boss, Ray leaves his superior dumfounded as he makes his way to a conference room where Dr. Harry Edwards, sports sociologist and architect of the 1968 Summer Olympic Games boycott, awaits him. Ray steps into the room and the door closes to the meeting. Just as you think that this meeting of the minds is where the film ends, *High Flying Bird* holds its storied pace as the camera cuts to a tracking shot that keeps us and the narrative moving with Erick and Ray's ex-assistant Sam (Zazie Beetz) heading back to his apartment. Once there, the camera reveals that the envelope ("Chekhov's gun") from the opening scene rests on the dining table. While Erick showers, Sam opens the package and accesses its contents, revealing that it holds the fiftieth anniversary edition of Harry Edwards's *The Revolt of the Black Athlete* (figure 25). As Sam begins to read it, Erick joins her in the living room. When he questions what she is doing, Sam tells Erick he must read this book, and the film ends.

Similar to *Hour Glass, High Flying Bird* rebels against "playing the game" on sports culture's hegemonic terms through a formal rejection of sports film tropes and thus becomes an anti-sports film, even while maintaining a pro–Black athletes stance throughout. Critic Andrew Chow accurately assesses this fact in his review of the film, which is worth quoting at length:

> In the same way that Edwards worked to debunk the rosy vision of sports presented by the Olympics, McCraney and Soderbergh use *High Flying Bird* to rebel against the utopian construct of sports movies. Films like *White Men Can't Jump, Glory Road* and *The Blind Side* propagate the idea that sports can drive equality; that class and race tensions vanish while on the hardwood or gridiron through a shared determination and perseverance. *High Flying Bird*, in contrast, is far

FIGURE 25. Sam opens the sealed package to find that Harry Edwards's 50th anniversary edition of *The Revolt of the Black Athlete* is the sacred text in *High Flying Bird* (Steven Soderbergh, 2019).

more cynical. "The league is a business," Ray reprimands Erick. "Business. We are in business." While Michael Jordan won his freedom through a buzzer beater in *Space Jam*, *High Flying Bird* quashes the notion that on-court victory even matters. The film's NBA isn't a conduit for greatness but rather a cold, unfeeling corporation in which MacLachlan's snot-rocketing executive profits off of black men scraping against each other in a zero-sum game. *High Flying Bird* could be called an anti-Sports Movie: its goal is not to uplift, but rather to provoke, mobilize and envision a future in which the players themselves own the league. And in contrast to the sweeping cinematography of other sports films, *High Flying Bird* was shot on an iPhone.[3]

High Flying Bird constructs sporting blackness and critical muscle memory as awareness of the zero-sum game and its sporting, social, and economic history. The characters, specifically Spence, center the history of Black professional basketball, drawing attention to the Harlem Rens, discussed in chapter 1, who innovated the game and made it their own. As evidenced by the cameo of Dr. Edwards and the inclusion of the anniversary edition of *The Revolt of the Black Athlete*, which is figured as a sacred text of social and sporting activism, *High Flying Bird* delves into the material, symbolic, and sporting ideas of resistant Black athletes to rethink the image and impact of Black basketballers in popular culture and public consciousness in the past as well as the present. While Soderbergh's use of the iPhone provides formally distinct cinematography different from most sports films, the film's melding of fiction and nonfiction modes helps to visualize and engage suppressed narratives and voices in sports discourses. In a manner akin to the Black sports documentaries I discuss in this book, the drama includes first-person documentary interviews within the diegesis, capturing current NBA players Reggie Jackson, Karl Anthony Towns, and Donovan Mitchell discussing their rookie-year experiences on and off the court. This nonfiction element—critical muscle memories of being young, Black, and male in the NBA—provides a critical dialogic between real Black athletes and the imagined world of soliloquized agency (via rich monologues) and athletics represented on screen. Attuned to Black vernacular in speech and song, the film's use of music, particularly the protest song "High Flying Bird," for example, underscores how sonic interpolations can recode the Black athletic body within new and potentially liberating paradigms. Overall, *High Flying Bird* reminds us that the Black athlete is both embodied and an abstraction, a historical figure and force that can compel us to think about sports, culture, and history in and at play in sports films.

The convergent, recurring, and potentially subversive nature of media representations of the Black athlete requires us to consider the "fitness" of sporting blackness, meaning the theoretical conditioning possible with this moving and contested discourse and performance by, of, and between Black sporting subjects. A fit mode and motor for representational and formal analysis, sporting blackness can help us consider the stakes of representation in classic sports films such as *Spirit of Youth* (Harry L. Fraser, 1938) and *The Jackie Robinson Story* (Alfred E. Green, 1950) as well as those that populate the contemporary sports media landscape. This includes the critically acclaimed and commercially successful boxing drama *Creed* (Ryan Coogler, 2015) and its sequel *Creed II* (Steven Caple Jr., 2018), both of which follow Apollo Creed's (Carl Weathers) son Adonis (Michael B. Jordan) as he vies for the light heavyweight title. As *Rocky* spin-offs, *Creed* and *Creed II* formally shadowbox with the racial representations and histories attached to the iconic film franchise. Or we can turn our attention to Spike Lee's *Livin' Da Dream* (2015), a film-within-the-game of *NBA 2K16*, where cinematic storytelling and "computational blackness" challenge the racial and procedural logics of video games in ways similar to his fictional sports film *He Got Game* (1998).[4] With documentaries and docuseries such as *Zion* (Floyd Russ, 2018) and *Last Chance U* (2016–present) to fiction films such as *Amateur* (Ryan Koo, 2018), *First Match* (Olivia Newman, 2018), and *High Flying Bird*, the streaming giant Netflix's foray into sports-related media indicates that stories about Black athletes are in demand (and on-demand) and, thus, demanding critical attention. From mainstream fare such as *Above the Rim* (Jeff Pollack, 1994), *The Hurricane* (Norman Jewison, 1999), or *The Express* (Gary Fleder, 2008) to more experimentalist, collage, and hybrid films such as *Hale County This Morning, This Evening* (RaMell Ross, 2018),

Marshawn Lynch: A History (David Shields, 2019), and *The Fits* (Anna Rose Holmer, 2015), my interdisciplinary and multi-discursive approach is meant to provide an enduring interpretive frame for those attempting to engage with how history and aesthetics always inform the rendering of blackness on screen.

In accounting for the fitness of sporting blackness, we also must think about the capacities of critical muscle memory as an associated analytic of the athletic Black body. Throughout this book, I have addressed how critical muscle memory reveals the embodied, kinesthetic, and cinematic histories that index, circulate, and/or engender counternarratives about Black sporting and non-sporting experiences on screen and in American society. At the same time, critical muscle memory's multivalent interpretive possibilities can be mobilized to think about and through Black spectatorial affects and collective experiences. This has been the case, for instance, in my reading of Big K.R.I.T.'s hip hop spectatorship, which remixes Boobie Miles's rhetorical grandstanding in *Friday Night Lights* as a form of cultural empowerment and subject formation as well as how aesthetic memories are embodied, looped, and recursively reexperienced in Black sports documentaries such as *This Is a Game, Ladies*. Both examples evince how sports films' forms, systems, structures, and resonances hinge upon the spectacle and signifying projections and receptive possibilities of the Black athlete. Critical muscle memory's capacities to contour connections to shared or similar histories and embodied experiences on screen and beyond make it particularly useful to account for the social, cultural, political forces acting out, in, and through popular culture and the public imagination.

Finally, as I think about spectatorial affects and collective experiences, I find myself not rounding to the finish line but poised at the starting block, as I end where I began with Serena Williams, whose sporting blackness reflects and projects Black sporting excellence in ways that compel, critique, and connect. Watching her play tennis (in my case, solely on television) has been an almost singular experience of feeling connected to an individual athlete and an imagined community of people—an instantiation of my own critical muscle memory—who are so moved by the embodied and historical force, fierceness, and "power" of her play, politics, and passions on and off the court.[5] To be so affected is to both revel in and be troubled by the mediated perils and pleasures associated with and delineated by sporting blackness and critical muscle memory. And for these reasons, we must be ready to unpack the sporting and social codes, conventions, and contests one match, one body, and one image at time. This is the challenge fitness of sporting blackness.

Notes

INTRODUCTION

1. Claudia Rankine, *Citizen: An American Lyric* (Minneapolis: Graywolf Press, 2014).

2. Kelly Caldwell, "Review of *Citizen: An American Lyric*," *MAKE Literary Magazine*, February 6, 2018, www.makemag.com/review-citizen-an-american-lyric/.

3. Nicole Fleetwood, *On Racial Icons: Blackness and the Public Imagination* (New Brunswick, NJ: Rutgers University Press, 2015), 99.

4. Fleetwood, *On Racial Icons*, 99.

5. Rankine, *Citizen*, 26.

6. Rankine, *Citizen*, 25.

7. Rankine, *Citizen*, 28. In 2004, umpire Mariana Alves was dismissed from officiating the finals of the US Open after making a series of inexplicably unjust calls against Williams in her semifinal match. In her assessment of the Grand Slam match, Rankine writes: "Though no one was saying anything explicitly about Serena's body, you are not the only viewer who thought it was getting in the way of Alves's sight lines." Rankine, *Citizen*, 27. Williams, while understandably upset by the loss, took the defeat in stride. However in 2009, the familiar event replayed itself on center court. During the semifinals of the US Open, Williams was called for a mysterious foot fault (one that video playback revealed did not occur), a penalty that decided the match in her opponent's favor. Livid, Williams turned to the offending lineswoman and shouted: "I swear to God I'm fucking going to take this fucking ball and shove it down your fucking throat; you hear that? I swear to God!" She not only lost the game for this outburst, but was also fined and placed on a two-year probation by the Grand Slam Committee. Rankine describes Williams's individual actions as indicative of systemic racial problems and structures that mirror the game itself, stating: "Perhaps the committee's decision is only about context, though context is not meaning. It is a public event being watched in homes across the world. In any case, it is difficult not to think if Serena lost context by abandoning all rules of civility, it could be

because her body, trapped in a racial imaginary, trapped in disbelief—code for being black in America—is being governed not by the tennis match she is participating in but by a collapsed relationship that had promised to play by the rules. Perhaps this is how racism feels no matter the context—randomly the rules everyone else gets to play by no longer apply to you, and to call this out by calling out 'I swear to God!' is to be called insane, crass, crazy. Bad sportsmanship." Rankine, *Citizen*, 30. Rankine's reading of this past moment is especially prescient when it comes to the backlash Williams faced following her loss to Naomi Osaka at the 2018 US Open final. The tennis champion was penalized for "cheating," smashing her racket, and her outburst toward the umpire. Racist and sexist accounts of the event labeled her a poor sportswoman and sore loser.

8. Rankine, *Citizen*, 32.

9. Claudia Rankine, "The Meaning of Serena Williams: On Tennis and Black Excellence," *New York Times Magazine*, August 25, 2015, 39.

10. Rankine, "The Meaning of Serena Williams," 39.

11. Serena Williams, "Serena Unretouched and in Her Own Words," *Harper's BAZAAR*, July 9, 2019, www.harpersbazaar.com/culture/features /a28209579/serena-williams-us-open-2018-essay/?fbclid=IwAR2B3ALyUvon ygPNq2sHQhBZ9xCyAfoGp9WLamjvVLcZbmRX6exSZ1sWyfY. The fact of Serena's dominance on the court puts into critical relief the notion of Black excellence in sports where racism abounds. To this point, Claudia Rankine writes that "Serena's grace comes because she won't be forced into stillness; she won't accept those racist projections onto her body without speaking back; she won't go gently into the white light of victory. Her excellence doesn't mask the struggle it takes to achieve each win. For black people, there is an unspoken script that demands the humble absorption of racist assaults, no matter the scale, because whites need to believe that it's no big deal. But Serena refuses to keep to that script. . . . I want Serena to win, but I know better than to think her winning can end something she didn't start. But Serena is providing a new script, one in which winning doesn't carry the burden of curing racism, in which we win just to win—knowing that it is simply her excellence, baby." Rankine, "The Meaning of Serena Williams," 39.

12. Here I am thinking alongside Judith Butler's reading of how tennis player Martina Navritalova's accomplishments transformed gender ideals. Butler argues that "Martina's accomplishments became increasingly apparent and consistent, exceeding the limits of women's tennis performance, setting new standards for play, helping to spawn a whole new generation of women tennis players. Many of those women (including Conchita [Martínez], who defeated her at Wimbledon) broke barriers of gender shame in assuming a muscularity and strength that were, for women, quite anomalous." Judith Butler, "Athletic Genders: Hyperbolic Instance and/or the Overcoming of Sexual Binarism," *Stanford Humanities Review* 6, no. 2 (1998): 103–11. Serena Williams's achievements operate in a similar manner; however, the specific ways in which gender ideals/norms are bisected with race connotes significant differences between her and Navritalova's experiences on and off the court.

13. Rankine, "The Meaning of Serena Williams," 39.

14. Fleetwood, *On Racial Icons*, 100.

15. Fleetwood, *On Racial Icons*, 100.

16. Alessandra Raengo, *Critical Race Theory and "Bamboozled"* (New York: Bloomsbury, 2016), 9.

17. Henry Louis Gates Jr., "Writing 'Race' and the Difference It Makes," in *Race, Writing, and Difference*, ed. Henry Louis Gates Jr. (Chicago: University of Chicago Press, 1986), 5.

18. Daniel Bernardi, "Introduction: Race and Hollywood Style," in *Classic Hollywood, Classic Whiteness*, ed. Daniel Bernardi (Minneapolis: University of Minnesota Press, 2001), xiii.

19. See Daniel Bernardi, ed., *The Birth of Whiteness: Race and the Emergence of U.S. Cinema* (New Brunswick, NJ: Rutgers University Press, 1996); Bernardi, ed., *Classic Hollywood, Classic Whiteness*; and Daniel Bernardi, ed., *The Persistence of Whiteness: Race and Contemporary Hollywood Cinema* (New York: Routledge, 2008).

20. Daniel Bernardi, "Introduction: Race and Contemporary Hollywood Cinema," in Bernardi, ed., *The Persistence of Whiteness*, xviii.

21. The action film, for example, uses the spectacle of the muscular white male body to project an idea/ideal of the United States as an exemplary body/nation. See Yvonne Tasker, *Spectacular Bodies: Gender, Genre, and the Action Film* (New York: Routledge, 1993).

22. Drawing on Susan Courtney, Linda Williams uses the term *color-mute* to signal how "no one is blind to visible racial differences, but the practice of politely ignoring them produces a condition of muteness that often impedes the ability to deal with racial inequality." Linda Williams, "Skin Flicks on the Racial Border: Pornography, Exploitation, and Interracial Lust," in *Porn Studies*, ed. Linda Williams (Durham, NC: Duke University Press, 2004), 303.

23. American cinema and US society's Anglocentrism results in the absorption of Anglophonic Caribbean immigrants and Caribbean Americans into the sporting genealogy and cinematic canon of Black sports films. However, documentaries such as *Roberto Clemente* (Bernardo Ruiz, 1988) and *Bragging Rights: Stickball Stories* (Sonia Gonzalez-Martinez, 2006), both of which centralize Black Puerto Rican figures and cultures, are left out of even quasi-diasporic readings of Black film cultures and canons.

24. Todd Boyd and Kenneth L. Shropshire, "Basketball Jones: A New World Order?," in *Basketball Jones: America above the Rim*, ed. Todd Boyd and Kenneth L. Shropshire (New York: New York University Press, 2000), 5. African Americans make up the majority of the players in both football and basketball's professional leagues. The National Football League (NFL) is 70 percent Black. The National Basketball Association (NBA) is 74.4 percent Black. Despite these large numbers of participation, both leagues are controlled by nearly all white ownership, management, and coaching staffs. Notwithstanding this lack of control of the sport, we cannot underestimate the impact Black athletes have had, post-integration, on the sports of football and basketball. Black sporting

excellence has shaped the style of play and popularity of both games in contemporary public imagination. For more on the time when baseball was the Black sports pastime, see Gerald Early, "Why Baseball Was the Black National Pastime," in Boyd and Shropshire, *Basketball Jones: America above the Rim*, 27–50. For more on African Americans and the boxing film, see Aaron Baker, *Contesting Identities: Sports in American Film* (Urbana: University of Illinois Press, 2003), 100–140. For more on the impact of Black athletes on football and basketball, see Charles K. Ross, *Outside the Lines: African Americans and the Integration of the National Football League* (New York: New York University Press, 2001); Charles K. Ross, *Mavericks, Money, and Men: The AFL, Black Players, and the Evolution of Modern Football* (Philadelphia: Temple University Press, 2016); and Howard Bryant, *The Heritage: Black Athletes, A Divided America, and the Politics of Patriotism* (Boston: Beacon Press, 2018).

25. My focus on basketball and football films is not meant to suggest that there are not significant Black films about other sports that can be studied in terms of sporting blackness and critical muscle memory. There are numerous films that could be analyzed (that this book's focused scope cannot discuss at length), including stories about baseball (e.g., *The Jackie Robinson Story*, *Soul of the Game*, *The Bingo Long Traveling All-Stars & Motor Kings*, and *42*); boxing (e.g., Jack Johnson's fight pictures, *Spirit of Youth*, *Keep Punching*, *The Greatest*, *Penitentiary*, *The Hurricane*, *Ali*, *Against the Ropes*, *Creed*, and *Creed II*); swimming (*Pride*); gymnastics (*The Gabby Douglas Story* and *The Simone Biles Story: Courage to Soar*); and track and field (*Race*), among other sports. The contemporary bent of my project means that sports traditionally privileged as sites of Black participation, excellence, and advancement (such as baseball and boxing) no longer fully dominate the cultural production of contemporary sports films as much as basketball- and football-themed works (though boxing films may be an important exception here).

26. In describing the genre's definition as "loose," I am drawing on Glen Jones's ambivalent categorical analysis of the sports film. Glen Jones, "In Praise of an 'Invisible Genre'? An Ambivalent Look at the Fictional Sports Feature Film," *Sport in Society* 11, no. 2 (2008): 117–29. For examples of scholarship engaged with race and ethnicity in genre criticism, see George Lipsitz, "Genre Anxiety and Racial Representation in 1970s Cinema," in *Refiguring American Film Genres*, ed. Nick Browne (Berkley: University of California Press, 1998), 208–32; Mark A. Reid, "The Black Gangster Film," in *Film Genre Reader III*, ed. Barry Keith Grant (Austin: University of Texas Press, 2005), 472–89; Nick Browne, "Race: The Political Unconscious in American Film," *East-West Film Journal* 6, no. 1 (January 1992): 5–16; Michael Boyce Gillespie, *Film Blackness: American Cinema and the Idea of Black Film* (Durham: Duke University Press, 2016), 83–118; and Robin Means Coleman, *Horror Noire: Blacks in American Horror Films from the 1890s to Present* (New York: Routledge, 2011).

27. Linda Williams, "Film Bodies: Gender, Genre, and Excess," *Film Quarterly* 44, no. 4 (Summer 1991): 2–13. Williams argues that "the bodies of women figured on the screen have functioned traditionally as the primary

embodiments of pleasure, fear, and pain," where gratuitous excess is represented by "the spectacle of the body caught in the grip of intense sensation or emotion" (4). I return to Williams's ideas of spectatorial excess in the conclusion's gesture toward critical muscle memory's spectatorial affects.

28. Harvey Young, *Embodying Black Experience: Stillness, Critical Memory, and the Black Body* (Ann Arbor: University of Michigan Press, 2010), 7.

29. Young, *Embodying Black Experience*, 10.

30. Frantz Fanon, *Black Skin, White Masks*, 1952, trans. Richard Philcox (New York: Grove Press, 2008).

31. My thoughts on sports films' blackness is inspired by Jason King's framing of blackness in literal and abstract terms of diasporic Black people's improvisational movement—mobility, immobility, direction, indirection, reorientation, disorientation. See Jason King, "Which Way Is Down? Improvisations on Black Mobility," *Women & Performance: A Journal of Feminist Theory* 14, no. 1 (2004), 28.

32. For example, the Jamaican bobsled comedy *Cool Runnings* (Jon Turteltaub, 1993) ends in a dignified loss for its Black competitors, including a "slow clap" started by one of the racist antagonists in the film that builds to a raucous round of applause, drawing tears (or eye-rolls) from viewers. This melodramatic scene and its revisionist history is maddening in its ability to emotionally move me every time I see it!

33. James Snead, *White Screens, Black Images: Hollywood from the Dark Side*, ed. Colin MacCabe and Cornel West (New York: Routledge, 1994), 8.

34. C. Richard King and David J. Leonard, "Why Sports Films Matter; or, Refusing a Happy Ending," in *Visual Economies of/in Motion: Sport and Film*, ed. C. Richard King and David J. Leonard (New York: Peter Lang, 2006), 228.

35. Samantha N. Sheppard, "Give and Go: The Double Movement of Shut Up and Dribble," *Los Angeles Review of Books*, February 12, 2019, www.lareviewofbooks.org/article/give-go-double-movement-shut-dribble/?fbclid=IwAR1LXURjKZPcuN2D2LCVffyze5kyCRcAdVymfoxoUKd-jnTYjolUWSpDFgs.

36. Baker, *Contesting Identities*, 2.

37. Linda Williams, *Playing the Race Card: Melodramas of Black and White from Uncle Tom to O.J. Simpson* (Princeton, NJ: Princeton University Press, 2001), 276.

38. A.O. Scott, "How the Goal Line Came to Replace the Color Line," *New York Times*, September 29, 2000, E00010. *The Blind Side* works through the Foucauldian idea that the Black body is docile, raw material that can be disciplined, manipulated, and used by white people for their needs. Michel Foucault, *Discipline & Punish: The Birth of the Prison* (New York: Vintage Books, 1995), 137. In a conversation with Michael Gillespie many years ago, he called *The Blind Side* an example of "Black Frankenstein Cinema," where white people create Black beasts. *The Blind Side* does exactly that but also teaches the viewer how to "tame" the beast as well. In *Remember The Titans*, the Titans' victories on the field are representative of their off-the-field victories, particularly their ability to break down racial barriers among each other and, by extension,

within their divided community. The film represents the field as a site for cultural conflict to be both played out and overcome. In sports films, the field is a privileged space, "often conceptualized as a separate, unconnected area in which athletic contests play themselves out in isolation from culture and history." Deborah Tudor, *Hollywood's Vision of Team Sports: Heroes, Race, and Gender* (New York: Garland Publishing, 1997), xxii–xxiii. *Remember the Titans* uses the field to not only connect to race issues but also to overcome racial issues.

39. Snead, *White Screens, Black Images*, 2.

40. Michael Rogin, *Black Face, White Noise: Jewish Immigrants in the Hollywood Melting Pot* (Berkley: University of California Press, 1996), 14.

41. Dan Streible, "Race and the Reception of Jack Johnson Fight Films," in *The Birth of Whiteness: Race and the Emergence of U.S. Cinema*, ed. Daniel Bernardi (New Brunswick, NJ: Rutgers University Press, 1996), 170.

42. Dan Streible, *Fight Pictures: A History of Boxing and Early Cinema* (Berkley: University of California Press, 2008), 195.

43. Ben Carrington, *Race, Sport and Politics: The Sporting Black Diaspora* (Los Angeles: Sage Publications, 2010), 85. His emphasis.

44. See Charlene Regester, "From the Gridiron and the Boxing Ring to the Cinema Screen: The African-American Athlete in pre-1950 Cinema," *Culture, Sport, Society: Cultures, Commerce, Media, Politics* 6 nos. 2–3 (2003): 270.

45. Stuart Hall, "What Is This 'Black' in Black Popular Culture," in *Black Popular Culture: A Project by Michele Wallace*, ed. Gina Dent (Seattle, WA: Bay Press, 1992), 27.

46. Carrington, *Race, Sport and Politics*, 67.

47. Carrington, *Race, Sport and Politics*, 85. His emphasis.

48. *Oxford English Dictionary*, s.v. "kinetics," www.oed.com.

49. Gretchen Reynolds, "How Exercise Can Help You Master New Skills," *New York Times*, September 26, 2012, www.well.blogs.nytimes.com/2012/09/26/how-exercise-can-help-you-master-new-skills/.

50. Qiang Liu and Erik Jorgensen, "Muscle Memory," *Journal of Physiology* 589, no. 4 (2011): 775–76.

51. Curtis L. Carter, "Arts and Cognition: Performance, Criticism, and Aesthetics," *Art Education* 33, no. 62 (1983): 61–67.

52. C.L.R. James, *Beyond a Boundary* (Durham, NC: Duke University Press, 1993), 196, 199.

53. James, *Beyond a Boundary*, 206–7.

54. Michelle Ann Stephens, *Skin Acts: Race, Psychoanalysis, and the Black Male Performer* (Durham, NC: Duke University Press, 2014), 80–85.

55. Frantz Fanon, *The Wretched of the Earth*, trans. Richard Philcox (New York: Grove Press, 2004), 17 and Darieck Scott, *Extravagant Abjection: Blackness, Power, and Sexuality in the African American Literary Imagination* (New York: New York University Press, 2010), 90.

56. Elizabeth Alexander, "'Can You Be BLACK and Look at This?' Reading the Rodney King Video(s)," *Public Culture* 7 (1994), 83. Elizabeth Alexander

explains that for many Black writers, including Audre Lorde, Toni Morrison, Bebe Moore Campbell, Gwendolyn Brooks, Anne Moody, Charlayne Hunter-Gault, and Shelby Steele, Emmett Till's body/story "was the basis for a rite of passage that indoctrinated these young people into understanding the vulnerability of their own black bodies, coming of age, and the way in which their fate was interchangeable with Till's" (87–88). Drawing on a passage from Muhammad Ali's autobiography *The Greatest*, Alexander calls attention to how the image of Till's murder was "a formative touchstone" that produced a "deep kinship" for Ali with Till, shaping Ali's "relationship between him and state power" (90). See Muhammad Ali with Richard Durham, *The Greatest: My Own Story* (New York: Random House, 1975): 34–35.

57. Young, *Embodying Black Experience*, 9. Harvey Young is drawing on Houston Baker's notion of critical memory as the capacity to think about the past and the agency of Black memory as a social, intellectual, and political site of struggle. See Houston A. Baker Jr., *Critical Memory: Public Spheres, African American Writing, and Black Fathers and Sons in America* (Athens: University of Georgia Press, 2001). In addition to Young's study of Black sports figures, Jamie Schultz's study of Black football players Jack Trice, Ozzie Simmons, and Johnny Bright provides a compelling history on racialized memory in sports. See Jaime Schultz, *Moments of Impact: Injury, Racialized Memory, and Reconciliation* (Lincoln: University of Nebraska Press, 2016).

58. Young, *Embodying Black Experience*, 6.

59. Young, *Embodying Black Experience*, 4.

60. Young, *Embodying Black Experience*, 4.

61. Young, *Embodying Black Experience*, 19.

62. Thank you to Alicia Imperiale for asking me "how deep is the color" when workshopping an early draft of this introduction.

63. Grant Farred, "When Kings Were (Anti-?)Colonials: Black Athletes in Film," *Sport in Society* 11, nos. 2–3 (March 2008): 242.

64. Farred, "When Kings Were (Anti-?)Colonials," 242.

65. I am drawing on Jennifer Doyle's invocation of the "athletic turn" from her forthcoming book *The Athletic Turn: Contemporary Art and the Sport Spectacle*. Some Black visual artists who have taken the "athletic turn have appropriated sports cinema into their artistic work to grapple with sports practices, cultural production, and the public imaginary. For example, this book's cover artist, Esmaa Mohamoud, in her installations *Heavy, Heavy (Hoop Dreams)* (2016) and *Glorious Bones*, references the films *Hoop Dreams* (Steve James, 1994) and *Remember the Titans* (Boaz Yakin, 2000). "Heavy, Heavy (Hoop Dreams)" is an installation of sixty solid concrete basketballs in various states of deflation that weigh thirty pounds each. The work references *Hoop Dreams*'s documentary protagonists' deflated dreams of making it to the NBA. I discuss *Hoop Dreams* in greater detail in chapter 1. "Glorious Bones" consists of forty-six mounted football helmets covered in African wax print. Surrounding the display is vinyl text printed on the gallery walls quoting the Disney football drama *Remember the Titans*. The quote is from Herman Boone

(played by Denzel Washington), who invokes the Battle of Gettysburg as a means to inspire brotherhood/racial harmony on his team on and off the gridiron. As football is often described as a battlefield, in the context of Mohamoud's installation, the text's war address comes into spatial contact and ideological conflict with the embellished helmets as the histories of racial violence against Black bodies in the NFL and beyond are portended in the space.

66. See Hank Willis Thomas, *Pitch Blackness* (New York: Aperture, 2008).

67. Richard Klein, *Hank Willis Thomas: Strange Fruit* (exhibition catalog) (Ridgefield, CT: The Aldrich Contemporary Art Museum, 2012), 6.

68. I was deeply moved by Alexis Pauline Gumbs's poetic description of the happening and unhappening of Black physical and metaphysical lifeworlds. See Alexis Pauline Gumbs, "Black Astrophysics: A Homemade Field of Love," in *We Travel the Space Ways: Black Imagination, Fragments, and Diffractions*, ed. Henriette Gunkel and kara lynch (New York: Transcript-Verlag, 2019), 15–20.

69. Klein, *Hank Willis Thomas*, 6.

70. See Tisa Bryant, *Unexplained Presence* (Providence, RI: Leon Works, 2007).

71. Billie Holiday, "Strange Fruit" (Commodore, Records April 20, 1939), 78 rpm.

72. Alessandra Raegno, *On the Sleeve of the Visual: Race as Face Value* (Hanover, NH: Dartmouth College Press, 2013), 116.

73. Young, *Embodying Black Experience*, 11.

74. Richard Klein draws connections to painters such as Michelangelo Merisi da Caravaggio and Francisco de Zurbarán, who used darkness and featureless voids to isolate and accentuate the theatricality of individuals and images. Klein, *Hank Willis Thomas*, 5–6.

75. Toni Morrison, *Playing in the Dark: Whiteness and the Literary Imagination* (Cambridge, MA: Harvard University Press, 1992).

76. Gumbs, "Black Astrophysics," 20.

77. Joshua Malitsky, "Knowing Sports: The Logic of the Contemporary Sports Documentary," *Journal of Sport History* 41, no. 2 (Summer 2014), 208.

78. Klein, *Hank Willis Thomas*, 5.

79. Baker, *Contesting Identities*, 24.

80. Baker, *Contesting Identities*, 24–27.

81. Regester, "From the Gridiron and the Boxing Ring to the Cinema Screen," 289.

82. The recurring casting of the same Black actor across a spectrum of sports films (as seen, for example, with actor Rob Brown, who goes from starring as high school basketball player Jamal Wallace in *Finding Forrester* [Gus Van Sant, 2000] to high school basketball player Kenyon Stone in *Coach Carter* [Thomas Carter, 2005] to collegiate football legend Ernie Davis in *The Express* [Gary Fleder, 2008]) suggests not only an industrial typecasting (and the limited roles available to Black actors) but also the ways in which the Black body is by default associated with athleticism. White actors are also cast on "type," and as Lester Friedman notes, Kevin Costner is the actor most associated with sports films,

having starred in ten sports films. The difference between this kind of typecasting is that Costner and other white actors are also afforded roles outside of the genre. Many of these Black actors, especially young Black male actors, play athletes (and/or criminals in police procedurals) without much variation from these two types. See Lester D. Friedman, *Sports Movies* (New Brunswick, NJ: Rutgers University Press, 2020), 24–26.

83. Jennifer Doyle, "Dirt off Her Shoulders," *GLQ: A Journal of Lesbian and Gay Studies* 13, no. 4 (2013), 420.

1. HISTORICAL CONTESTANTS IN BLACK SPORTS DOCUMENTARIES

1. Ben Carrington, *Race, Sport and Politics: The Sporting Black Diaspora* (Thousand Oaks, CA: Sage Publications, 2010), 5.

2. Nicole Fleetwood, *On Racial Icons: Blackness and the Public Imagination* (New Brunswick, NJ: Rutgers University Press, 2015), 84.

3. Joshua Malitsky, "Knowing Sports: The Logic of the Contemporary Sports Documentary," *Journal of Sport History* 41, no. 2 (Summer 2014), 211–12.

4. Vivian Sobchack, "Introduction: History Happens," in *The Persistence of History: Cinema, Television, and the Modern Event*, ed. Vivian Sobchack (New York: Routledge, 1996), 4. Malitsky, "*Knowing Sports*," 212.

5. Travis Vogan, "Institutionalizing and Industrializing Sport History in the Contemporary Sports Television Documentary," *Journal of Sport History* 41, no 2 (Summer 2014), 196.

6. Stuart Hall, "What Is This 'Black' in Black Popular Culture," in *Black Popular Culture: A Project by Michele Wallace*, ed. Gina Dent (Seattle, WA: Bay Press, 1992), 26.

7. Hall, "What Is This 'Black' in Black Popular Culture," 30.

8. Carrington, *Race, Sport and Politics*, 12.

9. Carrington, *Race, Sport and Politics*, 27 and 66. His emphasis.

10. Bill Nichols, *Representing Reality* (Bloomington: Indiana University Press, 1991), ix–x.

11. Nichols, *Representing Reality*, ix.

12. Nichols, *Representing Reality*, 3.

13. Nichols, *Representing Reality*, x.

14. Janet K. Cutler and Phyllis R. Klotman, "Introduction," in *Struggles for Representation: African American Documentary Film and Video*, ed. Phyllis R. Klotman and Janet K. Cutler (Bloomington: Indiana University Press, 1999), xix.

15. Cutler and Klotman, "Introduction," xv.

16. Clyde Taylor, "Paths of Enlightenment: Heroes, Rebels, and Thinkers," in *Struggles for Representation: African American Documentary Film and Video*, eds. Phyllis R. Klotman and Janet K. Cutler (Bloomington: Indiana University Press, 1999), 124.

17. Taylor, "Paths of Enlightenment," xiii.

18. Matt Richardson, "Our Stories Have Never Been Told: Preliminary Thoughts on Black Lesbian Cultural Production as Historiography in *The Watermelon Woman*," *Black Camera* 2, no. 2 (Spring 2011), 102.

19. Norbert Elias and Eric Dunning, *Quest for Excitement: Sport and Leisure in the Civilizing Process* (Oxford: Basil Blackwell, 1986).

20. Vogan, "Institutionalizing and Industrializing Sport History in the Contemporary Sports Television Documentary," 196.

21. As I have explained elsewhere, "A range of films about a variety of sports have been produced under the *30 for 30* banner, and many of them deal explicitly with Black sporting figures and histories, including, among others, Kirk Fraser's *Without Bias* (2009), Dan Klores' *Winning Time: Reggie Miller vs. The New York Knicks* (2010), Ice Cube's *Straight Outta L.A.* (2010), and Jonathan Hock's *The Best That Never Was* (2010). Since its initial launch in 2009, the *30 for 30* series has produced two additional volumes, shorts (*30 for 30* Shorts), spin-offs (*Soccer Stories*), and the *30 for 30* Podcast. While the series has won both a Peabody and an Emmy Award, Ezra Edelman's captivating mini-series *O. J.: Made in America* (2016), which was produced for *30 for 30*, cemented the series' critical acclaim and cultural relevance after winning the 2016 Academy Award for Best Documentary Feature." See Samantha N. Sheppard, "The Exception That Proves the Rule: Race, Place, and Meritocracy in *Rand University*," *Black Camera* 10, no. 1 (Fall 2018), 167–68. In addition to *30 for 30*, ESPN's *Nine for IX* documentary series and *Nine for IX* short documentaries focus on women in sports and are all directed by women.

22. Michael Renov states that documentary's function is to record, reveal or preserve; to persuade and promote; to analyze or interrogate; and to express. See Michael Renov, "Towards a Poetics of Documentary," in *Theorizing Documentary*, ed. Michael Renov (New York: Routledge, 1993), 12–36. Bill Nichols's six documentary modes include: poetic, expository, observational, participatory, reflexive, and performative. Nichols, *Representing Reality*, 32–75. Ian McDonald uses Nichols's classification to situate the sports documentary within a cinematic documentary tradition. See Ian McDonald, "Situating the Sport Documentary," *Journal of Sport & Social Issues* 31, no 3 (August 2007), 211–14.

23. McDonald, "Situating the Sport Documentary," 216.

24. Vogan, "Institutionalizing and Industrializing Sport History in the Contemporary Sports Television Documentary," 196.

25. Malitsky, "Knowing Sports," 206.

26. McDonald, "Situating the Sport Documentary," 208.

27. Michael Boyce Gillespie, *Film Blackness: American Cinema and the Idea of Black Film* (Durham, NC: Duke University Press, 2016), 16.

28. David J. Leonard describes the racial landscape in the NBA following the 2004 "Palace Brawl" between former Pistons player Ron Artest (currently known as Metta World Peace), Ben Wallace, and Pistons fans as the "after Artest" moment. Leonard explains that there was an "assault on blackness" during this

period that "mandated the transformation of NBA policy regarding the governance of black bodies." David J. Leonard, *After Artest: The NBA and the Assault on Blackness* (Albany: State University of New York Press, 2012), 3.

29. Kareem Abdul-Jabbar with Raymond Obstfeld, *On the Shoulders of Giants: My Journey through the Harlem Renaissance* (New York: Simon & Schuster, 2007).

30. Jay Caspian Kang, "What the World Got Wrong about Kareem Abdul-Jabbar," *New York Times Magazine*, September 17, 2015, 57.

31. Abdul Jabbar, *On the Shoulders of Giants*, 5–6.

32. Abdul Jabbar, *On the Shoulders of Giants*, 180–81.

33. Abdul Jabbar, *On the Shoulders of Giants*, 180.

34. Abdul Jabbar, *On the Shoulders of Giants*, 180.

35. Abdul Jabbar, *On the Shoulders of Giants*, 5.

36. Abdul Jabbar, *On the Shoulders of Giants*, 183.

37. Janet K. Cutler, "Rewritten on Film: Documenting the Artist," in *Struggles for Representation: African American Documentary Film and Video*, eds. Phyllis R. Klotman and Janet K. Cutler (Bloomington: Indiana University Press, 1999), 154.

38. Ava Rose and James Friedman, "Television Sports as Mas(s)culine Cult of Distraction," in *Out of Bounds: Sports, Media, and the Politics of Identity*, ed. Aaron Baker and Todd Boyd (Bloomington: Indiana University Press, 1997), 5.

39. While the book is coauthored by Raymond Obstfeld and the documentary directed by Abdul-Jabbar's longtime manager, Deborah Morales, it is Abdul-Jabbar's "personal as political" narrative framing of the Rens that structures both texts.

40. Klotman and Cutler, "Introduction," xxvi.

41. Valerie Smith, "The Documentary Impulse in Contemporary African-American Film," in *Black Popular Culture: A Project by Michele Wallace*, ed. Gina Dent (Seattle, WA: Bay Press, 1992), 61. As examples, Valerie Smith draws attention to Camille Billops and James V. Hatch's *Suzanne, Suzanne* (1982) and *Finding Christa* (1991); Marlon T. Rigg's *Tongues Untied* (1989) and *Color Adjustment* (1992); and Marco Williams's *In Search of Our Fathers* (1992). All of these documentaries experiment with artificiality and dramatic intensification, using combinations of reenactment, scripting, staging, performance pieces, televisual images, pantomime, fantasy, and composition "to defamiliarize assumptions about family, sexuality, gender, race, and identity" (62).

42. Ramin Zahed, "Calabash Animates *On Shoulders of Giants*," *Animation Magazine*, May 9, 2011, www.animationmagazine.net/features/calabash-animates-on-shoulders-of-giants/?doing_wp_cron=1464185400.71882295608520 50781250.

43. Klotman and Cutler, "Introduction," xxvi.

44. Renov, "Towards a Poetics of Documentary," 26.

45. Cutler, "Rewritten on Film," 152.

46. Susan Leigh Foster, "Choreographing History," in *Choreographing History*, ed. Susan Leigh Foster (Bloomington: Indiana University Press, 1995), 8.

47. Gwendolyn DuBois Shaw, *Seeing the Unspeakable: The Art of Kara Walker* (Durham, NC: Duke University Press, 2004), 6.

48. Thelma Golden, "My Brother," in *Black Male: Representations of Masculinity in Contemporary Art*, ed. Thelma Golden (New York: Whitney Museum of Art, 1994), 19.

49. The history behind the lynching images in *On the Shoulders of Giants* are detailed in James Allen's *Without Sanctuary: Lynching Photography in America* (Santa Fe, NM: Twins Palm Publishers, 2000). For more on the horrors of lynching that the film's imagery details, see Ida B. Wells-Barnett. "Southern Horrors: Lynch Law in All its Phases," in *Southern Horrors and Other Writings: The Anti-Lynching Campaign of Ida B. Wells, 1892–1900*, ed. Jacqueline Jones Royster (Boston: Bedford, 1997): 49–72; and Courtney R. Baker, *Humane Insight: Looking at Images of African American Suffering and Death* (Urbana: University of Illinois Press, 2015). The image of the noose resonates across a variety of sports films discussed in this book, including the introduction's analysis of *Overtime* and chapter 4's analysis of *Hour Glass*.

50. Amy Louise Wood, *Lynching and Spectacle: Witnessing Racial Violence in America, 1890–1940* (Chapel Hill, NC: University of North Carolina Press, 2009), 2.

51. Fleetwood, *On Racial Icons*, 110.

52. Taylor, "Paths of Enlightenment," 147. Clyde Taylor explains that "PBS-ification " describes what happens to Black documentaries made within and for the PBS system. According to Taylor, the "PBS documentary style imposed on black subjects comes across like the Negro spirituals sung after getting a college education and classical training" (143).

53. "The Filming," PBS, www.pbs.org/thisisagame/about/filming.htm.

54. "The Filming."

55. Aaron Baker discusses the genre hybrid of melodrama and the sports film in his treatment on the Black sports documentary *Venus Vs.* (Ava Duvernay, 2013). See Aaron Baker, "Intersectionality in *Venus Vs.*" in *Sporting Realities: Critical Readings on the Sports Documentary*, ed. Samantha N. Sheppard and Travis T. Vogan (Lincoln: University of Nebraska Press, 2020). Thank you, Aaron, for encouraging me to work with and through your ideas here.

56. In chapter 3 I discuss the marginalization of women's participation in sports, a consequence of the history of derision, sexism, and struggles against patriarchal control over women's bodies.

57. Susan K. Cahn, *Coming on Strong: Gender and Sexuality in Twentieth-Century Women's Sports* (New York: The Free Press, 1994), 83.

58. According to a 2013 study by Cheryl Cooky, Michael A. Messner, and Robin H. Hextrum, sports media has focused less than 10 percent of its coverage on women's sports despite the increase in participation of girls and women at all sporting levels. See Cheryl Cooky, Michael A. Messner, and Robin H.

Hextrum, "Women Play Sports, But Not on TV: A Longitudinal Study of Televised News Media," *Communication & Sport* 1, no. 3 (2013): 203–30.

59. Klotman and Cutler, "Introduction," xvii.

60. C. Vivian Stringer with Laura Tucker, *Standing Tall: A Memoir of Tragedy and Triumph* (New York: Three Rivers Press, 2008), 238.

61. Baker, "Intersectionality in *Venus Vs.*"

62. Clyde Taylor assesses many of these PBS (and the like) Black biographical documentaries. See Taylor, "Paths of Enlightenment," 122–50.

63. For more on television and domesticity, see Lynn Spiegel, *Make Room for TV: Television and the Family Ideal in Postwar America* (Chicago: University of Chicago Press, 1992). My analysis here of the scene where Stringer watches herself connects to my analysis in chapter 2 of the scene of Boobie Miles's injury in *Friday Night Lights* (Peter Berg, 2004), where the real-life Boobie in a cameo role watches his tragic fate replayed for him by actor Derek Luke.

64. The one profiled white player is Christina Fowler, the daughter of a pastor and the team's best outside shooter. Fowler had to redshirt the season due to multiple concussions. The following season, Fowler injured her back in practice, ending her college basketball playing career.

65. In her memoir, Stringer claims the title does not make sense to her, writing: "I still don't understand the title; as every one of my players can testify, what I'm known for saying is, 'It's *more* than a game, ladies.' For me, basketball is a way to address some of the bigger issues in life, a vehicle for me to take young girls and help them to become young women—women who will go on to become accomplished leaders. I think you see that very clearly in the documentary. If it were just a game, why would I call my team out for their apathy, lack of heart, and lackluster performance after a win with a margin in the double digits." Stringer, *Standing Tall*, 238.

66. While being a "lady" in Schnall's documentary is meant positively, the sporting connotation is often negatively associated with "playing like a girl," a concept I examine at greater length in my discussion of women's sports films in chapter 3.

67. Cahn, *Coming on Strong*, 127.

68. Cahn, *Coming on Strong*, 127–28.

69. Cahn, *Coming on Strong*, 118.

70. Evelyn Brooks Higginbotham, *Righteous Discontent: The Women's Movement in the Black Baptist Church, 1880–1920* (Cambridge, MA: Harvard University Press, 1993), 15.

71. Taylor, "Paths of Enlightenment," 147.

72. Taylor, "Paths of Enlightenment," 139.

73. Taylor, "Paths of Enlightenment," 148, 137.

74. Harvey Young, *Embodying Black Experience: Stillness, Critical Memory, and the Black Body* (Ann Arbor: University of Michigan Press, 2010), 21.

75. Stringer spoke for thirty-six minutes at the press conference followed by two players, one Black and one white. Eight out of the ten players on the Rutgers women's basketball team at the time were Black. In addition to the

press conference, there was widespread media coverage from various print and televised news outlets, giving way to national conversations about free speech and racism. The players also appeared via video on *The Oprah Winfrey Show*. The 2007 incident with Imus has followed Stringer and the team's reputation, much to Stringer's chagrin but also to her benefit. As Harvey Araton explains, Stringer was in the process of contract renegotiations with Rutgers when the incident occurred. In a profile of her, Araton notes: "Now Stringer's base pay of $450,000, more than doubled, equals that of the Rutgers's football savior, Greg Schiano. Now her compelling life story, still lacking a national championship, has a defining moment—thanks to the radio shock jock Don Imus, who couldn't let Stringer and her players enjoy their moment of celebrity and success. With his crude remarks, Imus unwittingly made Rutgers the most prominent team and Stringer the most recognizable coach in the women's game." Harvey Araton, "Dues Paid, Stringer Is Realizing Rewards," *New York Times*, April 26, 2007, D1.

76. Young, *Embodying Black Experience*, 21. His emphasis

77. Young, *Embodying Black Experience*, 21.

78. An image of Rutgers's Black women's basketball players at the 2007 conference is included in Claudia Rankine's *Citizen: An American Lyric*. Rankine juxtaposes the photo with a prose description of herself running late to meet a friend in Santa Monica and being called a nappy-headed ho. See Claudia Rankine, *Citizen: An American Lyric* (Minneapolis: Greywolf Press, 2014), 41.

79. Moya Bailey and Trudy, "On Misogynoir: Citation, Erasure, and Plagiarism," *Feminist Media Studies* 18, no. 4 (2018), 762.

80. Examples of the prospect sports documentary include *Through the Fire* (Alistair Christopher and Jonathan Hock, 2005), *More Than a Game* (Kristopher Belman, 2009) as well as docuseries such as *Last Chance U* (Netflix, 2016–present).

81. The filmmakers did produce a short film, *Higher Goals* (1993), to help raise money for *Hoop Dreams*'s production. Steve James recalls that they shot five days of the summer going into Gates's and Agee's freshman year, seven days during freshman year, ten days sophomore year, and forty days during junior year. Once they had funding from a MacArthur Grant, they shot one hundred days between the summer of junior year and the film's end. See Jason Guerrasio, "Hoop Dreams: An Oral History," *The Dissolve*, January 15, 2014, www.thedissolve.com/features/oral-history/360-an-oral-history-of-hoop-dreams-20-years-after-its-/?page=13.

82. *Hoop Dreams* was infamously snubbed in the Oscar's Best Documentary category but was nominated for its editing.

83. Cheryl L. Cole and Samantha King, "Representing Black Masculinity and Urban Possibilities: Racism, Realism, and *Hoop Dreams*," in *Sport and Postmodern Times*, ed. Geneviève Rail (Albany: State University of New York Press, 1998), 71.

84. Gates was perhaps the closest to achieving his "hoop dreams." In 2001, Guerrasio explains, "Gates was invited to try out with the NBA's Washington

Wizards through the pushing of Michael Jordan, who had come out of retirement to play for the team. Gates's comeback was halted when he injured his foot. Shortly after, Gates got the news that his brother Curtis was murdered." Guerrasio, "Hoop Dreams."

85. Cole and King, "Representing Black Masculinity and Urban Possibilities," 64. Roger Ebert lauded the film, writing: "A film like *Hoop Dreams* is what the movies are for. It takes us, shakes us, and make us think in new ways about the world around us. It gives us the impression of having touched life itself.... Many filmgoers are reluctant to see documentaries, for reasons I've never understood; the good ones are frequently more absorbing and entertaining than fiction. *Hoop Dreams*, however, is not only a documentary. It is also poetry and prose, muckraking and expose, journalism and polemic. It is one of the great moviegoing experiences of my lifetime." Roger Ebert, "*Hoop Dreams*," Roger Ebert.com, October 21, 1994, www.rogerebert.com /reviews/hoop-dreams-1994.

86. bell hooks, "Neo-colonial Fantasies of Conquest: Hoop Dreams," in *Reel to Real: Race, Class, and Sex at the Movies* (New York: Routledge, 1996), 78.

87. hooks, "Neo-colonial Fantasies of Conquest," 78.

88. Guerrasio, "*Hoop Dreams*."

89. Guerrasio, "*Hoop Dreams*."

90. William Gates has shied away from the spotlight after *Hoop Dreams*. He did not participate in the 2014 oral history of the film, which included the filmmakers, producers, and Agee. This absence is not all too surprising, in part, because Gates kept his personal life somewhat hidden from the filmmakers throughout the film. For example, they found out Gates had a child with his girlfriend Catherine well after the child had been born. James recalls: "So I talked to William after that on the phone, and he goes, 'Yeah.' And I wasn't pissed off, I was just surprised, and I asked, 'Why haven't we met Catherine?' He said, 'I didn't want to tell you guys, because I felt like for the film, I'd come off like I'm just another black teenage kid having babies out of wedlock, and that whole thing that people look down on.' So I asked him what his plan was, if he was going to marry Catherine. And he said yes. I told him, 'You guys are actually defying the stereotype, and that's something that should be in the film.' I don't remember if he agreed to it then, but obviously he agreed." Guerrasio, "*Hoop Dreams*."

91. hooks, "Neo-colonial Fantasies of Conquest," 81.

92. hooks, "Neo-colonial Fantasies of Conquest," 82.

93. hooks, "Neo-colonial Fantasies of Conquest," 81. Unlike Gates, Agee never shied away from the media or basketball's spotlight. Agee attempted a professional career on the court and on the big screen, including playing semi-professionally after college and booking roles in *Passing Glory* (Steve James, 1999), commercials, and a cameo in Spike Lee's *He Got Game* (1998).

94. Nichols, *Representing Reality*, 35.

95. Scoop Jackson, "'Hoop Reality' Gets Dream Postscript," ESPN, July 2, 2009, www.espn.com/chicago/columns/story?columnist=jackson_scoop&id=43

00069. The fact that Patrick Beverly finds success in the NBA does not affirm the "hoop dreams" ideology. Most of the effort (the labor, play, etc.) to get there takes place out of frame, requiring the filmmakers of *Hoop Reality* to tack on an affirmative ending. While Beverly has become a formidable player in the professional league, *Hoop Reality* reminds us that there is always this sense of contingency, possibility, and statistical probability that Beverly's "hoop dreams" could end at any time.

96. hooks, "Neo-colonial Fantasies of Conquest," 79.

97. Jared Sexton, "Black Box," *Docalogue*, January 2019, www.docalogue .com/january-minding-the-gap/.

98. Young, *Embodying Black Experience*, 19–20.

99. Cutler and Klotman, "Introduction," xvii.

100. Susan Foster, "Choreographies of Protest," *Theatre Journal* 55, no. 3 (October 2003), 395.

101. Cutler, "Rewritten on Film," 153.

102. Young, *Embodying Black Experience*, 20.

103. Diane Negra, *The Archive and the Repertoire: Performing Cultural Memory in the Americas* (Durham, NC: Duke University Press, 2003), 20.

104. Foster, "Choreographing History," 10.

105. Negra, *The Archive and the Repertoire*, 20.

106. "Doin' work" describes the process of skillfully dominating in a field of play and is a term used in the title of Spike Lee's sports documentary *Kobe Doin' Work* (2009).

2. RACIAL ICONICITY AND THE TRANSMEDIA BLACK ATHLETE

1. Big K.R.I.T., "Hometown Hero," *K.R.I.T. Wuz Here*, Cinematic Music Group, 2010.

2. H.G. Bissinger, *Friday Night Lights: A Town, A Team, A Dream*, 10th ed. (Cambridge, MA: Da Capo Press, 2000).

3. Bissinger, *Friday Night Lights*, xxxiii.

4. Bissinger, *Friday Night Lights*, xvii.

5. Ben Carrington, *Race, Sport and Politics: The Sporting Black Diaspora* (Thousand Oaks, CA: Sage, 2010), 113. His emphasis.

6. H.G. Bissinger, *After Friday Night Lights: When the Games Ended, Real Life Began. An Unlikely Love Story*. Kindle Edition (San Francisco: Byliner, Inc., 2012).

7. Bissinger, *After Friday Night Lights*.

8. Nicole R. Fleetwood, *On Racial Icons: Blackness and the Public Imagination* (New Brunswick, NJ: Rutgers University Press, 2015).

9. Fleetwood, *On Racial Icons*, 10. Her emphasis.

10. Jackie Robinson's transmedia character was first rendered on screen in the Arthur Mann biography *The Jackie Robinson Story*. Robinson travels across the biopics *The Jackie Robinson Story* (Alfred E. Green, 1950) and *42* (Brian Hegeland, 2013) and the made-for-television features *The Court Martial*

of Jackie Robinson (Larry Peerce, 1990) and *Soul of the Game* (Kevin Rodney Sullivan, 1996), among other media texts. Muhammad Ali's transmedia character begins with his autobiography *The Greatest: My Own Story* (1975), which was edited by Toni Morrison. The film was made into a biopic, *The Greatest* (Tom Gries, 1977), starring Ali. Prior to this, Ali (credited as Cassius Clay) had a cameo role in the film *Requiem for a Heavyweight* (Ralph Nelson, 1962). He also appeared as himself in Jeff Kanew's 1972 documentary *Black Rodeo* and is one the leads in Jan Kadar's 1978 film *Freedom Road*. Ali's storied career and world-historical impact in and out of the ring has been rendered is numerous documentaries and fiction films, including the Academy Award–winning documentary *When We Were Kings* (Leon Gast, 1996) and most recently the HBO docuseries *What's My Name: Muhammad Ali* (Antoine Fuqua, 2019).

11. Henry Jenkins, *Convergence Culture: Where Old and New Media Collide* (New York: New York University Press, 2006), 334. *Friday Night Lights* is a popular transmedia example and is often cited by those examining participatory culture and collective intelligence. For more on transmedia storytelling and the *Friday Night Lights* franchise, see Aaron Baker, "Transmedia Storytelling and *Friday Night Lights*" in *Sport im Films*, ed. Robert Gugutzer and Barbara Englert (Konstanz, Germany: UVK Publisher, 2014), 223–39.

12. Hortense Spillers, "Peter's Pans: Eating in the Diaspora," in *Black, White, and in Color: Essays on American Literature and Culture* (Chicago: University of Chicago Press, 2003), 21. Her emphasis.

13. Bissinger, *After Friday Night Lights*.

14. Jared Sexton, *Black Masculinity and the Cinema of Policing* (New York: Palgrave Macmillan, 2017), 28.

15. Robin Bernstein, "Dances with Things: Material Culture and the Performance of Race," *Social Text* 27, no. 4 (Winter 2009), 69.

16. Spillers, "Peter's Pans," 21.

17. Fleetwood, *On Racial Icons*, 8.

18. W.J.T. Mitchell, *Seeing through Race* (Cambridge, MA: Harvard University Press, 2012), 4.

19. Fleetwood, *On Racial Icons*, 12.

20. Beginning with famed boxer John "Jack" Johnson, the first Black heavyweight champion, Nicole Fleetwood provides a historical arc of the Black athlete. Johnson's defiant performance in the ring shattered the myth of Black athletic inferiority and countered notions of white dominance and supremacy in his victory over James "Jim" Jeffries in 1910. Fleetwood traces differentiations in professional Black athletes' iconicity, including "race man" Paul Robeson; activist athletes Muhammad Ali, Tommie Smith, and John Carlos; and corporate superstar and symbol Michael Jordan, ruminating finally on the contemporary careers and reception of basketball phenomenon LeBron James and tennis sensation Serena Williams. The polarized reactions to James's and Williams's sporting actions, career choices, and "defiant" behaviors evince the "the shifting dynamics of race, gender, corporatization, and superstar power." Fleetwood, *On Racial Icons*, 82. Their popularity vacillates as their transgressive actions and politics on

and off their respective courts define the coded precarity of the Black athlete as racial icon.

21. Kobena Mercer, *Welcome to the Jungle: New Positions in Black Cultural Studies* (New York: Routledge, 1994), 178.

22. Nicole R. Fleetwood, *Troubling Vision: Performance, Visuality, and Blackness* (Chicago: University of Chicago Press, 2011), 47.

23. Bissinger, *After Friday Night Lights.*

24. Fleetwood, *On Racial Icons,* 8.

25. Bissinger, *Friday Night Lights,* 39.

26. John Hoberman, *Darwin's Athletes: How Sport Has Damaged Black America and Preserved the Myth of Race* (New York: Houghton Mifflin Company, 1997), 12.

27. I am drawing on Mark Anthony Neal's interrogation of how "the 'legible' Black male body is continually recycled to serve the historical fictions of American culture." Mark Anthony Neal, *Looking for Leroy: Illegible Black Masculinities* (New York: New York University Press, 2013), 4. The Black athlete is a decidedly legible Black male body in popular culture, particularly media. Alongside television images of actual Black athletes in collegiate and professional sports, examples of fiction sports films that render the Black athlete legible include but are not limited to: *Cornbread, Earl and Me* (Joseph Manduke, 1975), *White Men Can't Jump* (Ron Shelton, 1992), *Above the Rim* (Jeff Pollack, 1994), *Rebound: The Legend of Earl "The Goat" Manigault* (Eriq La Salle, 1996), *He Got Game,* (Spike Lee, 1998), *The Hurricane* (Norman Jewison, 1999), *Any Given Sunday* (Oliver Stone, 1999), *Coach Carter* (Thomas Carter, 2005), *Glory Road* (James Gartner, 2006), *The Blind Side* (John Lee Hancock, 2009), *Creed* (Ryan Coogler, 2015), *Creed 2* (Steven Caple Jr., 2018), and *High Flying Bird* (Steven Soderbergh, 2019). As Neal's work suggests, the popularity of sports films about Black male athletes underscores the ways in which "black male bodies continue to function as tried and tested props" in American culture (4).

28. Bissinger, *Friday Night Lights,* 49.

29. Harvey Young, *Embodying Black Experience: Stillness, Critical Memory, and the Black Body* (Ann Arbor: University of Michigan Press, 2010), 7.

30. Bissinger, *Friday Night Lights,* 186.

31. Bissinger, *After Friday Night Lights.*

32. Lisa Kennedy, "Looking Back without Anger: The Black Familiar," *Village Voice,* October 16, 1990, 62.

33. Aaron Baker, *Contesting Identities: Sports in American Film* (Urbana: University of Illinois Press, 2003), 8.

34. James Snead, *White Screens, Black Images: Hollywood from the Dark Side* (New York: Routledge, 1994), 5.

35. Saidiya Hartmann quoted in Okwui Okpokwasili, "Beyoncé the Readymade," *Walker Art,* September 23, 2014, www.walkerart.org/magazine /beyonce-saidiya-hartment-ralph-lemon.

36. The 1976 box-office hit *Rocky* (John Avildsen) is perhaps the most popular example of a sports film narrative that ends in defeat. In *Rocky,* underdog Italian American fighter Rocky Balboa (Sylvester Stallone) overcomes emotional and physical obstacles to "go the distance" against Black heavyweight champion Apollo Creed (Carl Weathers). An American dream fable, Rocky narrowly loses the boxing match against Creed, and his defeat is framed as one of heroic whiteness where the American Dream—which like America itself is predicated on an institutional investment in whiteness—is both validated and reaffirmed. *Rocky* spawned six sequels, making the first film's ending of defeat a preface to the narrative of success represented in the franchise's subsequent four films. *Rocky II* through *Rocky V* ends in performances of triumph for Rocky. The final Rocky-specific film in the franchise, *Rocky Balboa* (Sylvester Stallone, 2006), is the exception, and the film ends with Rocky valiantly losing in a split-decision to a younger, faster world heavyweight champion. Coming full circle, *Rocky Balboa* provides Rocky a final chance to "go the distance" against another Black opponent. However, the reboot of the *Rocky* franchise to follow Apollo Creed's son, Adonis (played by Michael B. Jordan) in *Creed* and *Creed II,* continues and revises this narrative of defeat, with Adonis losing—like Rocky—in the first film and ultimately being triumphant in the sequel.

37. J. Jack Halberstam, *The Queer Art of Failure* (Durham, NC: Duke University Press), 93.

38. Halberstam, *The Queer Art of Failure,* 12.

39. Darieck Scott, *Extravagant Abjection: Blackness, Power, and Sexuality in the African American Literary Imagination* (New York: New York University Press, 2010), 17.

40. Snead, *White Screens, Black Images,* 2.

41. Snead, *White Screens, Black Images,* 4.

42. Sexton, *Black Masculinity and the Cinema of Policing,* 72.

43. Sexton, *Black Masculinity and the Cinema of Policing,* 69. His emphasis.

44. Hoberman, *Darwin's Athletes,* 5.

45. The preseason training sequence in *Friday Night Lights* is typical of many sports films that show athletes skills and abilities in practice situations. However, the sequence also shows the intersection of Black prowess and Black pain. While Boobie demonstrates his exceptional playing abilities, fellow Black teammate, Ivory, is forced during the preseason practice to do a "bull-in-the-ring" drill, where he stands in the middle of a circle of players who each take turns hitting him. Ivory is barely left standing following this gladiatorial contest turned football contact/tackling drill. The violence of each hit underscores the destructive, debilitating, and deadly concussion crisis that plagues football at all levels but especially the NFL. This violence is powerfully rendered and critiqued in Josh Begley's alternative highlight reel *Concussion Protocol* (2018), which captures the 280 concussions (traumatic brain injuries) in the 2017–2018 NFL season.

46. bell hooks, "Neo-colonial Fantasies of Conquest: *Hoop Dreams,*" in *Reel to Real: Race, Class, and Sex at the Movies* (New York: Routledge, 1996), 80.

47. William C. Rhoden, *Forty Million Dollar Slaves: The Rise, Fall, and Redemption of the Black Athlete* (New York: Three Rivers Press, 2006), 174.

48. Mercer, *Welcome to the Jungle*, 176.

49. Fleetwood, *On Racial Icons*, 81.

50. Gayatri Chakravorty Spivak, *The Post-Colonial Critic: Interviews, Strategies, Dialogues* (New York: Routledge, 1990), 108.

51. Hoberman, *Darwin's Athletes*, 6.

52. hooks, "Neo-colonial Fantasies of Conquest," 79.

53. Sexton, *Black Masculinity and the Cinema of Policing*, 70. His emphasis.

54. Fleetwood, *Troubling Vision*, 6.

55. Imogen Tyler, *Revolting Subjects: Social Abjection and Resistance in Neoliberal Britain* (London: Zed Books, 2013), 21. Her emphasis.

56. Young, *Embodying Black Experience*, 18.

57. Bissinger, *Friday Night Lights*, 38.

58. Fleetwood, *Troubling Vision*, 2.

59. Alessandra Raengo, "A Necessary Signifier: The Adaptation of Robinson's Body-Image in 'The Jackie Robinson Story,' *Adaptation* 1 (2008), 80.

60. Raengo, "A Necessary Signifier," 88.

61. Young, *Embodying Black Experience*, 5.

62. Scott, *Extravagant Abjection*, 61. His emphasis.

63. Garry Whannel, "Winning and Losing Respect: Narratives of Identity in Sport Films," *Sport in Society: Cultures, Commerce, Media, Politics* 11, nos. 2–3 (2008), 201.

64. To celebrate *Friday Night Lights'* twenty-fifth anniversary, Bissinger's "where are they now?" update in *Sports Illustrated* reveals that Boobie, who has had continual legal troubles, is currently incarcerated with a ten-year prison sentence following a parole violation in 2012. Unlike his white counterparts, Boobie's injury on the field exacerbates the personal hardships that shape his life. The preparation for his article and the afterward were captured in the documentary *Buzz* (Andrew Shea, 2019) about the prolific writer. Bissinger visits Boobie in prison, where the former football player has been for the past two and a half years. The scene between the two is devastating to watch, as they both reflect on Boobie's fate, a tragedy made worse by the fact the last cinematic image of Boobie is of him behind bars. H.G. Bissinger, "Stars of Friday Night Lights Reunite to Relive Their Story 25 Years Later," *Sports Illustrated*, March 29, 2015, www.si.com/high-school/2015/07/29/friday-night-lights-25th-anniversary-hg-bissinger-book-excerpt.

65. Linda Williams, *Playing the Race Card: Melodramas of Black and White from Uncle Tom to O.J. Simpson* (Princeton, NJ: Princeton University Press, 2001), 296.

66. Fleetwood, *On Racial Icons*, 111.

67. Fleetwood, *On Racial Icons*, 111.

68. Bissinger, *After Friday Night Lights*.

69. "A New Spelling of My Name" references Audre Lorde's biomythography, which fuses history, mythology, and biography into a single work. Boobie's

body in and across *Friday Night Lights'* texts operate resonantly within the textual layers of history, mythology, and biography described by Lorde. See Audre Lorde, *Zami: A New Spelling of My Name* (Berkeley, CA: Crossing Press, 1992).

70. Peter Berg, quoted in "Behind the Scenes of '*Friday Night Lights*,'" *Fresh Air*, July 13, 2011, www.npr.org/2011/07/15/137826323/behind-the-scenes-of-friday-night-lights.

71. The show was shot on location in Austin and Pflugerville, Texas, without the use of sound stages and with almost no constructed sets, utilizing real locations, natural lighting, and nonprofessional actors as extras. These elements, which firmly root the series in the cultural geography of Texas, also provide a level of authenticity to the show. The scenes are broadly conceived, and the directors give very little direction on character blocking to the actors. Using handheld cameras, the director of photography and other camera people and crew react to the behaviors of the actors and their actions as they unfold. The show uses pronounced close-ups to give an impression of intimacy and subjectivity, while quick and jerky camera movements convey a sense of dramatic vérité. The show's scripts are sparse, operating as vague guidelines that allow for the actors to improvise dialogue based on the tone of the scene and how they feel their characters would react. This naturalistic kind of acting, while looking and feeling authentic, is in fact highly stylized, technical, and fictive, and it is employed, paradoxically, both in scenes with actors less adept at this style and scenes with those well-trained in dramatic improvisation.

72. Tricia Rose, *Black Noise: Rap Music and Black Culture in Contemporary America* (Hanover, NH: Wesleyan University Press, 1994), 2.

73. Charlene Regester, "From the Gridiron and the Boxing Ring to the Cinema Screen: The African American Athlete in pre-1950 Cinema," *Culture, Sport, Society: Cultures, Commerce, Media, Politics* 6, nos. 2–3 (2003), 270.

74. Henry Louis Gates Jr., *The Signifying Monkey: A Theory of African American Literary Criticism* (New York: Oxford University Press, 1988), xxv. While I call Big K.R.I.T. an underground hip hop artist, the ascendant rapper operates at multiple levels, selling out shows while also being relatively unknown to mainstream audiences. In the hip hop industry, he is praised for his lyrical abilities and southern rap roots. Despite having made thirteen mixtapes and four studio albums, Big K.R.I.T.'s lack of popularity in terms of radio play and crossover appeal structures his street credibility as much as his mainstream obscurity.

75. Thanks to Michael Gillespie for suggesting thinking through Big K.R.I.T.'s hip hop spectatorship.

76. Kennedy, "Looking Back without Anger."

77. I am extending Keith Harris's use of Lisa Kennedy's idea of the Black familiar, specifically where he discusses the inversion of stereotypes in Warrington and Reginald Hudlin's *House Party* (1990). Keith Harris, *Boys, Boyz, Bois: An Ethics of Black Masculinity in Film and Popular Media* (New York: Routledge, 2006), 88.

78. Kennedy, "Looking Back without Anger."

79. J. Pablo, "Q&A: Big K.R.I.T. on His Rise, Dedicating Songs to His Grandma, and Being Inspired by *Friday Night Lights*," *Village Voice*, March 15, 2012, www.villagevoice.com/2012/03/15/qa-big-k-r-i-t-on-his-rise-dedicating -songs-to-his-grandma-and-being-inspired-by-friday-night-lights/.

80. Benjammin, "#MYTOP5: BIG K.R.I.T. Names His Top 5 Movies" *The Source*, February 20, 2013, www.thesource.com/2013/02/20/mytop5-big-k-r-i -t-names-his-top-5-movies/. Big K.R.I.T. was asked what his top-five favorite films are by *The Source*. *Friday Night Lights* was chosen as number two, bested by *There Will Be Blood* (Paul Thomas Anderson, 2007), and followed by *No Country for Old Men* (Ethan and Joel Coen, 2007), *Malcolm X* (Spike Lee, 1992), and *Lincoln* (Steven Spielberg, 2012).

81. Fellow southern rapper J. Cole released the mixtape *Friday Night Lights* in 2012. Discussing the mixtape's use of the popular media text, J. Cole explains: "It still embodies that J. Cole character—that basketball, high school athlete, varsity feeling without making it specific to basketball. People usually associate *Friday Night Lights* with football. [. . .] Where I'm in my career is like how a high school basketball player feels before a game. It's excitement for the game, but it's a little bit of nervousness about the game. There's all these emotions— that's what I think about when I think about *Friday Night Lights*." Omar Burgess, "J. Cole Explains Album Delays, Talks 'Friday Night Lights,'" *Hip Hop DX*, November 8, 2010, www.hiphopdx.com/news/id.12903/title.j-cole-explains -album-delays-talks-friday-night-lights#.

82. Carrington, *Race, Sport and Politics*, 113.

83. Halberstam, *The Queer Art of Failure*, 15; Jenkins, *Convergence Culture*, 331 and 324.

84. Rose, *Black Noise*, 9–10.

85. Saidiya Hartman, *Lose Your Mother: A Journey along the Atlantic Slave Route* (New York: Farrar, Straus and Giroux, 2007), 6.

86. The "Third Coast" refers to southern hip hop. See Roni Sarig, *Third Coast: OutKast, Timbaland, and How Hip-Hop Became a Southern Thing* (Cambridge, MA: Da Capo Press, 2007).

87. Stuart Hall, "Cultural Identity and Cinematic Representation," *Framework: The Journal of Cinema and Media*, no. 36 (1989), 80.

88. Rose, *Black Noise*, 79. Big K.R.I.T.'s sampling of Boobie's dialogue in *Friday Night Lights* evinces the complex narrative reformulation in rap music and contemporary Black cultural production.

89. Rose, *Black Noise*, 79.

90. Rose, *Black Noise*, 90. "Hometown Hero" was released on a mixtape, which is different from a studio-produced album or a music streaming service like Spotify, Apple Music, or Tidal in that mixtapes are often released via an artist's website and are meant to recall the practice of selling hip hop mixtapes on the streets of New York City, St. Louis, New Orleans, Los Angeles, Atlanta, and Houston.

91. José Esteban Muñoz, *Cruising Utopia: The Then and There of Queer Futurity* (New York: New York University Press, 2009), 178.

92. Big K. R. I. T. quoted in XXL Staff, "Big K. R. I. T. Breaks Down *4eva N A Day,* Talks Debut Album, New Single & Boobie Miles," *XXL Magazine,* March 15, 2012, www.xxlmag.com/news/2012/03/big-k-r-i-t-breaks-down-4eva-n-a -day-talks-debut-album-new-single-boobie-miles/.

93. Bissinger, *After Friday Night Lights.*

94. Fleetwood, *On Racial Icons,* 4. Her emphasis.

95. Boobie's "#45" jersey is available for purchase online from distributors such as Amazon. This "unofficial" merchandise is not licensed by Permian High School, Bissinger, the film's production studio, or Boobie himself. A cursory look at "#boobiemiles" on Instagram reveals thousands of photos of fans wearing his jersey, quoting the film, or reciting Big K. R. I. T.'s song "Boobie Miles."

96. The play of signification across Boobie's mediated body will possibly continue in the future. In May of 2018, *Variety* reported that David Gordon Green is in final negotiations to direct a new film version of *Friday Night Lights:* "Sources tell *Variety* that the movie is not a sequel to Universal's 2004 film starring Billy Bob Thornton, nor is it based on NBC's TV series with Kyle Chandler. Instead, it's a new property, though still focused [on] H. G. Bissinger's non-fiction book about the 1988 Permian High School Panthers as the new Texas football team makes a run towards the state championship." Justin Kroll, "'Friday Night Lights' New Film Taps Director David Gordon Green," *Variety,* May 9, 2018, www.variety .com/2018/film/news/friday-night-light-david-gordon-green-1202720026/.

3. BLACK FEMALE INCOMMENSURABILITY AND ATHLETIC GENDERS

1. *A League of Their Own* is the only baseball movie to exceed the $100 million mark. See www.boxofficemojo.com/movies/?id=leagueoftheirown.htm and Brian Welk, "20 Highest-Grossing Baseball Movies, from '*A League of Their Own*' to '*Mr. 3000,*'" *The Wrap,* October 28, 2018, www.thewrap.com /the-highest-grossing-baseball-movies-photos/.

2. Susan K. Cahn, *Coming on Strong: Gender and Sexuality in Twentieth-Century Women's Sports* (New York: The Free Press, 1994), 147.

3. Cahn, *Coming on Strong,* 141.

4. The All-American Girls Professional Baseball League, "All-American Girls Professional Baseball League Rules of Conduct, 1943–1954," in *Women and Sports in the United States: A Documentary Reader,* ed. Susan K. Cahn and Jean O'Reilly (Boston: Northeastern University Press, 2007): 59–61.

5. Cahn, *Coming on Strong,* 140.

6. The imagined sequel quoted in the epigraph is a tweet by Matthew Cherry posted following the death of *A League of Their Own* director Penny Marshall in 2018. Matthew A. Cherry (@MatthewACherry), December 18, 2018, 12:04PM, Tweet.

7. Cahn, *Coming on Strong,* 151.

8. Cahn, *Coming on Strong,* 152.

9. Michele Wallace, *Invisibility Blues: From Pop to Theory* (New York: Verso, 1990), 217.

10. Wallace, *Invisibility Blues*, 218.

11. Wallace, *Invisibility Blues*, 218.

12. Wallace, *Invisibility Blues*, 218.

13. Amira Rose Davis, "No League of Their Own: Baseball, Black Women, and the Politics of Representation," *Radical History Review* 124 (May 2016), 74. Davis uses the scene from *A League of Their Own* as an introduction to the history of Stone, Morgan, and Johnson's participation in the Negro Leagues. While my investments are different, Davis similarly captures the paradox of visibility and invisibility that shapes Black women's representation in sports history and popular consciousness.

14. Davis, "No League of Their Own," 76.

15. Davis draws attention to the athletic careers of Toni Stone, Connie Morgan, and Mamie Johnson, considering how these players, their teams, and the Black press negotiated their representational significance in sports and society. "Laboring symbolically as cultural commodities," Davis notes, "Stone, Johnson, and Morgan sustained the NAL [Negro American League] while simultaneously embodying the death of a masculine black institution. Their stories, sanitized snapshots of their lives and playing days, continue to be etched into public memory. Whether they are presented as a historical footnote or as heroic individual actors, the context of Stone's, Johnson's, and Morgan's participation and the politics of their representation—both historically and today—are obscured. . . . However, underscoring the ways in which individuals and institutions have used black women's athletic bodies to advance their own financial and political interests offers a fuller picture of black women's physical and symbolic labor in the postwar era." Davis, "No League of Their Own," 91.

16. I am inspired here by Michele Wallace's deployment of Ralph Ellison's definition of invisibility from *Invisible Man* for my understanding of Black women's sporting blackness. As she describes, "For Ellison, 'invisibility' doesn't merely describe a metaphysical 'absence' but rather the peculiar impact that the denial of an Afro-American 'presence' has on the structure and process of American culture and history." Wallace, *Invisibility Blues*, 237. This concept of invisibility also reverberates with Toni Morrison's notion of "playing in the dark." See Toni Morrison, *Playing in the Dark: Whiteness and the Literary Imagination* (Cambridge, MA: Harvard University Press, 1992).

17. Kobena Mercer, *Welcome to the Jungle: New Positions in Black Cultural Studies* (New York: Routledge, 1994), 178.

18. Mercer, *Welcome to the Jungle*, 178.

19. Ben Carrington, "'Race,' Representation and the Sporting Body," Paper submitted to the Centre for Urban and Community Research's Occasional Paper Series, Goldsmith College, University of London, May 2002, 20, www.gold.ac.uk/media/documents-by-section/departments/research-centres-and-units/research-centres/centre-for-urban-and-comm/carrington.pdf.

20. Kimberlé Crenshaw, "Mapping the Margins: Intersectionality, Identity Politics, and Violence against Women of Color," *Stanford Law Review* 43, no. 6 (July 1991): 1241–29. As Aaron Baker reminded me, Serena Williams faces

double and unmitigated discrimination. In the world of tennis, Williams is seen as both the wrong race and the wrong kind of strong woman.

21. Nicole Fleetwood, *On Racial Icons: Blackness and the Public Imagination* (New Brunswick, NJ: Rutgers University Press, 2015), 99.

22. Stuart Hall, "New Ethnicities," in *Stuart Hall: Critical Dialogues in Cultural Studies*, ed. David Morley and Kuan-Hsing Chen (New York: Routledge, 1996), 441.

23. Stuart Hall, "The Spectacle of the 'Other,'" in *Representation: Cultural Representations and Signifying Practices*, ed. Stuart Hall (London: Sage Publications, 1997), 232.

24. Judith Butler, *Undoing Gender* (New York: Routledge, 2004), 1.

25. The lack of representation of Black female athletes is wholly unearned, as US Black women athletes have historically achieved international celebrity and success in the panoply of sporting games—basketball, tennis, track and field, gymnastics, and so on. To my knowledge, there are only thirteen fiction films about Black women athletes to date, five of which are made-for-television biopics—*Wilma* (Bud Greenspan, 1977), *Run for the Dream: The Gail Devers Story* (Neema Barnette, 1996), *The Loretta Claiborne Story* (Lee Grant, 2000), *The Gabby Douglas Story* (Gregg Champion, 2014), and *The Simone Biles Story: Courage to Soar* (Vanessa Parise, 2018)—and six of which are theatrically or straight-to-DVD/streaming films—*Twice as Nice* (Jessie Maple, 1989), *The Longshots* (Fred Durst, 2008), *Fast Girls* (Regan Hall, 2011), *Never Quit* (Jason Aleman, 2016), *First Match* (Olivia Newman, 2016), *Overcomer* (Alex Kendrick, 2019), *Love and Basketball*, and *Juwanna Mann*, the last of which is not regularly considered within this meager canon and would bring the number provisionally back down to twelve films. *Wilma, Run for the Dream, The Loretta Claiborne Story, The Gabby Douglas Story, The Simone Biles Story*, and *The Longshots* are based on real sportswomen: Olympic sprinter Wilma Rudolph; Olympic hurdler Gail Devers; Special Olympics athlete Loretta Claiborne; Olympic gymnasts Gabby Douglas and Simone Biles; and Jasmine Plummer, the first female quarterback to play in the Junior Pee Wee Division of the Pop Warner Super Bowl. *Twice as Nice* is a basketball drama about two twin collegiate athletes competing to go pro that co-starred WNBA legend Cynthia Cooper-Dyke. *Fast Girls* is a fictional British drama about professional sprinters. *Never Quit* is a low-budget Christian-themed drama about a teenage basketball player who loses her ability to play and must learn to trust God's plan for her life. *First Match* is about a teenage girl who joins an all-boys wrestling team to reconcile with her estranged father. *Overcomer* is, also, a Christian-production about a Black cross-country runner who finds religion and her long-thought-to-be-dead father. In my counting of fiction films, I am not including the film *Bring It On* (Peyton Reed, 2002) or any of its sequels in the list of sports films about Black women because the narrative and screen time favors the white cheerleading team (and yes, while up for debate by some, competitive cheerleading is a sport). I also am not including the two films where Black women portray sports coaches, which are *Eddie* (Steve Rash, 1996) and

From the Rough (Pierre Bagley, 2011), or work for a sports organization in some capacity, such as *Just Wright* (Sanaa Hamri, 2010). I do not include films that are non-aerobic games such as the billiard film *Kiss Shot* (1989), the spelling bee film *Akeelah and the Bee* (Doug Atchison, 2006), and the chess movie *Queen of Katwe* (Mira Nair, 2016). I also am not including competition-based dance films such as *How She Move* (Ian Iqbal Rashid, 2007). In contrast, but still limited in number, there are a range of sports documentaries about Black female athletes (though they are easily outpaced by the number of documentaries about Black male athletes). Examples include: *Mo'ne Davis: Throw Like a Girl* (2014), *Venus Vs.* (Ava DuVernay, 2013), *Swoopes* (Hannah Storm, 2013), *Coach* (Bess Kargman, 2013), *Venus and Serena* (Maiken Baird and Michelle Major, 2013), *This Is a Game Ladies* (Peter Schnall, 2004), *Heart of the Game* (Ward Serrill, 2005), *The Anderson Monarchs* (Eugene Martin, 2013), *Training Rules* (Dee Mosbacher and Fawn Yacker, 2009), *Marion Jones: Press Pause* (John Singleton, 2010), and the HBO docuseries *Being Serena* (2018). Finally, on television, the FOX series *Pitch* (2016), which starred a Black woman as the first woman in the MLB, was cancelled after its first season.

26. Ed Guerrero, "The Black Man on Our Screens and the Empty Space in Representation," *Callaloo* 18, no. 2 (Spring 1995): 395–400.

27. Michele Wallace explains that "the highly visible success of a few black women writers serves to completely obscure the profound nature of the challenge black feminist creativity might pose to white cultural hegemony." Wallace, *Invisibility Blues*, 219.

28. Wallace, *Invisibility Blues*, 228.

29. Dayna B. Daniels, "You Throw Like a Girl: Sports and Misogyny on the Silver Screen," in *All-Stars and Movie Stars: Sports in Film and History*, ed. Ron Briley, Michael K. Schoenecke, and Deborah A. Carmichael (Lexington: University of Kentucky Press, 2008), 115. The gendering of sport shapes the gendering of the sports film genre, where men's physical competencies dominate, narrow conscriptions of masculinity are flaunted, and heterosexuality is the unquestioned modus operandi. In the construction of the male athlete as hero, gender conflict is defined by men's interactions with women in secondary roles as "easily thwarted antagonist. As [Ronald] Bergen puts it, 'In sports movies, if women did not exist, there would be no need to invent them.'" Jean O'Reilly, "The Woman's Sports Film as the New Melodrama," in *Women and Sports in the United States: A Documentary Reader*, ed. Jean O'Reilly and Susan K. Cahn (Boston: Northeastern University Press, 2007), 285.

30. M. Ann Hall, *Feminism and Sporting Bodies: Essays on Theory and Practice* (Champaign, IL: Human Kinetics, 1996), xv.

31. Daniels, "You Throw Like a Girl," 105. Cahn, *Coming on Strong*, xv.

32. Daniels, "You Throw Like a Girl," 107.

33. Cahn, *Coming on Strong*, 112.

34. Daniels, "You Throw Like a Girl," 105. While many sports scholars have attempted to recuperate the histories of women in sports to challenge sports culture's mythologies, these stories still privilege and sometimes universalize

accounts of middle- and upper-class, heterosexual, able-bodied white women in the public imagination. See Cahn, *Coming on Strong*; Cheryl Cole, *Women in Sports: Issues and Controversies* (Thousand Oaks, CA: Sage, 1993); Pamela J. Creedon, *Women, Media, and Sport: Challenging Gender Values* (Thousand Oaks, CA: Sage, 1994); Hall, *Feminism and Sporting Bodies*; Susan Birrell and Mary G. McDonald, eds., *Reading Sport: Critical Essays on Power and Representation* (Boston: Northeastern University Press, 2000); Susan K. Cahn and Jean O'Reilly, eds., *Women and Sports in the United States: A Documentary History* (Boston: Northeastern University Press, 2007); and Jennifer Doyle, *The Sport Spectacle*, www.thesportspectacle.com/. Black women's sporting history is riddled with glaring gaps and omissions, and Black women athletes are treated as invisible or non-women in sports history. As a result, we have yet to fully understand how, as M. Ann Hall charges, "Black sportswomen are not simply subjected to more disadvantages than their white counterparts; their oppression, because of racism, is qualitatively different in kind." Hall, *Feminism and the Sporting Body*, 44. While some sports studies scholars, particularly women of color, have recognized and attempted to undo these historical oversights, the lack of stories has, as Daniels notes, created a foundation of myths that have animated certain sporting images within the public imagination and imaginative processes that, to paraphrase *But Some of Us Are Brave*, depict all the sporting women as white and all the Black sporting bodies as men. Gloria T. Hull, Patricia Bell Scott, and Barbara Smith, eds., *All the Women Are White, All the Blacks Are Men, But Some of Us Are Brave* (New York: The Feminist Press at The City University of New York, 1982). For examples of some of the sport studies scholarship on Black female athletes, see: Davis, "No League of Their Own"; Yevonne Smith, "Women of Color in Society and Sport," *Quest* 44, no. 2 (1992): 230–45. Ramona J. Bell, "Competing Identities: Representations of the Black Female Sporting Body from 1960 to the Present," PhD dissertation, Bowling Green State University, 2008; Nancy Spencer, "From 'Child's Play' to 'Party Crasher': Venus Williams, Racism, and Professional Women's Tennis," in *Sport Stars: The Cultural Politics of Sport Celebrity*, ed. David L. Andrews and Steven J. Jackson (London: Routledge, 2001): 87–10; Samantha King, "Contesting the Closet: Sheryl Swoopes, Racialized Sexuality, and Media Culture," in *Commodified and Criminalized: New Racism and African Americans in Contemporary Sports*, eds. David J. Leonard and C. Richard King (New York: Rowan & Littlefield Publishers, Inc., 2011): 203–22; Linda D. Williams, "Sportswomen in Black and White: Sports History From An Afro-American Perspective," in *Women, Media, and Sports: Challenging Gender Values*, ed. Pamela J. Creedon (Thousand Oaks, CA: Sage, 1994), 45–66; and Jennifer H. Lansbury, *A Spectacular Leap: Black Women Athletes in Twentieth-Century America* (Fayetteville: University of Arkansas Press, 2014).

35. Nicole Fleetwood, *Troubling Vision: Performance, Visuality, and Blackness* (Chicago: University of Chicago Press, 2011), 16.

36. When women athletes are sports film protagonists, they are most often represented within specific narrative treatments and often alongside and in

relation to men. At times, she is represented as the only woman on a male team, a point of gender panic in films such as *Little Giants* (Duwayne Durham, 1994) and *Necessary Roughness* (Stan Dragoti, 1991). Other times, she is depicted in relation to a male love interest who also plays sports, evidenced in the romantic dramas such as *Wimbledon* (Richard Loncraine, 2004) and *The Cutting Edge* (Paul Michael Glasser, 1992). On the rare occasion, she is the coach of an all-male team, as seen in *Wildcats* (Michael Ritchie, 1986), *Eddie* (Steve Rash, 1996), and *Sunset Park* (Steve Gomer, 1996). Few films deal complexly with women's sexuality; though *Personal Best* (Robert Towne, 1982) provides a significant albeit conflicting representation of two women pentathletes in a relationship. Since the 2000s, there has been a rise in women-centered sports films, such as *Blue Crush* (John Stockwell, 2002), *Bend It Like Beckham* (Gurinder Chadha, 2002), and *Million Dollar Baby* (Clint Eastwood, 2004); however, as Jean O'Reilly notes, these films "about strong women reveal a disturbing return to the stifling conventions of a much older, well-established Hollywood genre, the melodrama. Far from heralding the rightful place of women in sports, several of these films convey surprisingly subversive messages about the place for women in the sports arena, and in the world at large." Jean O'Reilly, "The Woman's Sports Film as the New Melodrama," 283–97.

37. As a televisual form, the made-for-television movie often engages with the contemporary moment (current happenings and sensational events) in popular culture, usually tackling controversial subjects or sentimental modern figures. For more on the made-for-television movie, see Laurie Jane Schulze, "*Getting Physical*: Text/Context/Reading and the Made-for-Television Movie," *Cinema Journal* 25, no. 2 (Winter 1986): 35–50 and Elayne Rapping, *The Movie of the Week: Private Stories, Public Lives* (Minneapolis: University of Minnesota Press, 1992). Blending sports films' generic tropes with the televisual form, made-for-television sports films about Black women sports heroes emphasize individual star performances, self-reliance, heterosexuality, and circumscribed female sporting ambition.

38. Susan K. Cahn addresses Black women's treatment in sports, explaining that "the long exclusion of both African American women and female athletes from categories of acceptable femininity encouraged the development of analogous mythologies. References to imitative 'animalistic' behavior had often been used to describe white female athletes, who by 'aping' male athletic behavior were suspected of unleashing animal instincts. Charges of mimicry found an even deeper congruence with racist views of African Americans as simian and imitative. Similarly, the charge that sport masculinized women physically and sexually resonated with scientific and popular portrayals of mannishness and sexual pathology among black women. The assertion that sport made women physically unattractive and sexually unappealing found its corollary in views of black women as less attractive and desirable than white women. The correspondence between stereotyped depictions of black womanhood and athletic females was nearly exact, and thus doubly resonant in the case of African American women athletes." Cahn, *Coming on Strong*, 127–28.

39. Jacquie Jones, "The Accusatory Space," in *Black Popular Culture: A Project by Michele Wallace*, ed. Gina Dent (Seattle, WA: Bay Press, 1992): 96. According to Jacquie Jones, the two categories in 1990s cinema were that of the bitch and the ho, which "assigned the accusatory space from which representation in the media, and more generally in society, can continually be reprogrammed along gender lines" (96).

40. Judith Butler, "Performative Acts and Gender Constitution: An Essay in Phenomenology and Feminist Theory," in *Writing on the Body: Female Embodiment and Feminist Theory*, ed. Katie Conboy, Nadia Median, and Sarah Stanbury (New York: Columbia University Press, 1997), 402.

41. Judith Butler, "Athletic Genders: Hyperbolic Instance and/or the Overcoming of Sexual Binarism," *Stanford Humanities Review* 6, no. 2 (1998): 103–11.

42. Butler, "Athletic Genders," 111.

43. Butler, "Performative Acts and Gender Constitution," 402.

44. J. Jack Halberstam, *Female Masculinity* (Durham, NC: Duke University Press, 1998), 8. Aaron Baker also makes the point (via Butler, Halberstam, and Sedgwick) to look at nonce taxonomies and female masculinities in regard to women's representation in sports film. See Aaron Baker, *Contesting Identities: Sports in American Film* (Urbana: University of Illinois Press, 2003), 77–78.

45. Tambay A. Obenson, "Watch 25-Minute Conversation with Gina Prince-Bythewood on '*Love & Basketball*' and Indie Filmmaking Challenges," *Indie Wire*, November 13, 2015, www.indiewire.com/2015/11/watch-25-min ute-conversation-with-gina-prince-bythewood-on-love-basketball-indie-film making-challenges-137636/.

46. O'Reilly, "The Women's Sports Film as the New Melodrama," 286.

47. O'Reilly, "The Women's Sports Film as the New Melodrama," 285–86.

48. Butler, "Athletic Genders," 104.

49. Jennifer Doyle, "Why Police the Border between Men and Women's Sports? (Repost w/ Comments about Caster Semenya)," *From A Left Wing*, August 21, 2009, www.fromaleftwing.blogspot.com/2009/08/why-police-border -between-mens-and.html. This idea of "ladylike" code of court conduct is then used by sports critics as a reason to challenge the credibility of women's basketball and deem it "unwatchable" because it lacks the intensities (physical for athletes and emotive for audiences) and entertainment value of the men's game. It also, as I explained in chapter 1, can be deployed rhetorically by Black women to push back against racial scripts that cast them as non-women in the realm of sports.

50. Dayna B. Daniels, *Polygendered and Ponytailed: The Dilemma of Femininity and the Female Athlete* (Toronto: Women's Press, 2009), 1.

51. Halberstam, *Female Masculinity*, 1.

52. Halberstam, *Female Masculinity*, 1.

53. Gwendolyn D. Pough, *Check It While I Wreck It: Black Womanhood, Hip-Hop Culture, and the Public Sphere* (Boston: Northeastern University, 2004), 12.

54. This scene plays on the dialectic between hip hop and basketball. Todd Boyd describes the relationship between hip hop and basketball as two Black cultural expressions connected by an urban aesthetic. For Boyd, hip hop and basketball "are two arenas where Black people have had the best opportunity to express themselves, and where there continues to be a critical mass of individuals who use the opportunity to influence the culture at large, and hopefully, make some money in the process. These are two rarified spaces where the most fundamental elements of Blackness are articulated and played out, both internally, and for the masses." Todd Boyd, *Young, Black, Rich and Famous: The Rise of the NBA, the Hip Hop Invasion, and the Transformation of American Culture* (Lincoln: University of Nebraska Press, 2003), 12. While Boyd offers an important evaluation about basketball's relationship to hip hop from the late 1970s to the present (though he does address basketball history prior to the 1970s), his book deals solely with the NBA, an all-male professional league. Therefore, this masculinist relationship between hip hop and basketball underscores the hegemonic gender constructions of both realms. A consideration of what women athletes and female MCs bring to both arenas goes unaddressed. In relation to music, several feminist scholars of hip hop have tried to revise this by tracing women's histories in rap culture. However, no one has discussed the relationship between hip hop and women's basketball.

55. Pough, *Check It While I Wreck It*, 85.

56. Mihaly Csikszentmihalyi and Susan A. Jackson, *Flow in Sports: The Keys to Optimal Success and Performance* (Champaign, IL: Human Kinetics, 1999), 5.

57. Judith Butler makes this case in her analysis of Martina Navratilova, and so does Jennifer Doyle and Tavia Nyong'o in their respective essays on Caster Semenya. See Butler, "Athletic Genders;" Tavia Nyong'o, "The Unforgivable Transgression of Being Caster Semenya," *Women & Performance: A Journal of Feminist Theory* 20, no. 1 (2010): 95–100; and Jennifer Doyle, "Dirt off Her Shoulders," *GLQ: A Journal of Lesbian and Gay Studies* 13, no. 4 (2013): 419–33.

58. Roger Ebert, "*Juwanna Mann*," Roger Ebert.com, June 21, 2002, www .rogerebert.com/reviews/juwanna-mann-2002; Dennis Harvey, "*Juwanna Mann*," *Variety*, June 20, 2002, www.variety.com/2002/film/reviews/juwanna -mann-1200547674/.

59. David Germain, "*Juwanna Mann*," *Desert News*, June 21, 2002, www .google.com/search?q=david+germain+juwanna+mann&rlz=1C1CHBF_enUS 743US743&oq=david&aqs=chrome.0.69i59j69i57j69i65l2j35i139j0.2431j0j7 &sourceid=chrome&ie=UTF-8.

60. Anna Smith, "*Juwanna Mann*," *Time Out*, February 9, 2006, www.time out.com/london/film/juwanna-mann.

61. Owen Gleiberman, "*Juwanna Mann*." *Entertainment Weekly*, July 2, 2002, www.ew.com/article/2002/07/02/juwanna-mann-3/.

62. Racquel J. Gates, *Double Negative: The Black Image and Popular Culture* (Durham, NC: Duke University Press, 2018), 23.

63. Sports film criticism books often ignore or only briefly mention *Juwanna Mann*. Viridiana Lieberman's work is the exception here. She dedicates a brief section of her chapter on drag/cross-dressing sports films to the film. Lieberman, surprisingly, reads *Juwanna Mann* as an improvement in the representation of women athletes because, she argues, the film celebrates skilled female athletes and notions of teamwork. See Viridiana Lieberman, *Sports Heroines on Film: A Critical Study of Cinematic Women Athletes, Coaches, and Owners* (Jefferson, NC: McFarland & Company, Inc., 2015), 114–17.

64. Gates, *Double Negative*, 23.

65. Gates, *Double Negative*, 19.

66. Gates, *Double Negative*, 20.

67. Sarah Banet-Weiser, "Hoop Dreams: Professional Basketball and the Politics of Race and Gender," *Journal of Sport & Social Issues* 23, no. 4 (November 1999), 403.

68. I am drawing on Judith Butler's engagement with Louis Althusser's notion of interpellation. Butler explains that "the reprimand does not merely repress or control the subject but forms a crucial part of the juridical and social *formation* of the subject. The call is formative if not *performative*, precisely because it initiates the individual subjected space of the subject." Judith Butler, *Bodies That Matter: On the Discursive Limits of "Sex"* (New York: Routledge, 1993), 121.

69. Butler, *Bodies That Matter*, 126.

70. Banet-Weiser, "Hoop Dreams," 405.

71. Banet-Weiser, "Hoop Dreams," 125.

72. Mia Mask, "Who's behind That Fat Suit? Momma, Madea, Rasputia and the Politics of Cross-Dressing," in *Contemporary Black American Cinema: Race, Gender and Sexuality at the Movies*, ed. Mia Mask (New York: Routledge, 2012), 162.

73. Cahn, *Coming on Strong*, 127.

74. Cahn, *Coming on Strong*, 111. The example of the racist and biologist attacks on South African sprinter Caster Semenya comes to mind. For more on Caster Semenya, see Tavia Nyong'o, "The Unforgivable Transgression of Being Caster Semenya," and Jennifer Doyle, "Dirt off Her Shoulders."

75. Dunking is actually quite dangerous and puts shooters at risk of injury. Many women opt for the lay-up. While it is certainly less common than in the NBA, women dunk in the professional and amateur levels. West Virginia University's Georgeann Wells was the first woman to dunk in collegiate play. The Los Angeles Sparks' Lisa Leslie was the first woman to dunk in the WNBA. In 2019, Fran Belibi became the second woman to win McDonald's All-American dunk contest.

76. Iris Marion Young, *Throwing Like a Girl and Other Essays in Feminist Philosophy and Social Theory* (Bloomington: Indiana University Press, 1990), 148.

77. Nyong'o, "The Unforgivable Transgression of Being Caster Semenya," 99.

78. Butler, *Bodies That Matter*, 129.

79. Nyong'o, "The Unforgivable Transgression of Being Caster Semenya," 98.

80. Nyong'o, "The Unforgivable Transgression of Being Caster Semenya," 99.

81. Hortense Spillers, "The Crisis of the Negro Intellectual: A Post-Date," in *Black, White, and in Color: Essays on American Literature and Culture* (Chicago: University of Chicago Press, 2003), 469.

82. Bryan Turner, "Preface," in *The Consuming Body*, ed. Paki Falk (London: Sage, 1994), viii.

83. C. Riley Snorton, *Black on Both Sides: A Racial History of Trans Identity* (Minneapolis: University of Minnesota Press, 2017), 2. My turn to Snorton here is not to say that either *Love and Basketball* or *Juwanna Mann* are transgender narratives but that transgender studies critiques vitally shape larger claims about blackness and racial narratives. I am responding to Snorton's call to "eschew binaristic logic that might reify a distinction between transgender and cisgender, black and white, disabled and abled, and so on, in an effort to think expansively about how blackness and black studies, and transness and trans studies, yield insights that surpass an additive logic" (7–8).

84. The historical and political argument evidenced in Hortense Spillers's spellbinding essay "Mama's Baby, Papa's Maybe: An American Grammar Book" can be useful here in thinking through how sporting blackness can be constituted by Black men and women who resist normative gender frames, in part, because of the history of gendering/ungendering that began with the institution of slavery. See Hortense Spillers, "Mama's Baby, Papa's Maybe: An American Grammar Book," in *Black, White, and in Color: Essays on American Literature and Culture* (Chicago: The University of Chicago Press, 2003), 203–29.

4. THE REVOLT OF THE CINEMATIC BLACK ATHLETE

1. Harry Edwards, *The Revolt of the Black Athlete* (New York: Free Press, 1971), xxvii.

2. Harry Edwards, *The Revolt of the Black Athlete*, 50th anniversary ed. (Urbana: University of Illinois Press, 2017), xii.

3. Edwards, *The Revolt of the Black Athlete*, 1971, xxvii. In chapter 2's analysis of Boobie Miles in *Friday Night Lights*, I discuss the disposability of Black athletes after they lose their sporting ability and, thus, value to their teams, coaches, and communities.

4. Harry Edwards describes the impetus for revolt as stemming from a range of social issues/struggles: "The roots of the revolt of the black athlete spring from the same seed that produced the sit-ins, the freedom rides, and the rebellions in Watts, Detroit, and Newark. The athletic revolt springs from a disgust and dissatisfaction with the same racist germ that infected the warped minds responsible for the bomb murders of four black girls as they prayed in a Birmingham, Alabama, church and that conceived and carried out the murders of Malcolm X, Martin Luther King Jr., and Medgar

Evers, among a multitude of others. The revolt of the black athlete arises also from his new awareness of his responsibilities in an increasingly more desperate, violent, and unstable America." Edwards, *The Revolt of the Black Athlete*, 1971, xxvii.

5. Dave Zirin, *What's My Name, Fool? Sports and Resistance in the United States* (Chicago: Haymarket Books, 2005), 77. This gendered politic of "reclaiming manhood," as Dave Zirin notes, "mirrored a deep flaw also found in other sections of the New Left and Black Power movement: women were largely shut out . . . as if African American women weren't victims of racism or couldn't be part of a strong voice against it" (77). While women athletes did organize and participate in the revolt, the call to arms was myopically aimed at Black male sporting figures, as Harry Edwards described, to "[react] in a human and masculine fashion to the disparities between the heady artificial world of newspaper clippings, photographs, and screaming spectators and the real world of degradation, humiliation, and horror." Edwards, *The Revolt of the Black Athlete*, 1971, xxvii. Edwards addresses, in hindsight, this flawed gendered politic in the 50th anniversary edition of his book, explaining: "Along with the acknowledgement of some mistakes and missteps, there is one glaring omission that must be addressed: the lack of due attention paid to the status, circumstances, outcomes, and contributions of Black women—either as athletes or in the struggles for change more generally" (xxi).

6. This is not the first attempt at encouraging Black athletes to boycott the Olympic Games. There were calls for Black athletes such as Jesse Owens to boycott the 1936 Summer Olympics in Berlin, Germany. Activist, comedian, and former collegiate athlete Dick Gregory called for a boycott of the 1964 Summer Olympics in Tokyo. Similar to Harry Edwards, Gregory wanted Black athletes to join in a larger campaign for Black civil rights through civil and sporting disobedience.

7. Harry Edwards, Lee Evans, and Tommie Smith, quoted in Dave Zirin, *What's My Name, Fool?*, 74.

8. John Carlos with Dave Zirin, *The John Carlos Story* (Chicago: Haymarket Books, 2011), 81–82.

9. Amy Bass, *Not the Triumph but the Struggle: The 1968 Olympics and the Making of the Black Athlete* (Minneapolis: University of Minnesota Press, 2002), 5.

10. OPHR's demands included the reinstatement of Muhammad Ali's heavyweight boxing title (he was stripped of his title and boxing license earlier that year after refusing to submit to the Vietnam War draft); the removal of Avery Brundage, a white supremacist who fought against the boycott of the 1936 Summer Olympics in Nazi Germany, from his post as Chairman of the International Olympic Committee; the limiting of participation for all-white teams and players from the apartheid nations of the Union of South Africa and Southern Rhodesia; the addition of at least two Black coaches to the US men's track and field staff for the 1968 Olympic team; the appointment of two Black people to policy-making positions on the US Olympic Committee; and the

desegregation of the New York Athletic Club. Edwards, *The Revolt of the Black Athlete*, 1971, 185.

11. Bass, *Not the Triumph but the Struggle*, 4.

12. The notion that the Olympics are an apolitical arena is false. As Jules Boykoff explains, "In reality the Olympics are political through and through. The marching, the flags, the national anthems, the alliances with corporate sponsors, the labor exploitation behind the athletic-apparel labels, the treatment of indigenous peoples, the marginalization of the poor and working class, the selection of Olympic host cities—all political. To say the Olympics transcends politics is to conjure fantasy." Jules Boykoff, *Power Games: A Political History of the Olympics* (London: Verso, 2016), 2.

13. Bass, *Not the Triumph but the Struggle*, 241.

14. John Carlos, quoted in Zirin, *What's My Name, Fool?*, 87.

15. Tommie Smith, quoted in Edwards, *The Revolt of the Black Athlete*, 1971, 104.

16. John Carlos, quoted in Zirin, *What's My Name Fool?*, 87.

17. John Carlos, quoted in Zirin, *What's My Name Fool?*, 88.

18. Tommie Smith, quoted in Edwards, *The Revolt of the Black Athlete*, 1971, 104.

19. Tommie Smith, quoted in Edwards, *The Revolt of the Black Athlete*, 1971, 104.

20. Toni Morrison, quoted in Bass, *Not the Triumph but the Struggle*, 239.

21. Tommie Smith with David Steele, *Silent Gesture* (Philadelphia: Temple University Press, 2007). Stuart Hall, "Race, Articulation and Societies Structured in Dominance," in *Black British Cultural Studies: A Reader*, ed. Houston A. Baker Jr., Manthia Diawara, and Ruth H. Lindeborg (Chicago: University of Chicago Press, 1996), 16.

22. Bass, *Not the Triumph but the Struggle*, 241.

23. Bass, *Not the Triumph but the Struggle*, 241.

24. Bass, *Not the Triumph but the Struggle*, 25. Her emphasis.

25. W.E.B. Du Bois, *The Souls of Black Folk* (1903; repr., New York: Dover, 1994), 4. Trinh T. Minh-ha, *When the Moon Waxes Red: Representation, Gender, and Cultural Politics* (New York: Routledge, 1991), 157.

26. Harry Edward explains that despite the actions taken by the US Olympic officials and coaching staff, "[thousands] of black people turned out to honor [Smith and Carlos] in Washington, D.C. Many Black leaders—H. Rap Brown, Stokely Carmichael, Adam Clayton Powell, and Elijah Muhammad—paid their personal respects." Edwards, *The Revolt of the Black Athlete*, 1971, 107. While embraced by parts of the Black community, Smith and Carlos received death threats, were ostracized, and found little support around them. Carlos believes that the lack of support within the Black community contributed to his wife's suicide in 1977, explaining: "'There was pride, but only from the less fortunate. What could they do but show their pride? But we had Black businessmen, we had Black political caucuses, and they never embraced Tommie Smith or John Carlos. When my wife took her life in 1977 they never said, "Let me help."'"

John Carlos, quoted in Dave Zirin, *A People's History of Sports in the United States: 250 Years of Politics, Protest, People, and Play* (New York: The New Press, 2008), 172–173.

27. Smith and Carlos's act of resistance has since been recuperated in America's celebrated sporting history. In fact, both men received the 2008 Arthur Ashe Courage Award at the Excellence in Sports Performance Yearly (ESPY) Awards. A statue of the two stands on the campus of San Jose State University, where both attended and ran track. A few documentaries have referenced or depicted their story, including HBO's *Fists of Freedom: The Story of the '68 Summer Games* (George Roy, 1999) and *Salute* (Matt Norman 2008). The former film details the event, while the latter focuses on Australian silver medalist Peter Norman, the uncle of director Matt Norman, and his life before and after the games, including his post-1968 lifetime friendship with Smith and Carlos, who were pallbearers at his funeral. There is still no fictional treatment of their heroic actions, but their mediated image exists as mise-en-scène in other sports films such as, for example, on a poster that instigates a fight between Black and white football teammates in *Remember the Titans* (Boaz Yakin, 2000).

28. The "postgame" refers to the fact that sporting blackness is related to but also extends after the game/sporting contest itself. As *Hour Glass's* sporting activity is confined to the first few minutes of the film, the postgame landscape, or off-the-court action, is central to our understanding of the protagonist's sporting blackness and critical muscle memory.

29. Haile Gerima, quoted in Steve Howard, "A Cinema of Transformation: The Films of Haile Gerima," *Cinéaste* 14, no. 1 (1985), 29.

30. Gerima, quoted in Steve Howard, "A Cinema of Transformation," 29.

31. Trinh T. Min-ha's *Surname Viet Given Name Nam* (1989) dramatizes "Vietnam's history through collective and individual gaps." Trinh T. Minh-ha, *Cinema Interval* (New York: Routledge, 1999), 23. In her documentary, Minh-ha insists upon telling this history via "popular memory, with its 'bold omissions and minute depictions'; through women's personal stories; through songs, proverbs, and sayings" (23).

32. Louis Althusser's notion of "symptomatic readings" drives this articulation of critical muscle memory as visual and sonic indicators of absent and yet present histories in Gerima's film. Louis Althusser and Étienne Balibar, *Reading Capital*, trans. Ben Brewster (London: Verso, 1970), 8.

33. Astria Suparak and Brett Kashmere, "A Non-Zero-Sum Game," *Incite: Journal of Experimental Media* nos. 7–8 (2016–2017), 10. In the special issue, Suparak and Kashmere provide a wonderful compendium of essays and a nearly comprehensive filmography of experimental sports media. Thank you to Brett Kashmere for bringing this issue to my attention and generously sharing a copy with me.

34. George Lipsitz, "Genre Anxiety and Racial Representation in 1970s Cinema," in *Refiguring American Film Genres*, ed. Nick Browne (Berkley: University of California Press, 1998), 208–232.

35. My attention to *Hour Glass's* rendering of sporting blackness not only underscores my critical move to expand the kinds of case studies mobilized in sports cinema studies to include experimental forms but also signals a larger and purposeful shift in L.A. Rebellion scholarship. Allyson Nadia Field, Jan-Christopher Horak, and Jacqueline Stewart's seminal collection *L.A. Rebellion: Creating a New Black Cinema* advocates for scholars to consider and apply new critical frameworks, objectives, contexts, and methodologies to films and filmmakers at the periphery of the group. While Gerima is one of the more well-known and studied filmmakers of the L.A. Rebellion, there has been little written about *Hour Glass* beyond the film's positioning as the first installment in his "cinema of decolonization." John L. Jackson Jr. and Haile Gerima, "Decolonizing the Filmic Mind: An Interview with Haile Gerima," *Callaloo* 33, no. 1 (Spring 2010): 25–36. There are two notable exceptions of critical work that provide some analysis (and not just plot synopsis) of *Hour Glass*. Allyson Nadia Field gives a critical overview of *Hour Glass* in her substantial study of L.A. Rebellion Project Ones and Greg Thomas briefly fleshes out some of the complexity of Black resistance in the film. See Allyson Nadia Field, "Rebellious Unlearning: UCLA Project One Films (1967–1978)," in *L.A. Rebellion: Creating a New Black Cinema*, ed. Allyson Nadia Field, Jan-Christopher Horak, and Jacqueline Najuma Stewart (Oakland: University of California Press, 2015), 83–118; Greg Thomas, "Close-Up: Dragons! George Jackson in the Cinema with Haile Gerima—from the Watts Films to *Teza*," *Black Camera* 4, no. 2 (Spring 2013): 55–83. While the scholarship on *Hour Glass* is scant, the film recently was presented by Art + Practice and The Broad in their 2019 exhibition *Time Is Running Out of Time: Experimental Film and Video from the L.A. Rebellion and Today*. The title of the exhibit comes from a line by The Last Poets in Gerima's film.

36. Mike Murashige, "Haile Gerima and the Political Economy of Cinematic Resistance," in *Representing Blackness: Issues in Film and Video*, ed. Valerie Smith (New Brunswick, NJ: Rutgers University Press, 2003), 184.

37. Clyde Taylor, "The L.A. Rebellion: A Turning Point in Black Cinema," in *Whitney Museum of American Art: The New American Filmmakers Series 26* (New York: Whitney Museum of Art, 1986), 1–2. L.A. Rebellion filmmakers are also sometimes referred to as "The Los Angeles School of Black Filmmakers." See Ntongela Masilela, "The Los Angeles School of Black Filmmakers," in *Black American Cinema*, ed. Manthia Diawara (New York: Routledge, 1993), 107–17.

38. Working with UCLA film school's first Black faculty member, Elyeso Taylor, and later Third World film theorist Teshome Gabriel, L.A. Rebellion filmmakers developed their craft while learning about emerging African, Latin American, and other international films in "Film and Social Change," a course created by Taylor and continued by his successor Gabriel. As Cynthia Young details about minority enrollment and recruitment: "Functioning outside the control of the film department, ethnocommunications recruited undergraduates and graduates from other departments who wanted to learn filmmaking. Though it lasted only four years, ethnocommunications recruited several

African American, Asian American, Native American, and Chicano students during that time. . . . The second spark was the formation of a multiracial group called the Media Urban Crisis Committee (MUCCERS) that held a series of protests and sit-ins until the film department agreed to reverse its racially exclusionary admission practices by reserving 25 percent of the undergraduate and graduate admission slots for racial minorities. These two initiatives helped to attract and train dozens of filmmakers, including those in the Asian American group Visual Communications (VC), and the founders of two public broadcasting consortia for minority filmmakers, the Latino Consortium and the National Asian American Tele-communications Association." Cynthia Young, *Soul Power: Culture, Radicalism, and the Making of a U.S. Third World Left* (Durham, NC: Duke University Press, 2006), 216.

39. L.A. Rebellion filmmaker's Third Cinema influences included Brazil's Cinema Novo, Cuban documentary, Argentinian revolutionary cinema, and African cinema. They were also influenced by national film movements such as Italian neorealism, French New Wave, New German Cinema, British Documentary, and Soviet Cinema. New American cinemas, particularly the work of avant-garde and independent filmmakers like Shirley Clarke, Jonas Mekas, and John Cassavetes, as well as independent Black filmmakers from Oscar Micheaux to Melvin Van Peebles shaped their work. Intellectually they were engaged with theories of Black cultural nationalism and internationalism in the writings of Richard Wright, Amiri Baraka, and Malcolm X and the tensions between the Black Arts Movement and the Black Panther Party's Black nationalism; Third World Marxism in the work of Frantz Fanon, Amilcar Cabral, and Ngugi wa Thiong'o; and Pan-Africanism in the work of Kwame Nkrumah and George Padmore. See Allyson Nadia Field, Jan-Christopher Horak, and Jacqueline Najuma Stewart, "Introduction: Emancipating the Image—The L.A. Rebellion of Black Filmmakers," in *L.A. Rebellion: Creating a New Black Cinema*, ed. Allyson Nadia Field, Jan-Christopher Horak, and Jacqueline Najuma Stewart (Oakland: University of California Press, 2015), 3; Masilela, "The Los Angeles School of Black Filmmakers," 108–9; and Young, *Soul Power*, 214.

40. Murashige, "Haile Gerima and the Political Economy of Cinematic Resistance," 198, 199.

41. Field, "Rebellious Unlearning," 84.

42. As Mary Ann Doane explains: "The fantasmatic visual space which the film constructs is supplemented by techniques designed to spatialize the voice, localize it, give it depth and thus lend to the characters the consistency of the real." Mary Ann Doane, "The Voice in the Cinema: The Articulation of Body and Space," *Yale French Studies*, no. 60 (1980): 36. The use of sound effects in Project One films counters the primacy of voice/dialogue as an anchor for bodies in space in traditional narrative cinema.

43. Field, "Rebellious Unlearning," 83.

44. Haile Gerima, quoted in Tony Safford and William Triplett, "Haile Gerima: Radical Departures to a New Black Cinema," *Journal of the University Film and Video Association* 35, no. 2 (Spring 1983), 62.

45. Hamid Naficy, *An Accented Cinema: Exilic and Diasporic Filmmaking* (Princeton, NJ: Princeton University Press, 2001).

46. James Snead, "Images of Blacks in Black Independent Films: A Brief Survey," in *Cinemas of the Black Diaspora: Diversity, Dependence, and Oppositionality*, ed. Michael T. Martin (Detroit: Wayne State University Press, 1994), 373.

47. Teshome H. Gabriel, *Third Cinema and the Third World: The Aesthetics of Liberation* (Ann Arbor, MI: UMI Research Press, 1982).

48. Ralph Ellison, *Invisible Man* (1952; repr. New York: Vintage Books, 1980), 240–41.

49. I am drawing on Michael Gillespie's application of the term "sonic visuality" in his presentation at the 2018 Society for Cinema and Media Studies Conference.

50. Bhaskar Sarkar, "The Mellifluous 'Illogics' of the 'Bollywood Musical,'" in *The Sound of Musicals*, ed. Steven Cohan (London: BFI Publishing, 2010), 48.

51. Judith Butler, "Performative Acts and Gender Constitution: An Essay in Phenomenology and Feminist Theory," in *Writing on the Body: Female Embodiment and Feminist Theory*, ed. Katie Conboy, Nadia Median, and Sarah Stanbury (New York: Columbia University Press, 1997), 404. The noose inflects what Judith Butler describes as a corporeal style that "*is* a historical situation" and "a manner of doing, dramatizing, and *reproducing* an historical situation" (404).

52. This similar connection between basketball and lynching is made in the introduction's analysis of Hank Willis Thomas's *Overtime* and chapter 1's analysis of Deborah Morales's *On the Shoulder of Giants*.

53. Carter Mathes, *Imagine the Sound: Experimental African American Literature after Civil Rights* (Minneapolis: University of Minnesota Press, 2015), 4. Mathes is drawing on Fred Moten's understanding that "off-set or off-rhythm animates audiovisuality (the arrhythmia of its multiple tracks) of the commodity in general." Fred Moten, *In the Break: The Aesthetics of the Black Radical Tradition* (Minneapolis: University of Minnesota Press, 2003), 216.

54. Mathes, *Imagine the Sound*, 3.

55. Imamu Amiri Baraka, *It's Nation Time* (Chicago: Third World Press, 1970).

56. Grant Farred, *In Motion, at Rest: The Event of the Athletic Body* (Minneapolis: University of Minnesota Press, 2014), 39.

57. M. Jacqui Alexander, *Pedagogies of Crossing: Meditations on Feminism, Sexual Politics, Memory, and the Sacred* (Durham, NC: Duke University Press, 2006), 189–96.

58. Farred, *In Motion, At Rest*, 40. Grant Farred analyzes the event of the Black body at rest through the immobile acts of former Pacers small forward Ron Artest (currently known as Metta World Peace), specifically his infamous moment of lying down during an NBA game between the Indiana Pacers and the Detroit Pistons that disrupted the flow of sports time. Known

as the Motown Melee or the Palace Brawl, the ensuing "event"—the violent exchange between Artest, who lay on the scorer's table, and the white male inebriated Pistons fans who assaulted him—provoked "a 'crisis' about sport, about sportsmanship, about player salaries and their concomitant privileges, and race. All of which produced, in a predictable convergence of these factors, an opportunistic attack on the culture of hip-hop and its influence on the NBA." Grant Farred, "The Event of the Black Body at Rest: Mêlée in Motown," *Cultural Critique* 66 (Spring 2007), 61. NBA Commissioner David Stern suspended Artest for the rest of the 2004–2005 NBA season, the longest suspension ever given to a player. Farred argues that Artest's immobile body produced an event that generated its own historical forces, concatenating Artest's performance of refusal (his opposition to move, perform, and play out a specific racialized sporting role) to that of other bodies that performed spectacular acts of stillness, from Rosa Parks (as I encouraged Farred to consider in our correspondence about his work, for which he later theorized via the notion of the "black bottom") to Emmett Till to Jackie Robinson to Tommie Smith and John Carlos. Farred's reading of the stilled Black sporting body connected to other embodied experiences directly relates to Harvey Young's analyses of the enforced stillness of the Black body in American boxing through the boxers Tom Molineaux, Jack Johnson, Joe Louis, and Muhammad Ali. Young explains that each boxer had a "direct connection to the experience of black captivity, faced societal caricatures and stereotypes of blackness, and attempted to create a different persona that differed from the prizefighters who preceded him." Young, *Embodying Black Experience*, 24.

59. Farred, "The Event of the Black Body at Rest," 71.

60. Field, "Rebellious Unlearning," 97–98.

61. Sarkar, "The Mellifluous 'Illogics' of the 'Bollywood Musical,'" 48.

62. Stuart Hall, "Notes on Deconstructing 'The Popular,'" in *People's History and Socialist Theory*, ed. Raphael Samuel (London: Routledge and Kegan Paul, 1981), 228.

63. J.C. Furnas, *Goodbye to Uncle Tom: An Analysis of the Myths Pertaining to the American Negro, from Their Origins to the Misconceptions of Today* (New York: William Sloane Associates, 1956).

64. Du Bois, *The Souls of Black Folk*; Eldridge Cleaver, *Soul on Ice* (New York: Dell Publishing, 1986); Frantz Fanon, *Black Skin, White Masks*, trans. Richard Philcox (1952; repr., New York: Grove Press, 2008); Frantz Fanon, *The Wretched of the Earth*, trans. Constance Farrington (1961; repr., New York: Grove Press, 1966); Frantz Fanon, *Toward the African Revolution*, trans. Haakon Chevalier (1964; repr., New York: Grove Press, 1994); and Immanuel Wallerstein, *Africa: The Politics of Independence* (New York: Vintage Books, 1961).

65. While imprisoned in Folsom State Prison, Eldridge Cleaver read Malcolm X, Niccolò Machiavelli, Tom Payne, Richard Wright, and Karl Marx, among others, to make sense of and through his identification with blackness.

Soul on Ice also directly comments on sports, particularly when Cleaver discusses the Muhammad Ali and Floyd Patterson prizefights. In the book, Cleaver laments the fact that "what white America demands in her black champions is a brilliant, powerful body and a dull, bestial mind—a tiger in the ring and a pussycat outside of it." Cleaver, *Soul on Ice*, 92. For Cleaver, Muhammad Ali was the first "free" Black champion to challenge white America, a conclusion that would resonate with *Hour Glass*'s newly defiant athlete.

66. Fanon, *Black Skin, White Masks*, 136.

67. The concept of combat breathing is useful to analyze the sonic atmosphere in Gerima's film. Fanon writes that "there is no occupation of territory, on the one hand, and independence of persons on the other. It is the country as a whole, its history, its daily pulsation that are contested, disfigured, in the hope of final destruction. Under this condition, the individual's breathing is an observed and occupied breathing. It is a combat breathing." Fanon, *Toward the African Revolution*, 65. *Hour Glass* has no dialogue and the protagonist never opens his mouth to mime speech; instead the film's focus is centralized on images of him breathing on and off the court.

68. Immanuel Wallerstein was a Marxist sociologist who is most known for developing "world-systems" theory, an episteme that breaks from first, second, and third world assignations for his understanding of colony, labor, capital, and empire. Wallerstein traveled throughout Africa during the ends of colonial rule and published the book, which examines African politics during the collapse of colonization, in 1961 after the Year of Africa was declared in 1960. This was a time when many remaining African nations went through decolonization proper, a process that began after World War II.

69. Field, "Rebellious Unlearning," 98–99.

70. Fanon, *Black Skin, White Masks*, 206.

71. Huey P. Newton, *Revolutionary Suicide* (New York: Harcourt Brace Jovanovich, 1973).

72. Leerom Medovoi, "Theorizing Historicity, or the Many Meanings of *Blacula*," *Screen* 39, no. 1 (Spring 1998), 19. His emphasis.

73. Medovoi, "Theorizing Historicity, or the Many Meanings of *Blacula*," 16. His emphasis.

74. In her summary and analysis of the film, Allyson Nadia Field also makes the point that *Hour Glass* draws on Gerima's experiences, athletes' histories, the events at UCLA, and the broader social landscape. My initial insights are aided by her summation but expanded, clarified, and deepened for my own readings of critical muscle memory as symptomatic through unrepresented but also subtly referenced historical moments. Field, "Rebellious Unlearning," 98.

75. Q&A with Haile Gerima and Allyson Nadia Field, UCLA Film & Television Archive, Hammer Museum's Billy Wilder Theater, Los Angeles, California, October 23, 2011.

76. Haile Gerima, quoted in Safford and Triplett, "Haile Gerima," 62. His emphasis.

77. Young, *Soul Power*, 232.

78. Masilela, "The Los Angeles School of Black Filmmakers," 109.

79. The Watts Rebellion (also known as the Watts Uprising or the Watts Riot) began on August 11, 1965. The rebellion was the result of long-standing acts of racism, residential segregation, disenfranchisement, and police discrimination against Watts's Black residents. The Los Angeles Police Department stopped motorist Marquette Frye, and the incident, escalated into a fight, with the police officers assaulting and arresting Frye, his mother, and brother. This act of brutality was the tipping point for Watts's residents fed up with their treatment by the police. The Watts Rebellion lasted until August 15, the nation witnessing the violence on television. Thirty-four people died (all but five were Black), and thousands were arrested. The US National Guard was brought in to stop the rebellion, which resulted in more than $200 million in property damage. Gerald Horne, *Fire This Time: The Watts Uprising and the 1960s* (Charlottesville: University of Virginia Press, 1995), 3.

80. Kareem Abdul-Jabbar, quoted in Douglas Hartmann, *Race, Culture, and the Revolt of the Black Athlete: The 1968 Olympic Protests and Their Aftermath* (Chicago: University of Chicago Press, 2004), 56.

81. Kareem Abdul-Jabbar, quoted in Douglas Hartmann, *Race, Culture, and the Revolt of the Black Athlete*, 52.

82. Chet Walker, quoted in Zirin, *A People's History of Sports in the United States*, 281.

83. The nationally televised story of the "Black 14" is a reminder that narratives and images of Black athletes in revolt in the late 1960s were circulating beyond the defining moment of Smith and Carlos at the Olympic Games. The controversy, which divided the school and town, was captured by mainstream networks and alternative broadcast shows. Darius Clark Monroe deliberately wanted to tell the "Black 14's" story through the ample aired and unaired television footage shot by ABC News, NBC, and *Black Journal*, foregoing the use of talking heads and present-day one-on-one interviews to detail the story. This formal choice allows for the "Black 14" to speak for themselves. For example, there is a moment when ABC reporter John Davenport asks de facto leader Guillermo "Willie" Hysaw if he and the group are being influenced by an outside force to instigate protest as a test case for other schools. Willie responds: "I think this is typical, and if I might use the term, something a typical white person would say. Now, since a Black man stands up for what he believes, they think that automatically that some other guy had to come in and instigate this thing. But this is something that is going to be happening throughout the rest of this century." While giving space to the institutional voices that wanted to silence the Black football players through the mainstream footage, the documentary also centers the point of view of the "Black 14," specifically Willie's impassioned recounting of the events and the group's intentions, treatment, and expectations. As a result, the first-person archival footage feels immediate and prophetic. For example, at the end of the documentary, Willie explains: "I'm going to meet Coach Eaten again. He might not be fifty-two years old. He might not be a football coach. But I'm going to meet him again, and from this

experience I'm going to be prepared for the next Coach Eaten. And I'm going to solve it firsthand, you know. 'Cause I made a mistake by sitting there and letting this man holler at me and my other Black brothers, but I'd be damned if he walked in here now." Black athletes today still must confront the "next Coach Eaten" in their sporting world.

84. Medovoi, "Theorizing Historicity, or the Many Meanings of *Blacula*," 13. My unpacking of *Hour Glass*'s performativity draws on Leerom Medovoi's reading of the historicity of William Crain's 1972 film *Blacula*.

85. Michael Gillespie's focus is specifically on film noir and Bill Duke's *Deep Cover* (1992). Michael Boyce Gillespie, *Film Blackness: American Cinema and the Idea of Black Film* (Durham, NC: Duke University Press, 2016), 83–84.

86. George Lipsitz, "Genre Anxiety and Racial Representation in 1970s Cinema," 209.

87. George Lipsitz, "Genre Anxiety and Racial Representation in 1970s Cinema," 209.

88. George Lipsitz, "Genre Anxiety and Racial Representation in 1970s Cinema," 210.

89. Radhika Mohanram, *Black Body: Women, Colonialism, and Space* (Minneapolis: University of Minnesota Press, 1999), xiv.

90. Mypheduh Films is a production and distribution company formed in 1982 by Gerima, his partner Shirikiana Aina, and his sister Salome Gerima to control the distribution of his extensive filmography.

91. A preservation project that was part of the Getty Foundation's "Pacific Standard Time: Art in L.A. 1945–1980," UCLA's Film & Television Archive helped locate, identify, restore, catalog, preserve, and exhibit the films made by L.A. Rebellion filmmakers via film prints and in digital formats. The Archive maintains an extensive website on the L.A. Rebellion, including access to the story/history of the group; filmmaker bios and filmographies; films and videos (Project One films and interviews) for streaming; information on the 2011 film exhibition and symposium; and links to the book *L.A. Rebellion: Creating a New Black Cinema* and free DVD anthology, which includes twenty-five films.

92. Clyde Taylor, "Once upon a Time in the West ... L.A. Rebellion," in *L.A. Rebellion: Creating a New Black Cinema*, ed. Allyson Nadia Field, Jan-Christopher Horak, and Jacqueline Najuma Stewart (Oakland: University of California Press, 2015), xxiv. Framing the import and impact of L.A. Rebellion films, Clyde Taylor notes, "Those who might dismiss the preservation of these films as something like storing a time capsule are mistaken. These films are still radioactive in the present cultural landscape" (xxiv).

93. For more on *Shut Up and Dribble*, see Samantha N. Sheppard, "Give and Go: The Double Movement of *Shut Up and Dribble*," *Los Angeles Review of Books*, February 12, 2019, www.lareviewofbooks.org/article/give-go-double-movement-shut-dribble/?fbclid=IwAR1LXURjKZPcuN2D2LCVffyze5kyCRcAdVymfoxoUKd-jnTYjolUWSpDFgs.

94. Muhammad Ali was a global sports icon whose influence and humanitarian work extended beyond the world of sports. He was an inimitable figure

associated with Black sporting resistance. A skillful boxer, he fused verbal dexterity and Black vernacular traditions, making him a rebellious, countercultural athlete. Ali's sporting blackness made him a politicized, antiestablishment hero (and for some an antihero) whose performances of dissent were refusals to be "the people's champ" as defined by others, particularly the US government's agenda to use him as a pawn in their imperial foreign policy. Citing his religious belief, Ali refused to enlist in the US Armed Forces, famously not stepping forward when his named was called at the induction ceremony in Houston, Texas, on April 28, 1967. His radical act of stillness in that moment led to him being arrested, fined $10,000, stripped of his heavyweight title, and denied his passport. On June 28, 1971, the Supreme Court overturned Ali's conviction, setting the stage for his boxing comeback and the famous "Rumble in the Jungle" fight in 1974 against George Foreman, where he regained the heavyweight title. As a sports figure, Ali—the person/athlete—fits squarely within this chapter's framing of the revolt of the Black athlete. However, his cinematic depictions, ranging from *The Greatest* (Tom Gries, 1977) for which he stars as himself to *Ali* (Michael Man, 2001) starring Will Smith as the famous pugilist, are in tension (even if productively so) with my exploration of the revolt of the cinematic Black athlete, an engagement that considers not only the representation of resistance but also the formal modes of *un*convention. The fiction films about Ali appropriate many of the formal conventions of the boxing film, ones that dramatize the rise, fall, and redemption of the boxer. While these films do signal broader political and cultural struggles that center around Ali, they also demonstrate the tendency of sports films to individualize conflict and tout individual achievement above all else. As a result, the fictional boxing films about Ali do not have the same kind of representation of sporting blackness and/as formal *un*convention evinced in *Hour Glass*. The numerous sports documentaries about Ali, however, are interesting examples of discourses of and about critical muscle memory, an insight about Black sports documentaries I examine at length in chapter 1.

95. There are a number of interesting parallels between Colin Kaepernick and the protagonist in *Hour Glass*, including growing up in a white adoptive family, going from athletic participation to protest, and being advised/influenced by Harry Edwards. Both Kaepernick and the student-athlete in *Hour Glass* end up having to leave their sport and look to the Black community for support.

96. Samantha N. Sheppard, "Close-Up: Sports, Race, and the Power of Narrative—Introduction," *Black Camera* 10, no. 1 (Fall 2018), 158.

97. The "Dream Crazy" commercial includes footage of sports pros Nyjah Huston, Zeina Nassar, Kai Lenny, Eliud Kipchoge, Serena Williams, Odell Beckham Jr., Alphonso Davies, LeBron James, Colin Kaepernick, US Soccer's Women's National Team, Shaquem Griffin, and Lacey Baker alongside amateur athletes Isaiah Bird, Megan Blunk, Alicia Woollcott, and Charlie Jabaley. All are considered athletes who have overcome adversity to excel in their respective sports. The overarching theme is that greatness in sports and life requires one to "dream crazy."

98. The celebration over Nike's new advertising campaign with Colin Kaepernick should, however, be tempered. "Dream Crazy" is no *Hour Glass*. The commercial does not mention Black Lives Matter nor the kneeling protest specifically. Nike's use of Kaepernick was a calculated risk, driven less by fears of angering the NFL (they have been partners with Nike since 2012) and more by market logics for the clout and credibility to be gained by young, urban consumers. See Julie Creswell, Kevin Draper, and Sapna Maheshwari, "Nike Nearly Dropped Colin Kaepernick before Embracing Him," *New York Times*, September 27, 2018, B9. Similar to my critique of *Shut up and Dribble*, "Dream Crazy" reifies and capitulates to the sports industrial complex, underscoring how "every critique doubles as a celebration." Sheppard, "Give and Go."

99. J. Jack Halberstam, "Success, Failure, and Everything in Between," in *Asian American Sporting Cultures*, ed. Stanley I. Thangaraj, Constancio R. Arnaldo Jr., and Christina B. Chin (New York: New York University Press, 2016), viii.

CONCLUSION

1. Stuart Hall, "What Is This 'Black' in Black Popular Culture," in *Black Popular Culture: A Project by Michele Wallace*, ed. Gina Dent (Seattle, WA: Bay Press, 1992), 27.

2. A.O. Scott, "A Thrilling Dunk on Capitalism," *New York Times*, February 7, 2019, C1.

3. Andrew R. Chow, "How Netflix's *High Flying Bird* Upends the Conventional Sports Movie," *Time*, February 8, 2019, www.time.com/5524677/high-flying-bird-netflix-sports-movies/.

4. See TreaAndrea M. Russworm, "Computational Blackness: The Procedural Logics of Race, Game, and Cinema, or How Spike Lee's *Livin' Da Dream* Productively "Broke" a Popular Video Game," *Black Camera: An International Film Journal* 10, no. 1 (Fall 2018): 193–212.

5. I am not alone in thinking about the magnitude of what it means to witness Serena in this era of tennis. Almost immediately after her 2019 defeat at the US Open, the *New York Times* published the op-ed "The Power of Serena Williams" by Dr. Tera W. Hunter, described as a historian and avid tennis fan. This account and other writings alongside countless posts on social media attest to how watching Serena play (for most of us on television) is a unique individualized and shared media experience of sporting blackness that shapes our critical muscle memory of tennis, sports, and Black excellence. See Tera W. Hunter, "The Power of Serena Williams," *New York Times*, September 7, 2019, www.nytimes.com/2019/09/07/opinion/serena-williams-us-open-tennis.html?action=click&module=Opinion&pgtype=Homepage&fbclid=IwAR1mOXaa6 7osDScaY-Dx9rdXvJxlBJ-qyPgcBTo52OFaEQzV7EGPldHjEoE.

Bibliography

Abdul-Jabbar, Kareem. *On the Shoulders of Giants: My Journey Through the Harlem Renaissance*. New York: Simon and Schuster, 2007.

Alexander, Elizabeth. "Can You be BLACK and Look at This?": Reading the Rodney King Video(s)." *Public Culture* 7 (1994): 77–94.

Alexander, M. Jacqui. *Pedagogies of Crossing: Meditations on Feminism, Sexual Politics, Memory, and the Sacred*. Durham, NC: Duke University Press, 2006.

Ali, Muhmmad with Richard Durham. *The Greatest: My Own Story*. New York: Random House, 1975.

All-American Girls Professional Baseball League. "The All-American Girls Professional Baseball League Rules of Conduct, 1943–1954." In *Women and Sports in the United States: A Documentary Reader*, edited by Susan K. Cahn and Jean O'Reilly, 59–61. Boston: Northeastern University Press, 2007.

Allen, James. *Without Sanctuary: Lynching Photography in America*. Santa Fe: Twins Palm Publishers, 2000.

Althusser, Louis, and Etinne Balibar. *Reading Capital*. Translated by Ben Brewster. London: Verso, 1970.

Bailey, Moya, and Trudy. "On Misogynoir: Citation, Erasure, and Plagiarism." *Feminist Media Studies* 18, no. 4 (2018): 762–68.

Baker, Aaron. *Contesting Identities: Sports in American Film*. Urbana: University of Illinois Press, 2003.

———. "Intersectionality in *Venus Vs.*" In *Sporting Realities: Critical Readings on the Sports Documentary*, edited by Samantha N. Sheppard and Travis T. Vogan. Lincoln: University of Nebraska Press, 2020.

———. "Transmedia Storytelling and Friday Night Lights." In *Sport im Films*, edited by Robert Gugutzer and Barbara Englert, 223–39. Konstanz, Germany: UVK Publisher, 2014.

Baker, Courtney R. *Humane Insight: Looking at Images of African American Suffering and Death*. Chicago: University of Illinois Press, 2015.

Baker, Houston A. Jr. *Critical Memory: Public Spheres, African American Writing, and Black Fathers and Sons in America*. Athens: University of Georgia Press, 2001.

Banet-Weiser, Sarah. "Hoop Dreams: Professional Basketball and the Politics of Race and Gender." *Journal of Sport & Social Issues* 23, no. 4 (November 1999): 403–20.

Baraka, Imamu Amiri. *It's Nation Time*. Chicago: Third World Press, 1970.

Bass, Amy. *Not the Triumph but the Struggle: The 1968 Olympics and the Making of the Black Athlete*. Minneapolis: University of Minnesota Press, 2002.

"Behind the Scenes of '*Friday Night Lights*.'" *Fresh Air*, July 13, 2011. www.npr.org/2011/07/15/137826323/behind-the-scenes-of-friday-night-lights.

Bell, Ramona J. "Competing Identities: Representations of the Black Female Sporting Body from 1960 to the Present." PhD diss. Bowling Green State University, 2008.

Benjammin. "#MYTOP5: BIG K.R.I.T. Names His Top 5 Movies." *The Source*, February 20, 2013. www.thesource.com/2013/02/20/mytop5-big-k-r-i-t-names-his-top-5-movies/.

Bernardi, Daniel, ed. *The Birth of Whiteness: Race and the Emergence of U.S. Cinema*. New Brunswick, NJ: Rutgers University Press, 1996.

———. *Classic Hollywood, Classic Whiteness*. Minneapolis: University of Minnesota Press, 2001.

———. *The Persistence of Whiteness: Race and Contemporary Hollywood Cinema*. New York: Routledge, 2008.

Bernstein, Robin. "Dances with Things: Material Culture and the Performance of Race." *Social Text* 27, no. 4 (2009): 67–94.

Birrell, Susan, and Mary G. McDonald, eds. *Reading Sport: Critical Essays on Power and Representation*. Boston: Northeastern University Press, 2000.

Bissinger, H.G. *After Friday Night Lights: When the Games Ended, Real Life Began. An Unlikely Love Story*. Kindle Edition. New York: Byliner Inc, 2012.

———. *Friday Night Lights: A Town, a Team, and a Dream*. New York: De Capo Press, 2000.

———. "Stars of Friday Night Lights Reunite to Relive Their Story 25 Years Later." *Sports Illustrated*, July 29, 2015. www.si.com/high-school/2015/07/29/friday-night-lights-25th-anniversary-hg-bissinger-book-excerpt.

Boyd, Todd. *Young, Black, Rich, and Famous: The Rise of the NBA, the Hip Hop Invasion, and the Transformation of American Culture*. Lincoln: University of Nebraska Press, 2003.

Boyd, Todd, and Kenneth L. Shropshire. "Basketball Jones: A New World Order?" In *Basketball Jones: America Above the Rim*, edited by Todd Boyd and Kenneth L. Shropshire, 1–11. New York: New York University Press, 2000.

Boykoff, Jules. *Power Games: A Political History of the Olympics*. London: Verso, 2016.

Browne, Nick. "Race: The Political Unconscious in American Film." *East-West Film Journal* 6, no. 1 (January 1992): 5–16.

Bryant, Howard. *The Heritage: Black Athletes, a Divided America, and the Politics of Patriotism*. Boston: Beacon Press, 2018.

Bryant, Tisa. *Unexplained Presence*. Providence: Leon Works, 2007.

Burgess, Omar. "J. Cole Explains Album Delays, Talks 'Friday Night Lights.'" *HipHopDX*, November 8, 2010. www.hiphopdx.com/news/id.12903/title.j -cole-explains-album-delays-talks-friday-night-lights#.

Butler, Judith. "Athletic Genders: Hyperbolic Instance and/or the Overcoming of Sexual Binarism." *Stanford Humanities Review* 6, no. 2 (1998): 103–11.

———. *Bodies that Matter: On the Discursive Limits of Sex*. New York: Routledge, 1993.

———. "Performative Acts and Gender Constitution: An Essay in Phenomenology and Feminist Theory." In *Writing on the Body: Female Embodiment and Feminist Theory*, edited by Katie Conboy, Nadia Medina, and Sarah Stanbury, 401–18. New York: Columbia University Press, 1997.

———. *Undoing Gender*. New York: Routledge, 2004.

Cahn, Susan K. *Coming on Strong: Gender and Sexuality in Twentieth-Century Sport*. Cambridge, MA: Harvard University Press, 1998.

Cahn, Susan K., and Jean O'Reilly, eds. *Women and Sports in the United States: A Documentary Reader*. Boston: Northeastern University Press, 2007.

Caldwell, Kelly. "Review of Citizen: An American Lyric." *MAKE Literary Magazine*, February 6, 2018. www.makemag.com/review-citizen-an-american -lyric/.

Carlos, John, with Dave Zirin. *The John Carlos Story*. Chicago: Haymarket Books, 2011.

Carrington, Ben. "'Race,' Representation and the Sporting Body," Paper submitted to the Centre for Urban and Community Research's Occasional Paper series, Goldsmith College, University of London, May 2002. www .gold.ac.uk/media/documents-by-section/departments/research-centres -and-units/research-centres/centre-for-urban-and-comm/carrington.pdf.

———. *Race, Sport and Politics: The Sporting Black Diaspora*. Thousand Oaks, CA: Sage, 2010.

Carter, Curtis L. "Arts and Cognition: Performance, Criticism, and Aesthetics." *Art Education* 33, no. 62 (1983): 61–67.

Chow, Andrew R. "How Netflix's High Flying Bird Upends the Conventional Sports Movie." Time, February 8, 2019. www.time.com/5524677/high-flying -bird-netflix-sports-movies/.

Cleaver, Eldridge. *Soul on Ice*. New York: Dell, 1986.

Cole, Cheryl. *Women in Sports: Issues and Controversies*. Thousand Oaks, CA: Sage, 1993.

Cole, Cheryl, and Samantha King. "Representing Black Masculinity and Urban Possibilities: Racism, Realism, and Hoop Dreams." In *Sport and Postmodern Times*, edited by Geneviève Rail, 49–86. Albany: State University of New York Press, 1998.

Coleman, Robin Means. *Horror Noire: Blacks in American Horror Films from the 1890s to Present*. New York: Routledge, 2011.

Cooky, Cheryl, Michael A. Messner, and Robin H. Hextrum. "Women Play Sports, but Not on TV: A Longitudinal Study of Televised News Media." *Communication & Sport* 1, no. 3 (2013): 203–30.

Creedon, Pamela, ed. *Women, Media, and Sport: Challenging Gender Values.* Thousand Oaks, CA: Sage, 1994.

Crenshaw, Kimberlé. "Mapping the Margins: Intersectionality, Identity Politics, and Violence against Women of Color." *Stanford Law Review* 43, no. 6 (July 1991): 1241–29.

Creswell, Julie, Kevin Draper, and Sapna Maheshwari. "Nike Nearly Dropped Colin Kaepernick before Embracing Him." *New York Times.* September 27, 2018, B9.

Csikszentmihalyi, Mihaly, and Susan Jackson. *Flow in Sports: The Keys to Optimal Experiences and Performances.* Champaign, IL: Human Kinetics, 1999.

Cutler, Janet K. "Rewritten on Film: Documenting the Artist." In *Struggles for Representation: African American Documentary Film and Video,* edited by Phyllis R. Klotman and Janet K. Cutler, 151–210. Bloomington: Indiana University Press, 1999.

Cutler, Janet K., and Phyllis. R. Klotman. "Introduction." In *Struggles for Representation: African American Documentary Film and Video,* edited by Phyllis R. Klotman and Janet K. Cutler, xiii–xxxiii. Bloomington: Indiana University Press, 1999.

Daniels, Dayna B. *Polygendered and Ponytailed: The Dilemma of Femininity and the Female Athlete.* Toronto: Women's Press, 2009.

———. "You Throw Like a Girl: Sports and Misogyny on the Silver Screen." In *All-Stars and Movie Stars: Sports in Film and History,* edited by Ron Briley, Michael K. Schoenecke, and Deborah A. Carmichael, 105–28. Lexington: University of Kentucky Press, 2008.

Davis, Amira Rose. "No League of Their Own: Baseball, Black Women, and the Politics of Representation." *Radical History Review* 124 (May 2016): 74–96.

Doane, Mary Ann. "The Voice in the Cinema: The Articulation of Body and Space." *Yale French Studies* no. 60 (1980): 33–50.

Doyle, Jennifer. "Dirt off Her Shoulders." *GLQ: A Journal of Lesbian and Gay Studies.* 13, no. 4 (2013): 419–33.

———. "Why Police the Border between Men and Women's Sports? (Repost w/ Comments about Caster Semenya)." *From a Left Wing,* August 21, 2009. www.fromaleftwing.blogspot.com/2009/08/why-police-border-between -mens-and.html.

Du Bois, W. E. B. *The Souls of Black Folk.* 1903. New York: Dover, 1994.

Early, Gerald. "Why Baseball Was the Black National Pastime." In *Basketball Jones: America above the Rim,* edited by Todd Boyd and Kenneth L. Shropshire, 27–50. New York: New York University Press, 2000.

Ebert, Roger. "*Hoop Dreams.*" Roger Ebert.com, October 21, 1994. www.roger ebert.com/reviews/hoop-dreams-1994.

———. "*Juwanna Mann.*" Roger Ebert.com, June 21, 2002. www.rogerebert .com/reviews/juwanna-mann-2002.

Edwards, Harry. *The Revolt of the Black Athlete*. New York: Free Press, 1971.
———. *The Revolt of the Black Athlete*. 50th anniversary edition. Urbana: University of Illinois Press, 2017.
Elias, Norbert, and Eric Dunning. *Quest for Excitement: Sport and Leisure in the Civilizing Process*. Oxford: Basil Blackwell, 1986.
Ellison, Ralph. *Invisible Man*. 1952. New York: Vintage Books, 1980.
Fanon, Frantz. *Black Skin, White Masks*. Translated by Ricard Philcox. 1952. Reprint New York: Grove Press, 2008.
———. *Toward the African Revolution*. Translated by Haakon Chevalier. 1964. Reprint New York: Grove Press, 1994.
———. *The Wretched of the Earth*. Translated by Constance Farrington. 1961. Reprint New York: Grove Press, 1966.
Farred, Grant. "The Event of the Black Body at Rest: Mêlée in Motown." *Cultural Critique* 66 (Spring 2007): 58–77.
———. *In Motion, at Rest: The Event of the Athletic Body*. Minneapolis: University of Minnesota Press, 2014.
———. "When Kings Were (Anti-?)Colonials: Black Athletes in Film." *Sport in Society* 11, nos. 2–3 (March 2008): 240–52.
Field, Allyson Nadia. "Rebellious Unlearning: UCLA Project One Films (1967–1978)." In *L.A. Rebellion: Creating a New Black Cinema*, edited by Allyson Nadia Field, Jan-Christopher Horak, and Jacqueline Najuma Stewart, 83–118. Oakland: University of California Press, 2015.
Field, Allyson Nadia, Jan-Christopher Horak, and Jacqueline Najuma Stewart. "Introduction: Emancipating the Image—The L.A. Rebellion of Black Filmmakers." In *L.A. Rebellion: Creating a New Black Cinema*, edited by Allyson Nadia Field, Jan-Christopher Horak, and Jacqueline Najuma Stewart, 1–54. Oakland: University of California Press, 2015.
———, eds. *L.A. Rebellion: Creating a New Black Cinema*. Oakland: University of California Press, 2015.
Fleetwood, Nicole R. *On Racial Icons: Blackness and the Public Imagination*. New Brunswick, NJ: Rutgers University Press, 2015.
———. *Troubling Vision: Performance, Visuality, and Blackness*. Chicago: University of Chicago Press, 2011.
Foster, Susan Leigh. "Choreographies of Protest." *Theatre Journal* 55, no. 3 (October 2003): 395–412.
———, ed. *Choreographing History*. Bloomington: Indiana University Press, 1995.
Foucault, Michel. *Discipline and Punish: The Birth of the Prison*. New York: Vintage Books, 1995.
Friedman, Lester D. *Sports Movies*. New Brunswick, NJ: Rutgers University Press, 2020.
Furnas, J.C. *Goodbye to Uncle Tom: An Analysis of the Myths Pertaining to the American Negro, from Their Origins to the Misconceptions of Today*. New York: William Sloane Associates, 1956.
Gabriel, Teshome H. *Third Cinema and the Third World: The Aesthetics of Liberation*. Ann Arbor, MI: UMI Research Press, 1982.

Gates, Henry Louis Jr., ed. *"Race," Writing, and Difference*. Chicago: University of Chicago Press, 1986.

———. *The Signifying Monkey: A Theory of African American Literary Criticism*. New York: Oxford University Press, 1988.

Gates, Racquel J. *Double Negative: The Black Image & Popular Culture*. Durham: Duke University Press, 2018.

Germain, David. *"Juwanna Mann." Desert News*, June 21, 2002, www.google .com/search?q=david+germain+juwanna+mann&rlz=1C1CHBF_enUS743 US743&oq=david&aqs=chrome.0.69i59j69i57j69i65l2j35i39j0.2431j0j7 &sourceid=chrome&ie=UTF-8.

Gillespie, Michael Boyce. *Film Blackness: American Cinema and the Idea of Black Film*. Durham, NC: Duke University Press, 2016.

Gleiberman, Owen. *"Juwanna Mann." Entertainment Weekly*, July 2, 2002, www.ew.com/article/2002/07/02/juwanna-mann-3/.

Golden, Thelma. "My Brother." In *Black Male: Representations of Masculinity in Contemporary American Art*, edited by Thelma Golden, 19–43. New York: Whitney Museum of Art, 1994.

Guerrasio, Jason. "*Hoop Dreams*: An Oral History." *The Dissolve*. January 15, 2014. www.thedissolve.com/features/oral-history/360-an-oral-history-of -hoop-dreams-20-years-after-its-/?page=13.

Guerrero, Ed. "The Black Man on Our Screens and the Empty Space in Representation." *Callaloo* 18, no. 2 (Spring 1995): 395–400.

Gumbs, Alexis Pauline. "Black Astrophysics: A Homemade Field of Love." In *We Travel the Space Ways: Black Imagination, Fragments, and Diffractions*, edited by Henriette Gunkel and kara lynch, 15–20. New York: Transcript-Verlag, 2019.

Halberstam, J. Jack. "Success, Failure, and Everything in Between." In *Asian American Sporting Cultures*, edited by Stanley I. Thangaraj, Constancio R. Arnaldo Jr., and Christina B. Chin, vii–x. New York: New York University Press, 2016.

Halberstam, Judith. *Female Masculinity*. Durham, NC: Duke University Press, 1998.

———. *The Queer Art of Failure*. Durham, NC: Duke University Press, 2011.

Hall, M. Ann. *Feminism and Sporting Bodies: Essays on Theory and Practice*. Champaign, IL: Human Kinetics, 1996.

Hall, Stuart. "Cultural Identity and Cinematic Representation." *Framework: The Journal of Cinema and Media* no. 36 (1989): 68–81.

———. "New Ethnicities." In *Stuart Hall: Critical Dialogues in Cultural Studies*, edited by David Morley and Kuan-Hsing Chen. New York: Routledge, 1996. 441–49.

———. "Notes on Deconstructing 'The Popular.'" In *People's History and Socialist Theory*, edited by Raphael Samuel, 227–40. London: Routledge and Kegan Paul, 1981.

———. "Race, Articulation and Societies Structured in Dominance." In *Black British Cultural Studies: A Reader*, edited by Houston A. Baker Jr., Manthia

Diawara, and Ruth H. Lindeborg, 16–60. Chicago: University of Chicago Press, 1996.

———. "The Spectacle of the 'Other.'" In *Representation: Cultural Representations and Signifying Practices*, edited by Stuart Hall, 223–90. London: Sage, 1997.

———. "What Is This 'Black' in Black Popular Culture." In *Black Popular Culture: A Project by Michele Wallace*, edited by Gina Dent, 21–33. Seattle: Bay Press, 1992.

Harris, Keith M. *Boys, Boyz, Bois: An Ethics of Black Masculinity in Film and Popular Media*. New York: Routledge, 2006.

Hartman, Saidiya. *Lose Your Mother: A Journey along the Atlantic Slave Route*. New York: Farrar, Straus, and Giroux, 2007.

Hartmann, Douglas. *Race, Culture, and the Revolt of the Black Athlete: The 1968 Olympic Protests and Their Aftermath*. Chicago: University of Chicago Press, 2004.

Harvey, Dennis. "*Juwanna Mann*." *Variety*, June 20, 2002. www.variety .com/2002/film/reviews/juwanna-mann-1200547674/.

Higginbotham, Evelyn Brooks. *Righteous Discontent: The Women's Movement in the Black Baptist Church, 1880–1920*. Cambridge, MA: Harvard University Press, 1993.

Hoberman, John. *Darwin's Athletes: How Sport Has Damaged Black America and Preserved the Myth of Race*. Boston: Mariner, 1997.

hooks, bell. *Reel to Real: Race, Class, and Sex at the Movies*. New York: Routledge, 1996.

Horne, Gerald. *Fire This Time: The Watts Uprising and the 1960s*. Charlottesville: University of Virginia Press, 1995.

Howard, Steve. "A Cinema of Transformation: The Films of Haile Gerima." *Cinéaste* 14, no. 1 (1985): 28–29, 39.

Hull, Gloria T., Patricia Bell Scott, and Barbara Smith, eds. *All the Women Are White, All the Blacks Are Men, but Some of Us Are Brave*. New York: The Feminist Press, 1982.

Hunter, Tera W. "The Power of Serena Williams." *New York Times*, September 7, 2019. www.nytimes.com/2019/09/07/opinion/serena-williams-us-open -tennis.html?action=click&module=Opinion&pgtype=Homepage&fbclid=Iw AR1mOXaa67osDScaY-Dx9rdXvJxlBJ-qyPgcBT052OFaEQzV7EGPldHjEoE.

Jackson, John L. Jr., and Haile Gerima. "Decolonizing the Filmic Mind: An Interview with Haile Gerima." *Callaloo* 33, no. 1 (Spring 2010): 25–36.

Jackson, Scoop. "'Hoop Reality' Gets Dream Postscript." ESPN. July 2, 2009. www.espn.com/chicago/columns/story?columnist=jackson_scoop&id =4300069.

James, C. L. R. *Beyond a Boundary*. Durham, NC: Duke University Press, 1993.

Jenkins, Henry. *Convergence Culture: Where Old and New Media Collide*. New York: New York University Press, 2006.

Jones, Glen. "In Praise of an 'Invisible Genre'? An Ambivalent Look at the Fictional Sports Feature Film." *Sport in Society* 11, no. 2 (2008): 117–29.

Jones, Jacquie. "The Accusatory Space." In *Black Popular Culture: A Project by Michele Wallace,* edited by Gina Dent, 95–98. Seattle: Bay Press, 1992.

Jorgenson, Erik, and Qiang Liu. "Muscle Memory." *Journal of Physiology* 589, no. 4 (2011): 775–76.

Kang, Jay Caspian. "What the World Got Wrong about Kareem Abdul-Jabbar." *New York Times Magazine,* September 17, 2015, 57.

Kennedy, Lisa. "Looking Back without Anger: The Black Familiar." *Village Voice* 16 (October 1990): 62.

King, C. Richard, and David J. Leonard. "Screening the Social: An Introduction to Sport Cinema." In *Visual Economies of/in Motion: Sport and Film,* edited by C. Richard King and David J. Leonard, 1–22. New York: Peter Lang, 2006.

———. *Visual Economies of/in Motion: Sport and Film.* New York: Peter Lang, 2006.

King, Jason. "Which Way Is Down? Improvisations on Black Mobility." *Women & Performance: A Journal of Feminist Theory* 14, no. 1 (2004): 25–45.

King, Samantha. "Contesting the Closet: Sheryl Swoopes, Racialized Sexuality, and Media Culture." In *Commodified and Criminalized: New Racism and African Americans in Contemporary Sports,* edited by David J. Leonard and C. Richard King, 203–21. Lanham, MD: Rowman & Littlefield, 2011.

Klein, Richard. *Hank Willis Thomas: Strange Fruit* (exhibition catalog). Ridgefield, CT: The Aldrich Contemporary Art Museum, 2012.

Kroll, Justin. "'Friday Night Lights' New Film Taps Director David Gordon Green." *Variety,* May 9, 2018. www.variety.com/2018/film/news/friday -night-light-david-gordon-green-1202720026/.

Lansbury, Jennifer H. *A Spectacular Leap: Black Women Athletes in Twentieth-Century America.* Fayetteville: University of Arkansas Press, 2014.

Leonard, David J. *After Artest: The NBA and the Assault on Blackness.* Albany: State University of New York Press, 2012.

Lieberman, Viridiana. *Sports Heroines on Film: A Critical Study of Cinematic Women Athletes, Coaches, and Owners.* Jefferson, NC: McFarland & Company, Inc., 2015.

Lipsitz, George. "Genre Anxiety and Racial Representation in 1970s Cinema." In *Refiguring American Film Genres,* edited by Nick Browne, 208–32. Berkley: University of California Press, 1998.

Lorde, Audre. *Zami: A New Spelling of My Name.* Berkeley, CA: Crossing Press, 1982.

Malitsky, Joshua. "Knowing Sports: The Logic of the Contemporary Sports Documentary." *Journal of Sport History* 41, no. 2 (Summer 2014): 205–14.

Masilela, Ntongela. "The Los Angeles School of Black Filmmakers." In *Black American Cinema,* edited by Manthia Diawara, 107–17. New York: Routledge, 1993.

Mask, Mia. "Who's behind That Fat Suit? Momma, Madea, Rasputia and the Politics of Cross-Dressing." In *Contemporary Black American Cinema: Race, Gender and Sexuality at the Movies,* edited by Mia Mask, 155–74. New York: Routledge, 2012.

Mathes, Carter. *Imagine the Sound: Experimental African American Literature after Civil Rights*. Minneapolis: University of Minnesota Press, 2015.

McDonald, Ian. "Situating the Sport Documentary." *Journal of Sport & Social Issues* 31, no 3 (2007): 208–25.

Medovoi, Leerom. "Theorizing Historicity, or the Many Meanings of *Blacula*." *Screen* 39, no. 1 (Spring 1998): 1–28.

Mercer, Kobena. *Welcome to the Jungle: New Positions in Black Cultural Studies*. New York: Routledge, 1994.

Minh-ha, Trinh T. *Cinema Interval*. New York: Routledge, 1999.

———. *When the Moon Waxes Read: Representation, Gender, and Cultural Politics*. New York: Routledge, 1991.

Mitchell, W.J.T. *Seeing through Race*. Cambridge, MA: Harvard University Press, 2012.

Mohanram, Radhika. *Black Body: Women, Colonialism, and Space*. Minneapolis: University of Minnesota Press, 1999.

Morrison, Toni. *Playing in the Dark: Whiteness and the Literary Imagination*. Cambridge, MA: Harvard University Press, 1992.

Moten, Fred. *In the Break: The Aesthetics of the Black Radical Tradition*. Minneapolis: University of Minnesota Press, 2003.

Muñoz, José Esteban. *Cruising Utopia: The Then and There of Queer Futurity*. New York: New York University Press, 2009.

Murashige, Mike. "Haile Gerima and the Political Economy of Cinematic Resistance." In *Representing Blackness: Issues in Film and Video*, edited by Valerie Smith, 183–204. New Brunswick, NJ: Rutgers University Press, 2003.

Naficy, Hamid. *An Accented Cinema: Exilic and Diasporic Filmmaking*. Princeton, NJ: Princeton University Press, 2001.

Neal, Mark Anthony. *Looking for Leroy: Illegible Black Masculinities*. New York: New York University Press, 2013.

Negra, Diane. *The Archive and the Repertoire: Performing Cultural Memory in the Americas*. Durham, NC: Duke University Press, 2003.

Newton, Huey P. *Revolutionary Suicide*. New York: Harcourt Brace Jovanovich, 1973.

Nichols, Bill. *Representing Reality*. Bloomington: Indiana University Press, 1991.

Nyong'o, Tavia. "The Unforgivable Transgression of Being Caster Semenya." *Women & Performance: A Journal of Feminist Theory* 20, no. 1 (2010): 95–100.

Obenson, Tambay A. "Watch 25-Minute Conversation with Gina Prince-Bythewood on '*Love & Basketball*' and Indie Filmmaking Challenges." *Indie Wire*, November 13, 2015. www.indiewire.com/2015/11/watch-25-minute-conversation-with-gina-prince-bythewood-on-love-basketball-indie-filmmaking-challenges-137636/.

Okpokwasili, Okwui. "Beyoncé the Readymade." *Walker Art*, September 23, 2014. www.walkerart.org/magazine/beyonce-saidiya-hartment-ralph-lemon.

O'Reilly, Jean. "The Woman's Sports as the New Melodrama." In *Women and Sports in the United States: A Documentary Reader*, edited by Jean O'Reilly and Susan K. Cahn, 283–97. Boston: Northeastern University Press, 2007.

Pablo, J. "Q&A: Big K.R.I.T. on His Rise, Dedicating Songs to His Grandma, and Being Inspired by *Friday Night Lights*." *Village Voice*, March 15, 2012. www.villagevoice.com/2012/03/15/qa-big-k-r-i-t-on-his-rise-dedicating -songs-to-his-grandma-and-being-inspired-by-friday-night-lights/.

Pough, Gwendolyn D. *Check It While I Wreck It: Black Womanhood, Hip Hop Culture, and the Public Sphere*. Boston: Northeastern University Press, 2004.

Raengo, Alessandra. *Critical Race Theory and "Bamboozled."* New York: Bloomsbury, 2016.

———. "A Necessary Signifier: The Adaption of Robinson's Body-Image in 'The Jackie Robinson Story.'" *Adaptation* 1 (2008): 79–105.

———. *On the Sleeve of the Visual: Race as Face Value*. Hanover: Dartmouth University Press, 2013.

Rankine, Claudia. *Citizen: An American Lyric*. Minneapolis: Graywolf Press, 2014.

———. "The Meaning of Serena Williams: On Tennis and Black Excellence." *New York Times Magazine* August 25, 2015, 39.

Rapping, Elayne. *The Movie of the Week: Private Stories, Public Lives*. Minneapolis: University of Minnesota Press, 1992.

Regester, Charlene. "From the Gridiron and the Boxing Ring to the Cinema Screen: The African-American Athlete in pre-1950 Cinema." *Culture, Sport, Society: Cultures, Commerce, Media, Politics* 6, nos. 2–3 (2003): 269–92.

Reid, Mark A. "The Black Gangster Film." In *Film Genre Reader III*, edited by Barry Keith Grant, 472–89. Austin: University of Texas Press, 2005.

Renov, Michael. "Towards a Poetics of Documentary." In *Theorizing Documentary*, edited by Michael Renov, 12–36. New York: Routledge, 1993.

Reynolds, Gretchen. "How Exercise Can Help You Master New Skills." *New York Times*, September 26, 2012. www.well.blogs.nytimes.com/2012/09/26 /how-exercise-can-help-you-master-new-skills/.

Rhoden, William C. *Forty Million Dollar Slaves: The Rise, Fall, and Redemption of the Black Athlete*. New York: Three Rivers Press, 2006.

Richardson, Mark. "Our Stories Have Never Been Told: Preliminary Thoughts on Black Lesbian Cultural Production as Historiography in *The Watermelon Woman*." *Black Camera* 2, no. 2 (2011): 100–113.

Rogin, Michael. *Black Face, White Noise: Jewish Immigrants in the Hollywood Melting Pot*. Berkley: University of California Press, 1996.

Rose, Ava, and James Friedman. "Television Sports as Mas(s)culine Cult of Distraction." In *Out of Bounds: Sports, Media, and the Politics of Identity*, edited by Aaron Baker and Todd Boyd, 1–15. Bloomington: Indiana University Press, 1997.

Rose, Tricia. *Black Noise: Rap Music and Black Culture in Contemporary America*. Hanover, NH: Wesleyan University Press, 1994.

Ross, Charles K. *Mavericks, Money, and Men: The AFL, Black Players, and the Evolution of Modern Football.* Philadelphia: Temple University Press, 2016.

———. *Outside the Lines: African Americans and the Integration of the National Football League.* New York: New York University Press, 2001.

Russworm, TreaAndrea M. "Computational Blackness: The Procedural Logics of Race, Game, and Cinema, or How Spike Lee's *Livin' Da Dream* Productively 'Broke' a Popular Video Game." *Black Camera* 10, no. 1 (Fall 2018): 193–212.

Safford, Tony, and William Triplett. "Haile Gerima: Radical Departures to a New Black Cinema." *Journal of the University Film and Video Association* 35, no. 2 (Spring 1983): 59–65.

Sarig, Roni. *Third Coast: OutKast, Timbaland, and How Hip-Hop Became a Southern Thing.* Cambridge, MA: Da Capo Press, 2007.

Sarkar, Bhaskar. "The Mellifluous 'Illogics' of the 'Bollywood Musical.'" In *The Sound of Musicals,* edited by Steven Cohan, 41–53. London: BFI Publishing, 2010.

Schultz, Jaime. *Moments of Impact: Injury, Racialized Memory, and Reconciliation.* Lincoln: University of Nebraska Press, 2016.

Schulze, Laurie Jane. "*Getting Physical*: Text/Context/Reading and the Made-for-Television Movie." *Cinema Journal* 25, no. 2 (Winter 1986): 35–50.

Scott, A.O. "How the Goal Line Came to Replace the Color Line." *New York Times.* September 29, 2000, E00010.

———. "A Thrilling Dunk on Capitalism." *New York Times,* February 7, 2019, C1.

Scott, Darieck. *Extravagant Abjection: Blackness, Power, and Sexuality in the African American Literary Imagination.* New York: New York University Press, 2010.

Sexton, Jared. "Black Box." *Docalogue,* January 2019. www.docalogue.com /january-minding-the-gap/.

———. *Black Masculinity and the Cinema of Policing.* New York: Palgrave Macmillan, 2017.

Shaw, Gwendolyn DuBois. *Seeing the Unspeakable: The Art of Kara Walker.* Durham, NC: Duke University Press, 2004.

Sheppard, Samantha N. "Close-Up: Sports, Race, and the Power of Narrative—Introduction." *Black Camera* 10, no. 1 (Fall 2018): 156–61.

———. "The Exception That Proves the Rule: Race, Place, and Meritocracy in Rand University." *Black Camera* 10, no. 1 (Fall 2018): 162–76.

———. "Give and Go: The Double Movement of *Shut Up and Dribble.*" *Los Angeles Review of Books,* February 12, 2019. www.lareviewofbooks.org /article/give-go-double-movement-shut-dribble/?fbclid=IwAR1LXURjKZ PcuN2D2LCVffyze5kyCRcAdVymfoxoUKd-jnTYjolUWSpDFgs.

———. "Introduction to 'Sport and Failure.'" *Journal of Sport and Social Issues.* 43, no. 4 (2019): 267–75.

Smith, Anna. "*Juwanna Mann.*" *Time Out,* February 9, 2006. www.timeout .com/london/film/juwanna-mann.

Smith, Tommie, with David Steele. *Silent Gesture*. Philadelphia: Temple University Press, 2007.

Smith, Valerie. "The Documentary Impulse in Contemporary African-American Film." In *Black Popular Culture: A Project by Michele Wallace*, edited by Gina Dent, 56–64. Seattle: Bay Press, 1992.

Smith, Yevonne. "Women of Color in Sport and Society." *Quest* 44, no. 2 (1992): 230–45.

Snead, James. "Images of Blacks in Black Independent Films: A Brief Survey." In *Cinemas of the Black Diaspora: Diversity, Dependence, and Oppositionality*, edited by Michael T. Martin, 365–75. Detroit: Wayne State University Press, 1994.

———. *White Screens, Black Images: Hollywood from the Dark Side*. New York: Routledge, 1994.

Snorton, C. Riley. *Black on Both Sides: A Racial History of Trans Identity*. Minneapolis: University of Minnesota Press, 2017.

Sobchack, Vivian, ed. *The Persistence of History: Cinema, Television, and the Modern Event*. New York: Routledge, 1996.

Spencer, Nancy. "From 'Child's Play' to 'Party Crasher': Venus Williams, Racism, and Professional Women's Tennis." In *Sport Starts: The Cultural Politics of Sport Celebrity*, edited by David L. Andrews and Steven J. Jackson, 87–101. London: Routledge, 2001.

Spiegel, Lynn. *Make Room for TV: Television and the Family Ideal in Postwar America*. Chicago: University of Chicago Press, 1992.

Spillers, Hortense. *Black, White, and in Color: Essays on American Literature and Culture*. Chicago: University of Chicago Press, 2003.

Spivak, Gayatri Chakravorty. *The Post-Colonial Critic: Interviews, Strategies, Dialogues*. New York: Routledge, 1990.

Stephens, Michelle Ann. *Skin Acts: Race, Psychoanalysis and the Black Male Performer*. Durham, NC: Duke University Press, 2014.

Streible, Dan. *Fight Pictures: A History of Boxing and Early Cinema*. Berkley: University of California Press, 2008.

———. "Race and the Reception of Jack Johnson Fight Films." In *The Birth of Whiteness: Race and the Emergence of U.S. Cinema*, edited by Daniel Bernardi, 170–200. New Brunswick: Rutgers University Press, 1996.

Stringer, C. Vivian, with Laura Tucker. *Standing Tall: A Memoir of Tragedy and Triumph*. New York: Three Rivers Press, 2008.

Suparak, Astria, and Brett Kashmere. "A Non-Zero-Sum Game." *Incite: Journal of Experimental Media* nos. 7–8 (2016–2017): 6–10.

Tasker, Yvonne. *Spectacular Bodies: Gender, Genre, and the Action Film*. New York: Routledge, 1993.

Taylor, Clyde. "The L.A. Rebellion: A Turning Point in Black Cinema." In *Whitney Museum of American Art: The New American Filmmakers Series 26*, 1–2. New York: Whitney Museum of Art, 1986.

———. "Once Upon a Time in the West . . . L.A. Rebellion." In *L.A. Rebellion: Creating a New Black Cinema*, edited by Allyson Nadia Field, Jan-

Christopher Horak, and Jacqueline Najuma Stewart, ix–xxiv. Oakland: University of California Press, 2015.

———. "Paths of Enlightenment: Heroes, Rebels, and Thinkers." In *Struggles for Representation: African American Documentary Film and Video*, edited by Phyllis R. Klotman and Janet K. Cutler, 122–50. Bloomington: Indiana University Press, 1999.

Thomas, Greg. "Close-Up: Dragons! George Jackson in the Cinema with Haile Gerima—from the Watts Films to *Teza*." *Black Camera* 4, no. 2 (Spring 2013): 55–83.

Thomas, Hank Willis. *Pitch Blackness*. New York: Aperture, 2008.

Tudor, Deborah V. *Hollywood's Vision of Team Sports: Heroes, Race, and Gender*. New York: Garland Publishing, 1997.

Turner, Bryan. "Preface." In *The Consuming Body*, edited by Paki Falk. London: Sage, 1994.

Tyler, Imogen. *Revolting Subjects: Social Abjection and Resistance in Neoliberal Britain*. London: Zed Books, 2013.

Vogan, Travis. "Institutionalizing and Industrializing Sport History in the Contemporary Sports Television Documentary." *Journal of Sport History* 41, no. 2 (Summer 2014): 195–204.

Wallace, Michelle. *Invisibility Blues: From Pop to Theory*. New York: Verso, 1990.

Wallerstein, Immanuel. *Africa: The Politics of Independence*. New York: Vintage Books, 1961.

Welk, Brian. "20 Highest-Grossing Baseball Movies, from '*A League of Their Own*' to '*Mr. 3000*.'" *The Wrap*, October 28, 2018. www.thewrap.com/the-highest-grossing-baseball-movies-photos/.

Wells-Barnett, Ida B. "Southern Horrors: Lynch Law in All Its Phases." In *Southern Horrors and Other Writings: The Anti-Lynching Campaign of Ida B. Wells, 1892–1900*, edited by Jacqueline Jones Royster, 49–72. Boston: Bedford, 1997.

Whannel, Garry. "Winning and Losing Respect: Narratives of Identity in Sport Films." *Sport in Society: Cultures, Commerce, Media, Politics* 11, nos. 2–3 (2008): 195–208.

Williams, Linda. "Film Bodies: Gender, Genre, and Excess." *Film Quarterly* 44, no. 4 (Summer 1991): 2–13.

———. *Playing the Race Card: Melodramas of Black and White from Uncle Tom to O.J. Simpson*. Princeton, NJ: Princeton University Press, 2001.

———. "Skin Flicks on the Racial Border: Pornography, Exploitation, and Interracial Lust." In *Porn Studies*, edited by Linda Williams, 271–308. Durham, NC: Duke University Press, 2004.

———. "Sportswomen in Black and White: Sports History from An Afro-American Perspective." In *Women, Media and Sports: Challenging Gender Values*, edited by Pamela J. Creedon, 45–66. Thousand Oaks: Sage, 1994.

Williams, Serena. "Serena Unretouched and in Her Own Words." *Harper's Bazaar*, July 9, 2019. www.harpersbazaar.com/culture/features/a28209579

/serena-williams-us-open-2018-essay/?fbclid=IwAR2B3ALyUvonygPNq2s
HQhBZ9xCyAfoGp9WLamjvVLcZbmRX6exSZ1sWyfY.

Wood, Amy Louise. *Lynching and Spectacle: Witnessing Racial Violence in America, 1890–1940.* Chapel Hill: University of North Carolina Press, 2009.

XXL Staff. "Big K.R.I.T. Breaks Down *4eva N A Day,* Talks Debut Album, New Single & Boobie Miles." *XXL,* March 15, 2012. www.xxlmag.com/news/2012/03/big-k-r-i-t-breaks-down-4eva-n-a-day-talks-debut-album-new-single-boobie-miles/.

Young, Cynthia. *Soul Power: Culture, Radicalism, and the Making of a U.S. Third World Left.* Durham, NC: Duke University Press, 2006.

Young, Harvey. *Embodying Black Experience: Stillness, Critical Memory, and the Black Body.* Ann Arbor: University of Michigan Press, 2010.

Young, Iris Marion. *Throwing Like a Girl and Other Essays in Feminist Philosophy and Social Theory.* Bloomington: Indiana University Press, 1990.

Zahed, Ramin. "Calabash Animates *On Shoulders of Giants.*" *Animation Magazine,* May 9, 2011. www.animationmagazine.net/features/calabash-animates-on-shoulders-ofgiants/?doing_wp_cron=1464185400.718822956085205078125o.

Zirin, Dave. *A People's History of Sports in the United States: 250 Years of Politics, Protest, People, and Play.* New York: The New Press, 2008.

———. *What's My Name, Fool? Sports and Resistance in the United States.* Chicago: Haymarket Books, 2005.

Index

Founded in 1893,
UNIVERSITY OF CALIFORNIA PRESS
publishes bold, progressive books and journals
on topics in the arts, humanities, social sciences,
and natural sciences—with a focus on social
justice issues—that inspire thought and action
among readers worldwide.

The UC PRESS FOUNDATION
raises funds to uphold the press's vital role
as an independent, nonprofit publisher, and
receives philanthropic support from a wide
range of individuals and institutions—and from
committed readers like you. To learn more, visit
ucpress.edu/supportus.